EVALUATING CAPITAL PROJECTS

Ahmed Riahi-Belkaoui

Q

QUORUM BOOKS
Westport, Connecticut • London

Library of Congress Cataloging-in-Publication Data

Riahi-Belkaoui, Ahmed, 1943–
    Evaluating capital projects / Ahmed Riahi-Belkaoui.
        p. cm.
    Includes bibliographical references and index.
    ISBN 1–56720–357–4 (alk. paper)
    1. Capital budget. 2. Capital investments. I. Title.
HG4028.C4R465 2001
    658.15'4—dc21   00–042556

British Library Cataloguing in Publication Data is available.

Library of Congress Catalog Card Number: 00–042556
ISBN: 1–56720–357–4

First published in 2001

Quorum Books, 88 Post Road West, Westport, CT 06881
An imprint of Greenwood Publishing Group, Inc.
www.quorumbooks.com

Printed in the United States of America

The paper used in this book complies with the
Permanent Paper Standard issued by the National
Information Standards Organization (Z39.48–1984).

10 9 8 7 6 5 4 3 2 1

Copyright Acknowledgments

The author and publisher gratefully acknowledge permission for use of the following material:

Alan Sangster, "Capital Investment Appraisal Techniques: A Survey of Current Usage," *Journal of Business Finance and Accounting* 20, 3 (1993), pp. 307–332.

Arjun Chairath and Michael J. Seiler, "Capital Budgeting and the Stochastic Cost of Capital," *Managerial Finance* 23, 9 (1997), pp. 16–23.

George E. Pinches and Diane M. Lander, "The Use of NPV in Newly Industrialized and Developing Countries: a.k.a. What Have We Ignored?" *Managerial Finance* 23, 9 (1997), pp. 24–45.

To Dimitra

Contents

Exhibits

Preface

Evaluating Capital Projects examines the multidimensional scope of capital budgeting. Various facets, traditional and nontraditional, of capital budgeting are examined. The principles of true value of money and capital budgeting are examined in Chapters 1 and 2. Chapter 3, on advanced capital budgeting, examines the advanced issues of replacement decisions, capital rationing, and capital budgeting under uncertainty and inflation. Chapter 4 examines the issues associated with capital budgeting in a global context. Chapter 5 examines the determination of political risk and its use in capital budgeting internationally. Chapter 6 compares the techniques of leasing versus purchasing and their reliance on capital budgeting techniques. Chapter 7 examines the techniques of capital budgeting as applied to social projects. Finally, Chapter 8 examines the behavioral and cognitive implications of wealth measurement and distribution.

The book should be of interest to a variety of groups including accounting practitioners and managers, financial executives, controllers, and graduate and undergraduate students in management accounting and corporate finance classes.

Many people have helped in the development of this book. I received considerable assistance from the University of Illinois research assistants, especially Yukie Muria, Juliette Kim, and Brian Oliver. I also thank Eric Valentine and the entire production team at Quorum Books for their continuous and intelligent support.

Chapter 1

Time Value of Money

INTRODUCTION

When people must choose between receiving payment immediately or periodically over a number of periods, they show a preference for present satisfaction over future satisfaction. The preference for present payment is motivated by the possibility of either consuming the funds or investing them to provide greater amounts in the future, whereas the choice of receiving money in the future involves the sacrifice of waiting before it can be used. The compensation for waiting is the time value of money, called *interest*. Individuals require interest for postponing consumption.

COMPOUND VALUE

The *compound value* (CDV) is the future value of funds received today and invested at the prevalent interest rate. For example, assume an investment of $1,000 at 10 percent per year. The compound value at the end of year 1 is computed as follows:

$$CDV_1 = \$1,000 \ (1 + 0.10)^1 = \$1,100$$

Similarly, the compound value at the end of year 2 is computed as follows:

$$CDV_2 = \$1,100 \ (1 + 0.10)^1 = \$1,210$$

or

$$\text{CDV}_2 = \$1,000\ (1 + 0.10)^2 = \$1,210.$$

This can be generalized to yield the following formula, which applies to compute the compound value:

$$S_n = P(1 + r)^n,$$

where

S_n = Compound value at the end of year n = $1,210.
P = Beginning amount or present value = $1,000.
r = *Interest* rate or rate of return = 10%.
n = Number of years = 2.

Thus, the future value (FV) of $1, with n corresponding to the number of compounding periods, is

$$FV = (1 + r)^n.$$

The FV can be computed for any interest rate (r) and any number of compounding periods (n). Exhibit 1.1 shows the future value of $1 for a variety of interest rates and compounding periods.

PRESENT VALUE

In the previous example, if $1,000 compound at 10 percent per year becomes $1,210 at the end of two years, then $1,000 is the present value (PV) of $1,210 due at the end of two years. Finding the present value of a future value involves discounting the future value to the present. Discounting, then, is the opposite of compounding. The formula for the present value is the same as the formula for the future value, except it solves for P instead of S_n, which is known. Thus, if

$$S_n = P(1 + r)^n,$$

then

$$P = \frac{S_n}{(1 + r)^n}.$$

Inserting the illustrative numbers yields

$$P = \frac{\$1,210}{(1 + 0.10)^2} = \$1,000.$$

Exhibit 1.1
Future Value of $1 Payable in Period N

Year (N)	1%	2%	3%	4%	5%	6%	7%
1	1.010	1.020	1.030	1.040	1.050	1.060	1.070
2	1.020	1.040	1.061	1.082	1.102	1.124	1.145
3	1.030	1.061	1.093	1.125	1.158	1.191	1.225
4	1.041	1.082	1.126	1.170	1.216	1.262	1.311
5	1.051	1.104	1.159	1.217	1.276	1.338	1.403
6	1.062	1.126	1.194	1.265	1.340	1.419	1.501
7	1.072	1.149	1.230	1.316	1.407	1.504	1.606
8	1.083	1.172	1.267	1.369	1.477	1.594	1.718
9	1.094	1.195	1.305	1.423	1.551	1.689	1.838
10	1.105	1.219	1.344	1.480	1.629	1.791	1.967
11	1.116	1.243	1.384	1.539	1.710	1.898	2.105
12	1.127	1.268	1.426	1.601	1.796	2.012	2.252
13	1.138	1.294	1.469	1.665	1.886	2.133	2.410
14	1.149	1.319	1.513	1.732	1.980	2.261	2.579
15	1.161	1.346	1.558	1.801	2.079	2.397	2.759
16	1.173	1.373	1.605	1.873	2.183	2.540	2.952
17	1.184	1.400	1.653	1.948	2.292	2.693	3.159
18	1.196	1.428	1.702	2.026	2.407	2.854	3.380
19	1.208	1.457	1.754	2.107	2.527	3.026	3.617
20	1.220	1.486	1.806	2.191	2.653	3.207	3.870
25	1.282	1.641	2.094	2.666	3.386	4.292	5.427
30	1.348	1.811	2.427	3.243	4.322	5.743	7.612

Thus, the general formula for the present value of $1 is

$$PV = \frac{1}{(1 + r)^n}.$$

Exhibit 1.2 shows the present value of $1 for any interest rate (r) and any number of periods (n).

FUTURE VALUE OF AN ANNUITY IN ARREARS OF $1

An *annuity in arrears* is a series of periodic and equal payments (receipts) to be paid (received) at the end of successive similar periods. Assume, for example, that a firm is to receive annual payments of $1,000 at the end of each

Exhibit 1.1 (continued)

Year (N)	8%	9%	10%	12%	14%	15%	16%
1	1.080	1.090	1.100	1.120	1.140	1.150	1.160
2	1.166	1.188	1.210	1.254	1.30	1.322	1.346
3	1.260	1.295	1.331	1.405	1.482	1.521	1.561
4	1.360	1.412	1.464	1.574	1.689	1.749	1.811
5	1.469	1.539	1.611	1.762	1.925	2.011	2.10
6	1.587	1.677	1.772	1.974	2.195	2.313	2.436
7	1.714	1.828	1.949	2.211	2.502	2.660	2.826
8	1.851	1.993	2.144	2.476	2.853	3.059	3.278
9	1.999	2.172	2.358	2.773	3.252	3.518	3.803
10	2.159	2.367	2.594	3.106	3.707	4.046	4.411
11	2.332	2.580	2.853	3.479	4.226	4.652	5.117
12	2.518	2.813	3.138	3.896	4.818	5.350	5.936
13	2.720	3.066	3.452	4.363	5.492	6.153	6.886
14	2.937	3.342	3.797	4.887	6.261	7.076	7.988
15	3.172	3.642	4.177	5.474	7.138	8.137	9.266
16	3.426	3.970	4.595	6.130	8.137	9.358	10.748
17	3.70	4.328	5.054	6.866	9.276	10.761	12.468
18	3.996	4.717	5.560	7.690	10.575	12.375	14.463
19	4.316	5.142	6.116	8.613	12.056	14.232	16.777
20	4.661	5.604	6.728	9.646	13.743	16.367	19.461
25	6.848	8.623	10.835	17.000	26.462	32.919	40.874
30	10.063	13.268	17.449	29.960	50.950	66.212	85.850

year for three years and charges an interest rate of 10 percent. Using Exhibit 1.1, the pattern of compounding is as follows:

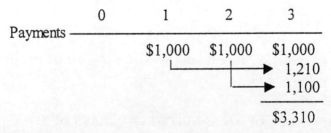

	0	1	2	3
Payments		$1,000	$1,000	$1,000
				1,210
				1,100
				$3,310

In other words, the future value of an annuity in arrears of $1,000 for three years at 10 percent is equal to

$$1,000 (1 + 0.10)^2 + 1,000 (1 + 0.10) + 1,000 = \$3,310$$

or

$$1,000 [1 + (1 + 0.10) + (1 + 0.10)^2] = \$3,310.$$

Therefore, the future value of an annuity in arrears can be determined from the following basic relationship:

$$S_n = a [(1 + r)^{n-1} + (1 + r)^{n-2} + \ldots + (1 + r)^1 + 1]$$

or

$$S_n = a \left[\frac{(1 + r)^n - 1}{r} \right]$$

where

S_n = The future value to which an annuity in arrears will accumulate.

a = The annuity.

$\dfrac{(1 + r)^n - 1}{r}$ = Annuity compound interest factor.

The annuity compound interest factor for an annuity in arrears of $1 can be computed for any interest rate and compounding period, as shown in Exhibit 1.3.

PRESENT VALUE OF AN ANNUITY IN ARREARS OF $1

Assume again that a firm is to receive annual payments of $1,000 at the end of each year for three years. At a 10 percent interest rate, what is the present value of those annual payments? Using Exhibit 1.2, the pattern of discounting is as follows:

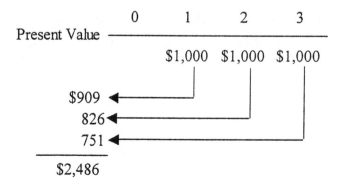

Exhibit 1.2
Present Value of $1 Received at the End of Period

Years Hence	1%	2%	4%	6%	8%	10%	12%	14%	15%	16%	18%
1	0.990	0.980	0.962	0.943	0.926	0.909	0.893	0.877	0.870	0.862	0.847
2	0.980	0.961	0.925	0.890	0.857	0.826	0.797	0.769	0.756	0.743	0.718
3	0.971	0.942	0.889	0.840	0.794	0.751	0.712	0.675	0.658	0.641	0.609
4	0.961	0.924	0.855	0.792	0.735	0.683	0.636	0.592	0.572	0.552	0.516
5	0.951	0.906	0.822	0.747	0.681	0.621	0.567	0.519	0.497	0.476	0.437
6	0.942	0.888	0.790	0.705	0.63	0.564	0.507	0.456	0.432	0.410	0.370
7	0.933	0.871	0.760	0.665	0.583	0.513	0.452	0.400	0.376	0.354	0.314
8	0.923	0.853	0.731	0.627	0.540	0.467	0.404	0.351	0.327	0.305	0.266
9	0.914	0.837	0.703	0.592	0.500	0.424	0.361	0.308	0.284	0.263	0.225
10	0.905	0.820	0.676	0.558	0.463	0.386	0.322	0.270	0.247	0.227	0.191
11	0.896	0.804	0.650	0.527	0.429	0.35	0.287	0.237	0.215	0.195	0.162
12	0.887	0.788	0.625	0.497	0.397	0.319	0.257	0.208	0.187	0.168	0.137
13	0.879	0.773	0.601	0.469	0.368	0.29	0.229	0.182	0.163	0.145	0.116
14	0.870	0.758	0.577	0.442	0.34	0.263	0.205	0.160	0.141	0.125	0.099
15	0.861	0.743	0.555	0.417	0.315	0.239	0.183	0.140	0.123	0.108	0.084
16	0.853	0.728	0.534	0.394	0.292	0.218	0.163	0.123	0.107	0.093	0.071
17	0.844	0.714	0.513	0.371	0.270	0.198	0.146	0.108	0.093	0.080	0.060
18	0.836	0.700	0.494	0.350	0.250	0.180	0.130	0.095	0.081	0.069	0.051
19	0.828	0.686	0.475	0.331	0.232	0.164	0.116	0.083	0.070	0.060	0.043
20	0.820	0.673	0.456	0.312	0.215	0.149	0.104	0.073	0.061	0.051	0.037
21	0.811	0.660	0.439	0.294	0.199	0.135	0.093	0.064	0.053	0.044	0.031
22	0.803	0.647	0.422	0.278	0.184	0.123	0.083	0.056	0.046	0.038	0.026
23	0.795	0.634	0.406	0.262	0.170	0.112	0.074	0.049	0.040	0.033	0.022
24	0.788	0.622	0.390	0.247	0.158	0.102	0.066	0.043	0.035	0.028	0.019
25	0.780	0.610	0.375	0.233	0.146	0.092	0.059	0.038	0.030	0.024	0.016
26	0.772	0.598	0.361	0.220	0.135	0.084	0.053	0.033	0.026	0.021	0.014
27	0.764	0.586	0.347	0.207	0.125	0.076	0.047	0.029	0.023	0.018	0.011
28	0.757	0.574	0.333	0.196	0.116	0.069	0.042	0.026	0.020	0.016	0.010
29	0.749	0.563	0.321	0.185	0.107	0.063	0.037	0.022	0.017	0.014	0.008
30	0.742	0.552	0.308	0.174	0.099	0.057	0.033	0.020	0.015	0.012	0.007
40	0.672	0.453	0.208	0.097	0.046	0.022	0.011	0.005	0.004	0.003	0.001
50	0.608	0.372	0.141	0.054	0.021	0.009	0.003	0.001	0.001	0.001	

Exhibit 1.2 (continued)

20%	22%	24%	25%	26%	28%	30%	35%	40%	45%	50%
0.833	0.820	0.806	0.800	0.794	0.781	0.769	0.741	0.714	0.690	0.667
0.694	0.672	0.650	0.640	0.630	0.610	0.592	0.549	0.510	0.476	0.444
0.579	0.551	0.524	0.512	0.5	0.477	0.455	0.406	0.364	0.328	0.296
0.482	0.451	0.423	0.410	0.397	0.373	0.350	0.301	0.260	0.226	0.198
0.402	0.370	0.341	0.328	0.315	0.291	0.269	0.223	0.186	0.156	0.132
0.335	0.303	0.275	0.262	0.25	0.227	0.207	0.165	0.133	0.108	0.088
0.279	0.249	0.222	0.210	0.198	0.178	0.159	0.122	0.095	0.074	0.059
0.233	0.204	0.179	0.168	0.157	0.139	0.123	0.091	0.068	0.051	0.039
0.194	0.167	0.144	0.134	0.125	0.108	0.094	0.067	0.048	0.035	0.026
0.162	0.137	0.116	0.107	0.099	0.085	0.073	0.05	0.035	0.024	0.017
0.135	0.112	0.094	0.086	0.079	0.066	0.056	0.037	0.025	0.017	0.012
0.112	0.092	0.076	0.069	0.062	0.052	0.043	0.027	0.018	0.012	0.008
0.093	0.075	0.061	0.055	0.05	0.040	0.033	0.020	0.013	0.008	0.005
0.078	0.062	0.049	0.044	0.039	0.032	0.025	0.015	0.009	0.006	0.003
0.065	0.051	0.040	0.035	0.031	0.025	0.02	0.011	0.006	0.004	0.002
0.054	0.042	0.032	0.028	0.025	0.019	0.015	0.008	0.005	0.003	0.002
0.045	0.034	0.026	0.023	0.02	0.015	0.012	0.006	0.003	0.002	0.001
0.038	0.028	0.021	0.018	0.016	0.012	0.009	0.005	0.002	0.001	0.001
0.031	0.023	0.017	0.014	0.012	0.009	0.007	0.003	0.002	0.001	
0.026	0.019	0.014	0.012	0.01	0.007	0.005	0.002	0.001	0.001	
0.022	0.015	0.011	0.009	0.008	0.006	0.004	0.002	0.001		
0.018	0.013	0.009	0.007	0.006	0.004	0.003	0.001	0.001		
0.015	0.010	0.007	0.006	0.005	0.003	0.002	0.001			
0.013	0.008	0.006	0.005	0.004	0.003	0.002	0.001			
0.01	0.007	0.005	0.004	0.003	0.002	0.001	0.001			
0.009	0.006	0.004	0.003	0.002	0.002	0.001				
0.007	0.005	0.003	0.002	0.002	0.001	0.001				
0.006	0.004	0.002	0.002	0.002	0.001	0.001				
0.005	0.003	0.002	0.002	0.001	0.001	0.001				
0.004	0.003	0.002	0.001	0.001	0.001					
0.001										

Exhibit 1.3
Future Value of Annuity in Arrears of $1 for N Periods

Year (N)	1%	2%	3%	4%	5%	6%
1	1.000	1.000	1.000	1.000	1.000	1.000
2	2.010	2.020	2.030	2.040	2.050	2.060
3	3.030	3.060	3.091	3.122	3.152	3.184
4	4.060	4.122	4.184	4.246	4.31	4.375
5	5.101	5.204	5.309	5.416	5.526	5.637
6	6.152	6.308	6.468	6.633	6.802	6.975
7	7.214	7.434	7.662	7.898	8.142	8.394
8	8.286	8.583	8.892	9.214	9.549	9.897
9	9.369	9.755	10.159	10.583	11.027	11.491
10	10.462	10.95	11.464	12.006	12.578	13.181
11	11.567	12.169	12.808	13.486	14.207	14.972
12	12.683	13.412	14.192	15.026	15.917	16.87
13	13.809	14.68	15.618	16.627	17.713	18.882
14	14.947	15.974	17.086	18.292	19.599	21.051
15	16.097	17.293	18.599	20.024	21.579	23.276
16	17.258	18.639	20.157	21.825	23.657	25.673
17	18.430	20.012	21.762	23.698	25.840	28.213
18	19.615	21.412	23.414	25.645	28.132	30.906
19	20.811	22.841	25.117	27.671	30.539	33.760
20	22.019	24.297	26.870	29.778	33.066	36.786
25	28.243	32.030	36.459 ¨	41.646	47.727	54.865
30	34.785	40.568	47.575	56.085	66.439	79.058

The present value of an annuity in arrears of $1,000 for three years at 10 percent is equal to

$$\$1{,}000\ (1 + 0.10)^{-1} + 1{,}000\ (1 + 0.10)^{-2} + 1{,}000\ (1 + 0.10)^{-3} = \$2{,}486$$

or

$$\$1{,}000\ [(1 + 0.10)^{-1} + (1 + 0.10)^{-2} + (1 + 0.10)^{-3}]$$

Therefore, the present value of an annuity in arrears can be generalized by the following formula:

Exhibit 1.3 (continued)

Year (N)	7%	8%	9%	10%	12%	14%
1	1.000	1.000	1.000	1.000	1.000	1.000
2	2.070	2.080	2.090	2.100	2.120	2.140
3	3.215	3.246	3.278	3.31	3.374	3.440
4	4.440	4.506	4.573	4.641	4.770	4.921
5	5.751	5.867	5.985	6.105	6.353	6.610
6	7.153	7.336	7.523	7.716	8.115	8.536
7	8.654	8.923	9.200	9.487	10.089	10.73
8	10.260	10.637	11.028	11.436	12.300	13.233
9	11.978	12.488	13.021	13.579	14.776	16.085
10	13.816	14.487	15.193	15.937	17.549	19.337
11	15.784	16.645	17.560	18.531	20.655	23.044
12	17.888	18.977	20.141	21.384	24.133	27.271
13	20.141	21.495	22.953	24.523	28.029	32.089
14	22.550	24.215	26.019	27.975	32.393	37.581
15	25.129	27.152	29.361	31.772	37.280	43.842
16	27.888	30.324	33.003	35.950	42.753	50.980
17	30.840	33.750	36.974	40.545	48.884	59.118
18	33.999	37.450	41.301	45.599	55.750	68.394
19	37.379	41.446	46.018	51.159	63.440	78.969
20	40.995	45.762	51.160	57.275	72.052	91.025
25	63.249	73.106	84.701	98.347	133.334	181.871
30	94.461	113.283	136.308	164.494	241.333	356.787

$$P_n = a \left[\frac{1 - \dfrac{1}{(1 + r)^n}}{r} \right],$$

where

P_n = Present value of the annuity in arrears.

a = Amount of the annuity.

r = Interest rate.

n = Number of years.

The annuity discount interest factor,

Exhibit 1.4

Present Value of $1 Received Annuity at the End of Each Period for N Periods

Year (N)	1%	2%	4%	6%	8%	10%	12%	14%	15%	16%
1	0.990	0.980	0.962	0.943	0.926	0.909	0.893	0.877	0.870	0.862
2	1.970	1.942	1.886	1.833	1.783	1.736	1.690	1.647	1.626	1.605
3	2.941	2.884	2.775	2.673	2.577	2.487	2.402	2.322	2.283	2.246
4	3.902	3.808	3.630	3.465	3.312	3.170	3.037	2.914	2.855	2.798
5	4.853	4.713	4.452	4.212	3.993	3.791	3.605	3.433	3.352	3.274
6	5.795	5.601	5.242	4.917	4.623	4.355	4.111	3.889	3.784	3.685
7	6.728	6.472	6.002	5.582	5.206	4.868	4.564	4.288	4.160	4.039
8	7.652	7.325	6.733	6.210	5.747	5.335	4.968	4.639	4.487	4.344
9	8.566	8.162	7.435	6.802	6.247	5.759	5.328	4.946	4.772	4.607
10	9.471	8.983	8.111	7.360	6.710	6.145	5.650	5.216	5.019	4.833
11	10.368	9.787	8.760	7.887	7.139	6.495	5.988	5.453	5.234	5.029
12	11.255	10.575	9.385	8.384	7.536	6.814	6.194	5.660	5.421	5.197
13	12.134	11.343	9.986	8.853	7.904	7.103	6.424	5.842	5.583	5.342
14	13.004	12.106	10.563	9.295	8.244	7.367	6.628	6.002	5.724	5.468
15	13.865	12.849	11.118	9.712	8.559	7.606	6.811	6.142	5.847	5.575
16	14.718	13.578	11.652	10.106	8.851	7.824	6.974	6.265	5.954	5.669
17	15.562	14.292	12.166	10.477	9.122	8.022	7.120	6.373	6.047	5.749
18	16.398	14.992	12.659	10.828	9.372	8.201	7.250	6.467	6.128	5.818
19	17.226	15.678	13.134	11.158	9.604	8.365	7.366	6.550	6.198	5.877
20	18.046	16.351	13.59	11.470	9.818	8.514	7.469	6.623	6.259	5.929
21	18.857	17.011	14.029	11.764	10.017	8.649	7.562	6.687	6.312	5.973
22	19.660	17.658	14.451	12.042	10.201	8.772	7.645	6.743	6.359	6.011
23	20.456	18.292	14.857	12.303	10.371	8.883	7.718	6.792	6.399	6.044
24	21.243	18.914	15.247	12.550	10.529	8.985	7.784	6.835	6.434	6.073
25	22.023	19.523	15.622	12.783	10.675	9.077	7.843	6.873	6.464	6.097
26	22.795	20.121	15.983	13.003	10.81	9.161	7.896	6.906	6.491	6.118
27	23.560	20.707	16.33	13.211	10.935	9.237	7.943	6.935	6.514	6.136
28	24.316	21.281	16.663	13.406	11.051	9.307	7.984	6.961	6.534	6.152
29	25.066	21.844	16.984	13.591	11.158	9.370	8.022	6.983	6.551	6.166
30	25.808	22.396	17.292	13.765	11.258	9.427	8.055	7.003	6.566	6.177
40	32.835	27.355	19.793	15.046	11.925	9.779	8.244	7.105	6.642	6.234
50	39.196	31.424	21.482	15.762	12.234	9.915	8.304	7.133	6.661	6.246

Exhibit 1.4 (continued)

18%	20%	22%	24%	25%	26%	28%	30%	35%	40%	45%	50%
0.847	0.833	0.820	0.806	0.80	0.794	0.781	0.769	0.741	0.714	0.690	0.667
1.566	1.528	1.492	1.457	1.440	1.424	1.392	1.361	1.289	1.224	1.165	1.111
2.174	2.106	2.042	1.981	1.952	1.923	1.868	1.816	1.696	1.589	1.493	1.407
2.69	2.589	2.494	2.404	2.362	2.320	2.241	2.166	1.997	1.849	1.720	1.605
3.127	2.991	2.864	2.745	2.689	2.635	2.532	2.436	2.220	2.035	1.876	1.737
3.498	3.326	3.167	3.020	2.951	2.885	2.759	2.643	2.385	2.168	1.983	1.824
3.812	3.605	3.416	3.242	3.161	3.083	2.937	2.802	2.508	2.263	2.057	1.883
4.078	3.837	3.619	3.421	3.329	3.241	3.076	2.925	2.598	2.331	2.108	1.922
4.303	4.031	3.786	3.566	3.463	3.366	3.184	3.019	2.665	2.379	2.144	1.948
4.494	4.192	3.923	3.682	3.571	3.465	3.269	3.092	2.715	2.414	2.168	1.965
4.656	4.327	4.035	3.776	3.656	3.544	3.335	3.147	2.752	2.438	2.185	1.977
4.793	4.439	4.127	3.851	3.725	3.606	3.387	3.190	2.779	2.456	2.196	1.985
4.910	4.533	4.203	3.912	3.78	3.656	3.427	3.223	2.799	2.468	2.204	1.990
5.008	4.611	4.265	3.962	3.824	3.695	3.459	3.249	2.814	2.477	2.210	1.993
5.092	4.675	4.315	4.001	3.859	3.726	3.483	3.268	2.825	2.484	2.214	1.995
5.162	4.730	4.357	4.003	3.887	3.751	3.503	3.283	2.834	2.489	2.216	1.997
5.222	4.775	4.391	4.059	3.910	3.771	3.518	3.295	2.840	2.492	2.218	1.998
5.273	4.812	4.419	4.080	3.928	3.786	3.529	3.304	2.844	2.494	2.219	1.999
5.316	4.844	4.442	4.097	3.942	3.799	3.539	3.311	2.848	2.496	2.220	1.999
5.353	4.870	4.460	4.110	3.954	3.808	3.546	3.316	2.850	2.497	2.221	1.999
5.384	4.891	4.476	4.121	3.963	3.816	3.551	3.320	2.852	2.498	2.221	2.000
5.410	4.909	4.488	4.130	3.970	3.822	3.556	3.323	2.853	2.498	2.222	2.000
5.432	4.925	4.499	4.137	3.976	3.827	3.559	3.325	2.854	2.499	2.222	2.000
5.451	4.937	4.507	4.143	3.981	3.831	3.562	3.327	2.855	2.499	2.222	2.000
5.467	4.948	4.514	4.147	3.985	3.834	3.564	3.329	2.856	2.499	2.222	2.000
5.480	4.956	4.520	4.151	3.988	3.837	3.566	3.330	2.856	2.500	2.222	2.000
5.492	4.964	4.524	4.154	3.990	3.839	3.567	3.331	2.856	2.500	2.222	2.000
5.502	4.970	4.528	4.157	3.992	3.840	3.568	3.331	2.857	2.500	2.222	2.000
5.510	4.975	4.531	4.159	3.994	3.841	3.569	3.332	2.857	2.500	2.222	2.000
5.517	4.979	4.534	4.160	3.995	3.842	3.569	3.332	2.857	2.500	2.222	2.000
5.548	4.997	4.544	4.166	3.999	3.846	3.571	3.333	2.857	2.500	2.222	2.000
5.554	4.999	4.545	4.167	4.000	3.846	3.571	3.333	2.857	2.500	2.222	2.000

$$\frac{1 - \dfrac{1}{(1 + r)^n}}{r}$$

can be computed for an annuity of $1 in arrears for any interest rate and discounting period, as shown in Exhibit 1.4.

Chapter 2

Principles of Capital Budgeting

INTRODUCTION

Management must often decide whether to add a product or buy a new machine. They make many general, nonrecurring investment decisions involving fixed assets, or *capital budgeting* decisions. Capital budgeting involves a current outlay or a series of outlays of cash resources in return for anticipated benefits to be received beyond one year in the future. The capital budgeting decision has three distinguishing characteristics: anticipated benefits, a time element, and a degree of risk associated with the realization of the benefits. In general, these characteristics can be described more specifically as anticipated cash benefits, a time lag between the initial capital investment and the realization of the cash benefits, and a degree of risk. Ideally, a firm with a profit maximization motive will seek an investment that will generate large benefits in a short period and with a minimum of risk. However, investments with potentially large benefits are generally possible only with high risk and may require more time than investments with lower benefits.

Given these less-than-ideal relationships between the dimensions of a capital budgeting decision, management should desire a trade-off between these elements in making a capital budgeting decision that will meet their objectives. Although various objective functions may be chosen by firms, the most useful for evaluating capital budgeting decisions is the stockholders' wealth maximization model (SWMM). Despite the fact that it represents a normative model, the SWMM provides a generally acceptable and meaningful criterion for the evaluation of capital budgeting proposals: the maximization of owners' wealth.

ADMINISTRATION OF CAPITAL BUDGETING

Although the administrative process of capital budgeting may differ from one firm to another, it involves five basic steps. The first step is the planning, or origination and specification, of capital investments. Because capital investments are considered essential to a firm's profitable long-run growth, managers constantly search for new methods processes, plants, and products. These projects usually come from various sources, including the following:

1. New products or markets, and the expansion of existing products or markets.
2. Research and development.
3. Replacement of fixed assets.
4. Other investments to reduce costs; improve the quality of the product; improve morale; or comply with government orders, labor agreements, insurance policy terms, and so forth.

The second step in capital budgeting is the evaluation of the proposed capital investments. Firms differ in their routine for processing capital budgets, but most evaluate and approve the projects at various managerial levels. For example, a request for capital investment made by the production department may be examined, evaluated, and approved by (1) the plant managers, (2) the vice-president for operations, and (3) a capital budget committee or department, which may submit recommendations to the president. The president, after adding recommendations, may submit the project to the board of directors. This routine is often complemented and simplified by a uniform policy and procedure manual presenting in detail the firm's capital budgeting philosophy and techniques.

The third step in capital budgeting is the decision making based on the results of the evaluation process. Depending on the size of the projects, some decisions may be made at a high level, such as the board of directors (if they are large projects), or at a lower level if they are small to medium-sized projects.

The fourth step is control. The firm includes each of the accepted projects in the capital budget and appropriates funds. Periodically, control is exercised over the expenditures made for the project. If the appropriated funds are insufficient, a budgetary review can be initiated to examine and approve the estimated overrun. The control step can be extended to include a continuous evaluation process to incorporate current information and check the validity of the original predictions.

The fifth capital budgeting step is the postaudit. This involves a comparison of the actual cash flows of a capital investment with those planned and included in the capital budget.

ESTIMATING CASH FLOWS

One of the most important capital budgeting tasks for the evaluation of the project capital investments is the estimation of the *relevant cash flows* for each project, which refers to the incremental cash flow arising from each project. Because companies rely on accrual accounting rather than cash accounting, adjustments are necessary to derive the cash flows from the conventional financial accounting records.

Cash and Accrual Accounting

Capital budgeting determines a project's potential incremental cash inflows and outflows compared with the flows if the project were not initiated. The receipt and payment of cash is the significant event in recording the cash inflows and outflows and determining the cash income of a project. This cash income, however, differs in the following ways from the accounting income owing to the timing differences arising from the use of accrual accounting for external reporting:

1. The first difference arises from the capitalization of the cost of a capital asset at the time of purchase and the recognition of depreciation expenses over the asset's economic life. In a capital budgeting context, the cost of a capital asset is a cash outflow when paid.
2. Accrual accounting rests on the application of the matching of revenues and expenses, which leads to the recognition of revenues when earned and costs when incurred, even if no cash has been received or paid. This leads to the recognition of accounts receivable, accounts payable, and various asset balances as the result of the timing differences between accounting income and cash income.

To determine the cash income, adjustments in the accounting income are necessary to correct for these timing differences. Some adjustments are illustrated in Exhibit 2.1.

Identifying the Project Cash Flows

Project cash flows are incremental cash flows arising from a project and are equal to the difference between the cash inflows and the cash outflows. The cash inflows include (1) after-tax net cash revenues, (2) savings in operating expenses, and (3) the salvage value of equipment from each project. The cash outflows include the cost of investment in each of the projects.

Effect of Charges on Cash Flows

Various charges affect the computation of cash flows. *Depreciation* and *amortization charges* are noncash expenses. However, they have an indirect influence on cash flow. Because depreciation is tax deductible, it provides a tax shield by protecting from taxation an amount of income equal to the depreciation deduction. The after-tax proceeds of a project are increased by the

Exhibit 2.1

Reconciliation of Cash Flow and Accounting Income

1. Accounting Income (Traditional Income Statement)

Assume that the purchase of a new machine costing $10,000 and having a ten-year life and disposal value is expected to earn the following for the first year:

Sales	$10,000
Less: Operating Expenses, Excluding Depreciation	$ 5,000
Depreciation (Straight-line)	1,000
Total expenses	$ 6,000
Operating Income before Income Taxes	$ 4,000
Less: Income Taxes at 40 Percent	1,600
Net Income after Taxes	$ 2,400

Other Accrual Information:
a. Sales are 40 percent cash.
b. The expenses, excluding depreciation, are 60 percent on credit.

2. Cash Flow (Cash Effects of Operations)

a. *Cash Inflow from Operations*	
Total Sales	$10,000
Less: Credit Sales: 60 Percent of $10,000 (Increase in Accounts Receivable)	6,000
Cash Collections from Sales	$ 4,000
b. *Cash Outflow from Operating Expenses*	
Total Expenses	$ 5,000
Less: Credit Expenditures: 60 Percent of $5,000 (Increase in Accounts Payable)	$ 3,000
Cash Payments for Operating Expenses	$ 2,000
c. *Net Cash Inflow:* $4,000 - $2,000	$ 2,000
d. *Income Tax Outflow*	$ 1,600
e. *After-Tax Net Cash Inflow*	$ 400
f. *Effect of Depreciation*	
Depreciation Expense	$ 1,000
Tax at 50%	500
Tax Shield	$ 500
g. *Total Cash Flow* (After-Tax Net Cash Inflow + Tax Shield)	$ 900

allowable depreciation times the tax rate. As shown by the following relationships:

$$
\begin{array}{l}
\text{After-tax} \\
\text{cash} \\
\text{proceeds}
\end{array}
=
\begin{array}{l}
\text{Expenses} \\
\text{other than} \\
\text{depreciation}
\end{array}
- \text{Income tax.}
\tag{1}
$$

The income tax can be determined as follows:

$$
\text{Income tax} = \text{Tax rate} \times \text{Taxable income}
\tag{2}
$$

or

$$
\text{Income tax} = \text{Tax rate} \times \left(\text{Revenues} -
\begin{array}{l}
\text{Expenses} \\
\text{other than} \\
\text{Depreciation}
\end{array}
- \text{Depreciation}\right).
\tag{3}
$$

Therefore, the higher the depreciation, the lower the income tax.

By substituting equation 3 into equation 1, the after-tax process can be expressed as follows:

$$
\begin{array}{l}
\text{After-tax} \\
\text{cash} \\
\text{proceeds}
\end{array}
= (1 - \text{Tax rate}) \left(\text{Revenues} -
\begin{array}{l}
\text{Expenses} \\
\text{other than} \\
\text{depreciation}
\end{array}\right) + (\text{Tax rate} \times \text{Depreciation}).
$$

Financing charges are excluded from the cash flow computation used in capital budgeting. First, the interest factor would be counted twice by the use of present value methods of evaluation (to be presented in the next section). Second, the evaluation of a capital project is separate from and independent of the financing aspects.

Opportunity costs of scarce resources diverted from other uses because of the capital project should be charged against the investment project. They can be measured by estimating how much the resource (personnel time or facility space) would earn if the investment project were not undertaken.

RANKING CAPITAL PROJECTS

The project evaluation phase consists of evaluating the attractiveness of the investment proposals. Managers first choose the project evaluation methods best suited to the capital budgeting decision. The most common are the *discounted cash flow (DCF) methods* (*internal rate of return [IRR] method, net present value [NPV] method*, and *profitability index [PI]*), the *payback method*, and the *accounting rate of return (ARR) method.* Each of these methods will be examined in the following sections.

DISCOUNTED CASH FLOW METHODS

The discounted cash flow methods consider the *time value of money* in the evaluation of capital budgeting proposals. A dollar received now is worth more than a dollar received in the future; a dollar in the hand today can be invested to earn a return. Hence, to understand the discounted cash flow methods, it is necessary to grasp the time value concepts.

The discounted cash flow methods focus on cash flows generated over the life of a project rather than the accounting income. These methods involve discounting the cash flow of a project to its *present value* using an appropriate discount rate. There are two basic discounted cash flow methods: (1) the internal rate of return (or time-adjusted rate of return) method and (2) the net present value method.

Internal Rate of Return Method

The IRR is the interest rate that equates the present value of an investment's cash flows and the cost of the investment. The IRR equation follows:

$$\sum_{t=0}^{n} \frac{C_t}{(1 + r)^t} = 0$$

where

> C_t = Cash flow for period t, whether it be a net inflow or a net outflow, including the initial investment at $t = 0$.
>
> n = Investment life, that is, the last period in which a cash flow is expected.
>
> r = IRR as the discount rate that equates the present value of cash flow C_t to zero.

If the initial cash outlay or cost occurs at a time 0, the IRR equation becomes

$$\sum_{t=1}^{n} \frac{C_t}{(1 + r)^t} = C_0 = 0.$$

Solving for r is on a trial-and-error basis; the procedures differ depending on whether the cash flows are uniform or nonuniform.

Uniform Cash Flows

To illustrate, assume a project considered by the Camelli Corporation requires a cash outlay of $39,100 and has an expected after-tax annual net cash savings of $10,000 for six years and no salvage value. Find the interest rate (r) that equates the present value of future annual cash flows of $10,000 and the initial outlay of $39,100 at time 0. Experimenting with two discount rates, 12 and 14 percent, you find

Discount Rate	Discount Factor	Cash Flow	Present Value of Stream
12%	4.1110	$10,000	$41,110
14%	3.8890	$10,000	$38,890

Thus, the IRR that equates the present value of the stream of annual savings and $39,100 is between 12 and 14 percent. This rate can be found by interpolating between 12 and 14 percent:

12%	$41,110 (Too large)
14%	38,890 (Too small)
2%	$ 2,220

$$\frac{\$41,110 - \$39,100}{\$2,220} = 0.905.$$

$$\text{IRR} = 12\% + (0.905 \times 2\%) = 13.81\%.$$

A trial-and-error process determines that 13.81 percent is the IRR that equates the present value of the stream of savings and the cost of the investment. This indicates that the investment will yield a return of 13.81 percent per year in addition to recovering the original cost of $39,100. Exhibit 2.2 depicts the amortization schedule of the investment: The six-year cash savings of $10,000 recovers the original investment plus an annual return of 13.81 percent on the investment.

The computation of the IRR does not determine if the project is to be accepted or rejected. To do so, the IRR generally is compared with a required rate of return. For example, if the IRR exceeds the required rate of return, the project is acceptable. The required rate of return, also known as a *cutoff rate* or *hurdle rate*, is the firm's cost of capital (the cost of acquiring funds). Passing this test does not mean the project will be funded, as funds may be rationed.

Nonuniform Cash Flows

The following example illustrates a project yielding cash flows that are not equal for all the periods of the project's life. We assume the machine considered by the Camelli Corporation costs $39,100 and yields the following cash savings:

Exhibit 2.2
Amortization Schedule: Proof for the Internal Rate of Return

Year	Unrecorded Investment at Beginning of Year	Annual Cash Savings	13.81% Return or Interest[a]	Cost Recovery[b]	Unrecorded Investment at End of Year[c]
1	$39,100.00	$10,000	$5,399.71	$4,600.29	$34,499.71
2	34,499.71	10,000	4764.41	5235.59	29,264.12
3	29,264.12	10,000	4041.38	5958.62	23,305.50
4	23,305.50	10,000	3218.49	6781.51	16,523.99
5	16,523.99	10,000	2281.96	7718.04	8,805.95
6	8,805.95	10,000	1216.10	8783.90	22.05[d]

[a]Return = Unrecorded investment $\times 13.81\%$.

[b]Cost recovery = Annual cash savings - Return.

[c]Unrecovered investment at the end of the year = Unrecorded investment at the beginning of the year − Cost recovery.

[d]Rounding error.

Year	Cash Savings
1	$20,000
2	14,000
3	10,000
4	6,000
5	5,000
6	4,000

Solving for the IRR that equates the present value of these savings and the cost of the investment also requires trial and error. First, experimenting with an interest rate of 16 percent, we find

Year	Discount Factor	×	Cash Savings	=	Present Value of Cash Savings
1	0.862		$20,000		$17,240
2	0.743		14,000		10,402
3	0.641		10,000		6,410
4	0.552		6,000		3,312

Year	Discount Factor	×	Cash Savings	=	Present Value of Cash Savings
5	0.476		5,000		2,380
6	0.410		4,000		1,640
Present Value of Cash Savings					$41,384
Present Value of Cash Outflow					
(Cost of the Machine)					39,100
Difference					$2,284

Given that the present value of cash savings is $2,284 higher than the present value of the cash outflow, the IRR must be higher than 16 percent.

Second, experimenting with an interest rate of 20 percent, we find

Year	Discount Factor	×	Cash Savings	=	Present Value of Cash Savings
1	0.833		$20,000		$16,660
2	0.694		14,000		9,716
3	0.579		10,000		5,716
4	0.482		6,000		2,892
5	0.402		5,000		2,010
6	0.335		4,000		1,340
Present Value of Cash Savings					$38,408
Present Value of Cash Outflow					
(Cost of the Machine)					39,100
Difference (NPV)					$(692)

Given that the present value of cash savings is $692 lower than the present value of the cash outflow, the IRR must be *between* 16 and 20 percent, and closer to 20 percent.

Third, experimenting with 19 percent we obtain

Year	Discount Factor	×	Cash Savings	=	Present Value of Cash Savings
1	0.840		$20,000		$16,800
2	0.706		14,000		9,884
3	0.593		10,000		5,930
4	0.499		6,000		2,994
5	0.419		5,000		2,095
6	0.352		4,000		1,408
Present Value of Cash Savings					$39,111
Present Value of Cash Outflow					
(Cost of the Machine)					39,100
Difference (NPV)					$11

Given that the present value of cash savings is only $11 higher than the cost of the machine, the IRR is approximately 19 percent.

Net Present Value Method

The NPV method compares the cost of an investment with the present value of the future cash flows of the investment at a selected rate of return, or hurdle rate. The NPV of an investment is

$$NPV = \sum_{t=1}^{n} \frac{C_t}{(1 + r)^t} - C_0,$$

where

C_t = Project cash flows.
r = Selected hurdle rate.
n = Project life.
C_0 = Cost of the investment.

If the NPV is greater than or equal to zero, the project is deemed acceptable, but it may not be funded if there is rationing. The required rate of return, or hurdle rate, is usually the cost of capital. The NPV procedure differs depending upon whether the cash flows are uniform or nonuniform.

Uniform Cash Flows

To illustrate the NPV method, let us return to the Camelli Corporation example in which a new machine costing \$39,100 would yield an annual cash savings of \$10,000 for the six years of its life. Assuming a cost of capital of 10 percent, the NPV of the project can be stated as follows:

$$NPV = \sum_{t=1}^{6} \frac{\$10,000}{(1 + 0.10)^6} - \$39,100.$$

The appropriate discount factor for the Camelli Corporation is 4.355. Thus, the NPV is computed as follows:

$$NPV = (\$10,000 \times 4.355) - \$39,100 = \$4,450.$$

Given that the NPV is greater than zero, the Camelli Corporation should accept the new machine proposal. The positive NPV indicates that the Camelli Corporation will earn a higher rate of return on its investment than its cost of capital.

Different NPVs result from different hurdle rates. For example,

NPV at an 8% required rate = (\$10,000 × 4.623) − \$39,100 = \$7,130.
NPV at a 14% required rate = (\$10,000 × 3.889) − \$39,100 = \$(210).

Exhibit 2.3
Amortization Schedule Underlying the Net Present Value

Option 1: Borrow and Invest in the Project

Year	Loan Balance at Beginning of Year	Interest at 10% per Year	Loan and Interest at End of Year	Cash Flow to Repay the Loan	Loan Balance at End of Year
1	$39,100.00	$3,910.00	$43,010.00	$10,000	$33,010.00
2	33,010.00	3,301.00	36,311.00	10,000	26,311.00
3	26,311.00	2,631.10	28,942.10	10,000	18,942.10
4	18,942.10	1,894.21	20,836.31	10,000	10,836.31
5	10,836.31	1,083.63	11,919.94	10,000	1,919.94
6	1,919.94	191.99	2,111.93	10,000	(7,888.06)

Option 2: Invest $4,450 at 10 Percent Rate of Return

Year	Investment Balance at Beginning of Year	Interest at 10% per Year	Investment and Interest at End of Year
1	$4,450.00	$445.00	$4,895.00
2	4,895.00	489.50	5,385.50
3	5,384.50	538.45	5,922.95
4	5,922.95	592.30	6,515.95
5	6,515.25	651.53	7,166.78
6	7,166.78	716.68	7883.46[a]

[a] The $4.60 difference between $7,888.06 and $7,883.46 is a rounding error.

Thus, given a stream of uniform cash flows, the higher the hurdle rate, the less attractive any investment proposal becomes.

The NPV method rests on two assumptions: (1) The cash flows are *certain* (this applies also to the IRR), and (2) the original investment can be viewed as either borrowed or loaned by the Camelli Corporation at the hurdle rate.

Thus, if the Camelli Corporation borrows $39,100 from the bank at 10 percent and uses the cash flows generated to repay the loan, it will obtain the same return as if it had invested $4,450 at the same rate. (See Exhibit 2.3.)

Nonuniform Cash Flows

The following example illustrates a project yielding cash flows that are not equal for all periods of the project's life. Assume again that the machine considered by the Camelli Corporation yields annual cash savings of $20,000, $14,000, $10,000, $6,000, $5,000, and $4,000 for the six years, respectively, and the cost of capital is 10 percent. The computation of the NPV follows:

Year	Discount Factor	×	Cash Savings	=	Present Value of Cash Savings
1	0.909		$20,000		$18,180
2	0.826		14,000		11,564
3	0.753		10,000		7,530
4	0.683		6,000		4,098
5	0.621		5,000		3,105
6	0.564		4,000		2,256
Present Value of Cash Savings					$46,733
Present Value of Cash Outflow (Cost of the Machine)					39,100
Difference (NPV)					$7,633

The NPV method is easier to apply than the IRR method with nonuniform cash flows, because it does not require iterative numerical methods.

Profitability Index

The PI, or benefit cost ratio, is another form of the NPV method. It is generally expressed as

$$PI = \frac{\text{Present value of cash inflows}}{\text{Present value of cash outflows}}$$

For the Camelli Corporation example with uniform cash flows, the PI would be

$$PI = \frac{\$43,550}{\$39,100} = 1.114.$$

For the Camelli Corporation example with nonuniform cash flows, the PI would be

$$PI = \frac{\$46,733}{\$39,100} = 1.195.$$

The decision rule when evaluating different projects is to choose the project with the highest PI.

The NPV and the PI result in the same acceptance or rejection decision for any given project. However, the NPV and the PI can give different rankings for mutually exclusive projects. In such a case, the NPV method is the preferred

Exhibit 2.4
Relationship between Net Present Value (NPV) and Internal Rate of Return (IRR)

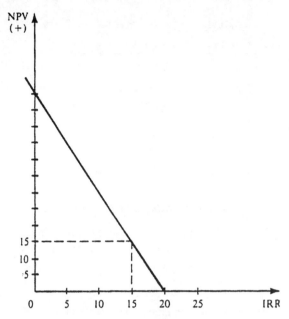

method; it expresses the absolute profitability of a project, whereas the PI expresses the relative profitability.

Comparison between Net Present Value and Internal Rate of Return

Acceptance or Rejection Decision

The IRR and NPV methods lead to the same acceptance or rejection decisions for independent projects with one or more periods of outlays followed *only* by periods of net cash inflows. Exhibit 2.4 illustrates both the NPV and IRR applied to a capital project. At the zero discount rate, the NPV is equal to the sum of the total cash inflows less the total cash outflows. As the discount rate increases, the NPV decreases. Where the NPV reaches zero, the discount rate corresponds to the IRR, which is 20 percent in the fictional example. The following situations are possible:

1. If the required rate of return used as a discount rate is less than the IRR, the project is acceptable under both methods. For example, if the required rate of return is 15 percent, the project is acceptable under both methods, given that at that rate Exhibit 2.4 shows an NPV superior to zero and a required rate inferior to the 20 percent IRR.

2. If the required rate of return is equal to the IRR, the project is acceptable under both

Exhibit 2.5
Mutually Exclusive Investments: Scale Effects

| | Initial | Cash Inflow | NPV | |
Project	Outlay	(End of Year 1)	at 15%	IRR
X	$8,333	$10,000	$362.70	20%
Y	$16,949	$20,000	$442.40	18%
W	$8,616	$10,000	$79.70	15.10%

methods. In such a case the NPV is equal to zero, and the required rate of return is equal to the IRR.

3. If the required rate of return is higher than the IRR, the project is not acceptable under either method.

Conflicts between Net Present Value and Internal Rate of Return

The NPV and the IRR methods may lead to conflicting rankings. Which method provides the best result? To answer this question, the main conflicts between NPV and IRR must be examined, along with the problems associated with each of the methods.

The conflicts arise mainly in comparing mutually exclusive projects (projects capable of performing the same function). The evaluation of mutually exclusive projects by the NPV and the IRR methods can lead to at least three problems:

1. The problem when the mutually exclusive projects have different initial outlays is called the *scale effects problem*.
2. The problem when the mutually exclusive projects have a different timing of cash flows is called the *timing effects problem*.
3. The problem when the mutually exclusive projects have different lives is called the *live effects problem*.

Other problems arise from possible *multiple rates of return* when using the IRR method.

Both the conflicts and problems identified will be examined before we judge which method provides the best ranking.

Scale Effects

The NPV and the IRR methods yield conflicting rankings when mutually exclusive projects having different initial outlays are compared. Consider the example in Exhibit 2.5, where project X is ranked better with the IRR method, and project Y is ranked better with the NPV method.

Given this conflicting result, which project should be chosen? Projects X and Y are incorrectly ranked by the IRR method because of the large difference in the cost of the projects. The incremental cost of $8,616 for project Y can be

Exhibit 2.6
Mutually Exclusive Investments: Timing Effects

		Cash Inflow	Cash Inflow		
	Initial	(End of	(End of	NPV	
Project	Outlay	Year 1)	Year 2)	at 10%	IRR
X	$2,310	$1,000	$2,000	$251.99	14%
Y	$2,310	$2,000	$ 788	$159.24	16%
W	$ 0	$1,000	$1,212	$101.82	21.19%

seen as an additional project W, which yields a positive NPV of $79.70 and an IRR of 15.10 percent, which is greater than the required rate of return of 15 percent. The incremental cost is acceptable under both the IRR and the NPV methods: thus, project Y should be selected. Since the NPV method has selected project Y, the NPV method is preferable.

Timing Effects

The NPV and IRR methods also yield conflicting results when mutually exclusive projects of equal size but with different timing of cash flows are compared. Consider the example in Exhibit 2.6, where project Y is ranked better with the IRR method, and project X is ranked better with the NPV method.

Given this conflicting result, should project X or Y be chosen? Again, use the incremental approach:

Year 0: $0 cash outlays for both projects.

Year 1: $1,000 project Y cash flow exceeds that of project X.

Year 2: $1,212 project X cash flow exceeds that of project Y.

This situation also can be conceived as an investment of $1,000 in year 1 yielding $1,212 in year 2. Such a project W will yield a positive NPV of $101.81 and an IRR of 21.19 percent. Thus, project X should be selected. Since the NPV method selected project X, it can again be concluded that the NPV method is preferable.

Live Effects: The Reinvestment Rate Assumption

The NPV and the IRR methods may yield conflicting results when mutually exclusive projects of equal sizes with different lives are compared. For example, consider the example in Exhibit 2.7, where project X is ranked better with the IRR method, whereas project Y is ranked better with the NPV method. This ranking difference is due to the difference in the investment rate assumption. The IRR method assumes a reinvestment rate equal to the internal rate, whereas

Exhibit 2.7
Mutually Exclusive Investments: Different Lives

	Initial	Cash Inflow			NPV	
Project	Outlay	Year 1	Year 2	Year 3	at 10%	IRR
X	$5,000	$5,750	—	—	$227.26	15%
Y	$5,000	—	—	$7,025	$277.95	12%

the NPV method assumes a reinvestment rate equal to the required rate of return used as a discount factor.

The two reinvestment assumptions can be illustrated by calculating the terminal values of project X under each of the two assumptions. The terminal value using 15 percent for two years is equal to $7,601.50. The terminal value using the required rate of return of 10 percent is equal to $6,957.50. If we compare these two terminal values to the $7,025 terminal value of project Y, we obtain two situations:

1. Using the IRR method, the terminal value of project X, $7,601.50, is greater than the terminal value of project Y, $7,025. The IRR method favors project X.

2. Using the NPV method, the terminal value of project X, $6,957.50, is lower than the terminal value of project Y, $7,025. The NPV method favors project Y.

The assumption of reinvestment at the required rate of return implied in the NPV method is considered to be the better one, the cost of capital being the minimum return acceptable to the firm.

Multiple Internal Rates of Return

Another problem with the IRR method arises from the possibility of multiple IRRs for "abnormal" projects. A "normal" project has one or more outflows followed by a series of inflows. An abnormal project is one that has negative cash flows in periods after the first positive cash flow. With abnormal projects, there may be several different returns that fit the equation, one for each change of the sign of the cash flows.

For example, suppose a capital project requires the following cash flows:

Year	Cash Flow
0	$(1,600)
1	10,000
2	(10,000)

Solving for the IRR, we find two rates: 25 and 400 percent. Neither rate is correct because neither measures investment value. Instead, the NPV method will give the correct decision and avoid the problem of multiple rates of return associated with some abnormal projects.

PAYBACK METHOD

The payback method, also called the *payout method*, is simply the number of years before the initial cash outlay of a project is fully recovered by its future cash inflows. For example, assume a firm is considering purchasing at $15,000 a delivery truck expected to save $5,000 per year in shipping expenses for four years. The payback formula is

$$\text{Payback} = \frac{\text{Initial cost of the project}}{\text{Annual net cash flows}}$$
$$= \frac{\$15,000}{\$5,000}$$
$$= 3 \text{ years.}$$

In other words, the cost of the delivery truck will be recovered in three years. If the payback period calculated is less than an acceptable maximum payback period, the firm should accept the truck proposal.

For projects with nonuniform cash flows the procedure is slightly different. For example, assume the yearly cash savings are $4,000 in year 1, $5,000 in year 2, $3,000 in year 3, $3,000 in year 4, and $6,000 in year 5. It takes up to year 4 to recover a cumulative cash savings equal to the initial cost of the truck. Therefore, the payback period is four years.

An extension of the payback method is the *bailout method*, which takes into account both the cash savings and the salvage value needed to recover the initial cost of a project. Going back to the first example of the $15,000 truck with an expected savings of $5,000 per year in shipping expenses, assume also that the salvage value is estimated to be $8,000 at the end of year 1 and $5,000 at the end of year 2. The cash savings and salvage value of the truck for the next two years, then, are as follows:

Year	Cash Savings	Salvage Value	Cumulative Cash Savings and Salvage Value
1	$5,000	$8,000	$13,000 = $5,000 + $8,000
2	$5,000	$5,000	$15,000 = $5,000 + $5,000 + $5,000

Thus, at the end of year 2, the total of the cumulative cash savings and the salvage value is equal to the initial cost of the truck. The bailout period is two years.

Businesses commonly use the payback method to provide a quick ranking of capital projects. Some of its features follow, including both advantages and disadvantages:

1. It is easy to calculate and provide a quick answer to the question: How many years will it take before the initial cash outlay is completely recovered?
2. The payback method does not take into account the time value of money. The annual cash flows are given the same weight from one year to another. While the first feature can be interpreted as one of the strengths of the method, this feature is definitely a weakness.
3. The payback method ignores both the cash flows occurring after the payback period and the project's total physical life plan.
4. The payback period can be used to compute the *payback reciprocal*, which is equal to the IRR of the project, provided the project's expected cash flows are constant and are anticipated to continue until infinity. Although projects rarely, if ever, have a perpetual life, a rule of thumb states that the payback reciprocal yields a reasonable approximation of the IRR. The formula for the payback reciprocal is

$$\text{Payback reciprocal} = \frac{r}{\text{Payback period}}$$

ACCOUNTING RATE OF RETURN

The ARR method is a capital budgeting evaluation technique that uses the ratio of the average annual profit after taxes to the investment of the project. The ARR formula based on initial investment is

$$\text{ARR} = \frac{\text{Annual revenue from the project} - \text{Annual expenses of the project}}{\text{Initial investment}}$$

The ARR formula based on average investment is

$$\text{ARR} = \frac{\text{Annual revenue from the project} - \text{Annual expenses of the project}}{\text{Average investment}}$$

These computed ARR values are compared with a cutoff rate before an acceptance or rejection decision is made. For example, assume the Saxon Company is contemplating the purchase of a new machine costing $20,000 and having a five-year useful life and no salvage value. The new machine is expected to generate annual operating revenues of $7,000 and annual expenses of $5,000. The ARR can be computed as follows:

$$\text{ARR based on initial investment:} \quad \frac{\$7,000 - \$5,000}{\$20,000} = 10\%.$$

$$\text{ARR based on average investment} = \frac{\dfrac{\$7,000 - \$5,000}{\$20,000 + 0}}{2} = 20\%.$$

The ARR, then, depends on the choice of an initial or average investment base. Using an average investment base leads to substantially higher rates of return. This can be corrected, however, by choosing a higher required cutoff ARR.

The principal strength of the ARR may be its simplicity. It can be computed easily from the accounting records. Since this same characteristic can be perceived as a weakness, the ARR relies on accounting income rather than cash flows. It fails to take into account the timing of cash flows and the time value of money.

METHODS OF CALCULATING DEPRECIATION

The three widely used depreciation methods are the straight-line (SL), sum-of-the-years'-digits (SYD), and double declining balance (DDB) methods. Depreciation charges under the straight-line method are constant over an asset's useful life. Depreciation charges under the latter two methods are higher in the early years of an asset's useful life and taper off rapidly in later years. The best method for tax depreciation maximizes the present value of the depreciation tax shield (that is, reduces income taxes resulting from depreciation expense). The Economic Recovery Act of 1981 introduced new tax lives and an accelerated depreciation method labeled the *Accelerated Cost Recovery System (ACRS)*, which in most cases results in the highest tax shield.

To determine which of the three depreciation methods maximizes the present value of the tax shield, let us use the example of a machine costing $100,000 with a ten-year useful life and no expected salvage value. The required rate of return (r) is 10 percent, and the marginal tax rate (T) is 40 percent.

Straight-Line Depreciation

The annual straight-line depreciation charge is the difference between the cost of an asset (C) and its future salvage value (S) divided by the asset's useful life (N), where $t = $ year:

$$\begin{aligned}\text{Annual SL depreciation charge} &= SL_t \\ &= \frac{C - S}{N} \\ &= \frac{\$100,000}{10} \\ &= \$10,000.\end{aligned}$$

$$\text{Annual SL depreciation rate} = SLR_6$$

$$= \frac{SL_t}{C - S}$$

$$= \frac{\$10,000}{100,000} = 10\%.$$

$$\text{Depreciation tax shield} = \sum_{t=1}^{N} \frac{SL_t \times T}{(1 + r)^t}$$

$$= \sum_{t=1}^{N} \frac{\$100,000 \times 0.40}{(1 + 0.10)^t}$$

$$= \$24,580.$$

Double Declining Balance Depreciation

Under the double declining balance method, twice the straight-line rate is applied to the book value of the asset each year until the salvage value is reached:

$$\text{Annual DDB depreciation} = DDB_t = \frac{2}{N} \left(C - \sum_{i=1}^{n} DDB_i \right).$$

$$\text{Annual DDB rate} = \frac{2}{N} = \frac{2}{10} = 20\%.$$

$$\text{Depreciation tax shield} = \sum_{t=1}^{n} \frac{DDB \times T}{(1 + r)^t}.$$

Applying these formulae yields the following results:

1 Year	2 Book Value before Depreciation	3 Depreciation	4 Tax Shield (Col. 3 × 40%)	5 Discount Factor at 10%	6 Present Value (Col. 4 × Col. 5)
1	$100,000	$20,000	$8,000	0.909	$7,272
2	80,000	16,000	6,400	0.826	5,286
3	64,000	12,800	5,120	0.751	3,845
4	51,200	10,240	4,096	0.683	2,798
5	40,960	8,192	3,277	0.621	2,035
6	32,768	6,554[1]	2,622	0.564	1,479
7	26,214	6,553	2,621	0.513	1,345
8	19,661	6,554	2,622	0.467	1,224
9	13,107	6,553	2,621	0.424	1,111
10	6,554	6,554	2,621	0.386	1,012
Present Value Tax Shield					$27,407

Sum-of-the-Years'-Digits Depreciation

Under the sum-of-the-years'-digits method, a mathematical fraction is applied to the base. The numerator for a given year is the number of years remaining in the life of the project taken from the beginning of the year. The denominator is the sum of the series of numbers representing the years of useful life. The sum of the numbers 1 through 10 is equal to 55. $N=$ useful life, $t =$ year, $S =$ salvage value, $T =$ tax rate, and $C =$ acquisition price.

Annual SYD depreciation $= SYD_t$

$$= (C - S) \frac{\dfrac{N - t}{N(N + 1)}}{2}$$

$$= (C - S) \frac{\dfrac{2(N - t)}{N(N + 1)}}{2}$$

$$\text{Annual SYD rate} = \frac{SYD_t}{C - S}$$

$$\text{Depreciation tax shield} = \sum_{i=1}^{N} \frac{SYD_t \times T}{(1 + r)^t}.$$

Applying these formulae yields the following results:

1 Year	2 Fraction	3 Depreciation	4 Tax Shield (Col.3 × 40%)	5 Discount Factor at 10%	6 Present Value (Col. 4 × Col. 5)
1	10/55	$18,182	$7,273	0.909	$6,611
2	9/55	16,364	6,546	0.826	5,407
3	8/55	14,545	5,818	0.751	4,369
4	7/55	12,727	5,091	0.683	3,477
5	6/55	10,909	4,364	0.621	2,710
6	5/55	9,091	3,636	0.564	2,051
7	4/55	7,273	2,909	0.513	1,492
8	3/55	5,455	2,182	0.467	1,019
9	2/55	3,636	1,455	0.424	617
10	1/55	1,818	727	0.386	281
Present Value of Tax Shield					$28,033

The present value of the tax shield under each depreciation method has been found to be

Straight-Line	$24,580
Double Declining Balance	27,407
Sum-of-the-Years'-Digits	28,033

Therefore, the present value of the tax shield is highest under the sum-of-the-years'-digits method for this example, and this method should be used for tax depreciation.

CAPITAL BUDGETING ILLUSTRATIONS

Problems

1. Payback Method. A project being planned will cost $30,000. The annual cash inflow net of income taxes for the next five years is as follows:

Period	Cash Flow
1	$8,000
2	4,000
3	12,000
4	14,000
5	6,000

Required: Compute the payback period of the project.

2. Multiple Internal Rate of Return. A project calls for the outlay of $20,000,000 to develop a strip mine. The mine will produce a cash flow of $90,000,000 at the end of year 1. At the end of year 2, $80,000,000 will be used to restore the land to its original condition. Compute the IRR of the project.

3. Internal Rate of Return. A project offers an initial cash outflow of $33,000, an annual expected cash inflow of $10,000 for five years, and no salvage value. Compute the IRR for the project.

4. Mutually Exclusive Projects: Different Outlays. The Baski Company is considering two mutually exclusive, one-year projects. A and B require outlays of $1,000 and $1,500, respectively. Project A will generate a return of $1,250 at the end of the first year, and project B will generate a return of $1,830 at the end of the second year. The cost of capital is 10 percent.

Required:

1. Utilizing the NPV method, which project would the Baksi Company accept?
2. Utilizing the IRR method, which project would the company accept?
3. Which ranking is better?

5. Mutually Exclusive Projects: Differential Timing of Cash Flows. The Beauchemin Company is considering two mutually exclusive, two-year projects. Projects A and B require an outlay of $1,000 each. Project A promises a return of $200 at the end of year 1 and $1,290 at the end of year 2. Project B promises a return at $1,100 at the end of year 1 and $245 at the end of year 2. The cost of capital is 10 percent.

Required:

1. Using the NPV method, which project would the Beauchemin Company accept?
2. Using the IRR method, which project would the Beauchemin Company accept?
3. Which ranking is better?

6. *Mutually Exclusive Projects: Different Lives.* The Express Company is considering two mutually exclusive projects. Project A and B require an outlay of $1,000 each. Project A promises a return of $1,200 at the end of year 1, and project B promises only a return of $1,520 at the end of year 3. The cost of capital is 10 percent.

Required:

1. Using the NPV method, which project would the Express Company accept?
2. Using the IRR method, which project would the company accept?
3. Which ranking is better?

7. *Accounting Treatment of Accelerated Depreciation.* The McIntosh Company is considering the purchase of a piece of equipment for $100,000. The equipment will have a ten-year useful life and no salvage value, and the tax rate is 10 percent. The equipment is expected to generate an annual net income before taxes and depreciation of $50,000. The McIntosh Company expects to take advantage of double declining balance depreciation for tax purposes, and for reporting purposes it expects to issue financial statements based on straight-line depreciation. The two approaches are reconciled by setting up a deferred tax credit account.

Required:

1. Determine the annual tax liability under straight-line depreciation.
2. Determine the annual tax liability under double declining balance depreciation.
3. Make the annual entries to recognize the tax expense and the tax payable.

8. *Cash Flow and Accrual Accounting.* The Slattery Corporation purchased a new machine, which is expected to earn an accounting profit of $2,000 in 19X1, computed as follows:

Sales	$18,000
− Operating Expenses (8,000) and Depreciation (6,000)	14,000
= Operating Income before Tax	$4,000
− Income Tax Expense (50%)	2,000
= Operating Income after Tax	$2,000

Related accrual information includes the following:

Uncollected sales total $400 at year-end.

Unpaid wages amount to $800 at year-end.

The tax return depreciation is $12,000 for 19X1.

 Required: Determine the cash flow for 19X1.

 9. *NPV Technique*. The Stefanski Company is considering the initiation of a new project. This project has a three-year life and initial outflow, or project cost, of $60,000. Revenues and expenses for the first year are estimated to be $100,000 and $50,000, respectively. It is assumed that an inflation rate of 10 percent per year will cause similar increases in cash revenues and cash expenses. The tax rate is assumed to be 40 percent.

 Required:

1. Compute the income statements of the new project for each of the three years. (Assume a straight-line depreciation and no salvage.)

2. Compute the after-tax cash inflow for each of the three years.

3. Assuming that the before-tax borrowing rate is 15 percent, determine the NPV of the project.

Solutions

 1. *Payback.* Evaluating the project with unequal cash flow using payback, we find:

Year	Cash Flow	Cumulative Cash Flow
1	$8,000	$8,000
2	4,000	12,000
3	12,000	24,000
4	12,000	36,000
5	6,000	42,000

In year 3, the cumulative cash flow for the project is:

Year 1	Year 2		Year 3	
$8,000	$4,000	+	$12,000	= $24,000

Since the recovery of the investment falls between the third and fourth year, the payback period is 3 and a fraction years. To calculate that fraction divide the amount of funds needed to recover the investment in year 4 by the amount of cash flow in that year. Since the cumulative cash flow in year 3 is $24,000, we need \$6,000 to recover the investment of \$30,000. The annual cash flow in year 4 is \$12,000. The payback fraction is then $\frac{\$6,000}{\$12,000}$, or .5. The payback for the project is 3.5 years.

2. *Multiple Internal Rate of Return.* We can find the rates that are the solutions to this problem by solving the following equation:

$$\$20,000,000 = \frac{\$90,000,000}{(1 + r)^2} - \frac{\$80,000,000}{(1 + r)^2}$$

Let $(1 + r) = X$ and divide both sides of the equation by 10,000,000. We then obtain:

$$2 = \frac{9}{x} - \frac{8}{x^2} \quad \text{or} \quad 2x^2 - 9x + 8 = 0$$

This type of equation has two roots, which can be computed as follows:

$$x = \frac{-b \pm \sqrt{b^2 - 4ac}}{2a}$$

The solutions are:

$$x_1 = 3.285 \text{ and } x_2 = 1.215$$

Since $x = (1 + r)$, the multiple internal rates of return for this project are 21.5% and 228.5%.

3. *Internal Rate of Return.* Experimenting with three discount rates, 14 percent, 15 percent, and 16 percent, we find:

Discount Rate	Discount Factor	Cash Flow Each Year	Present Value of Stream
16%	3.274	\$10,000	\$32,740
15%	3.352	\$10,000	\$33,520
14%	3.4331	\$10,000	\$34,331

Thus, the internal rate necessary to discount the stream to \$33,000 falls between 15 and 16 percent. To approximate the actual rate, we interpole between 15 and 16 percent:

15%	\$33,520
16%	\$32,740
1%	\$780

$$\frac{520}{789} = .66$$

Then $15\% + .66 = 15.66\%$

IRR = 15.66%

4. Mutually Exclusive Projects: Different Outlays. The relevant results for the three questions are in the following table:

Project	Initial Outlay	Cash Flow Year 1	NPV at 10%	IRR
A	$1,000	$1,250	$136	25%
B	$1,500	$1,830	$163	22%

1. The projects are ranked B with NPV.
2. The projects are ranked A B with IRR.
3. The two projects are ranked incorrectly by the IRR method because the size of the initial outlays is ignored. The incremental outlay of $500 for project B provides an incremental cash inflow of $580, which gives an IRR of 16 percent on the incremental investment. An IRR of 16 percent is obviously acceptable for a company with a cost of capital of 10 percent. Thus, the incremental approach with IRR gives the same result as NPV; project B should be selected over project A. (Adapted with permission from James A. Hendricks. "Capital Budgeting Decisions: NPV or IRR?" *Cost and Management*, March-April 1980, pp. 16–20.)

5. Mutually Exclusive Projects: Differential Timing of Cash Flows. The relevant results for the three questions are in the following table:

Cash Flows

Project	Outlay	Year 1	Year 2	NPV at 10%	IRR
A	$1,000	$200	$1,290	$247	24%
B	$1,000	1,100	245	202	29%

1. The projects are ranked AB with NPV.
2. The projects are ranked BA with IRR.
3. The incremental approach with IRR will be useful:

Year 0	$0	Cash outlays are the same
Year 1	$900	Project B cash flow exceeds that of A
Year 2	$1,045	Project A cash flow exceeds that of B

In year 1, the cash flow of project B exceeds that of project A by $900, while in year 2, the cash flow of project A exceeds that of project B by $1,045. This can be considered to be an investment of $900 that returns $1,045 after one year. The IRR on an investment of $900 that returns $1,045 after one year is

16.1 percent, which is advantageous if the cost of capital is 10 percent. Thus, the incremental approach with IRR confirms what NPV revealed immediately—project A should be selected over project B. (Adapted with permission from James A. Hendricks, "Capital Budgeting Decisions: NPV or IRR?" *Cost and Management*, March-April 1980, pp. 16–20.)

6. *Mutually Exclusive Projects: Different Lives.* Consider the following results:

Cash Inflows

Project	Outlay	Year 1	Year 2	Year 3	NPV at 10%	IRR
A	$1,000	$1,200	—	—	$91	20%
B	$1,000	—	—	$1,520	$142	15%

1. The projects are ranked BA using NPV.
2. The projects are ranked AB using IRR.
3. The different rankings of projects A and B are caused by different assumptions about the reinvestment of the cash proceeds from project A at the end of year 1. The IRR proceeds from project A at the end of year 1. The IRR technique implicitly assumes that these funds can be reinvested at the calculated IRR, 20 percent, while the NPV technique implicitly assumes that these funds can be reinvested at 10 percent, the cost of capital. Which reinvestment assumption should be adopted? Ideally, both assumptions should be rejected and management should predict an explicit reinvestment rate for the time between the end of the short-lived project and of the project of larger life.

7. *Accounting Treatment of Accelerated Depreciation.*
1. The tax liability under the straight line depreciation is as follows:

Year	Net Income Before Taxes & Depreciation	Depreciation	Taxable Income	Tax Liability
1	$50,000	$10,000	$40,000	$16,000

Entries are the same each year.

2. The tax liability under the double declining balance depreciation is as follows:

Year	Net Income Before Taxes & Depreciation	Depreciation	Taxable Income	Tax Liability
1	$50,000	$20,000	$30,000	$12,000
2	50,000	16,000	34,000	13,600
3	50,000	12,800	37,200	14,880
4	50,000	10,240	39,760	15,904
5	50,000	8,192	41,808	16,723.2

Year	Net Income Before Taxes & Depreciation	Depreciation	Taxable Income	Tax Liability
6*	50,000	6,554	43,446	17,378.4
7	50,000	6,554	43,446	17,378.4
8	50,000	6,554	43,446	17,378.4
9	50,000	6,554	43,446	17,378.4
10	50,000	6,554	43,446	17,378.4
		6,554	43,446	17,378.4

*Switch to straight line

3. Entry Year One

Tax Expense	$16,000	
Tax Liability		$12,000
Deferred Tax Credits		4,000
and so on through year 4		
Year 5		
Tax Expense	$16,000	
Deferred Tax Credit	723.2	
Tax Payable		$16,723.2
Year 6 through Year 10		
Tax Expense	$16,000	
Deferred Tax Credits	1,378.4	
Tax Payable		$17,378.4

8. Cash Flow and Accrual Accounting.
Cash Flow:

1. Cash Receipts from Sales
Sales	$18,000
Less Uncollected Sales	400
	$17,600
2. Cash Payments for Operating Expenses | $8,000
Total Expenses	800
Less Unpaid Wages	$ 7,200
3. Net Cash Inflow	$10,400
4. Income Tax Expense	2,000
5. After-Tax Net Cash Inflow	$8,400
6. Effect of Depreciation
Tax reduction due to excess of tax return
depreciation ($12,000) over accounting
depreciation ($6,000) at a 50% rate	$3,000
	$11,400

9. Net Present Value Technique.

1. Income Statement

	Year 1	Year 2	Year 3
Revenues	$100,000	$110,000	$121,000
Expenses	50,000	55,000	60,500
Depreciation	20,000	20,000	20,000
Taxable Income	30,000	35,000	40,500
Taxes at 40%	12,000	14,000	16,200
Net Income	$18,000	$21,000	$24,300

2. After-Tax Cash Inflow

	Year 1	Year 2	Year 3
Net Income	$18,000	$21,000	$24,300
Depreciation	20,000	20,000	20,000
Cash Inflow	$38,000	$41,000	$44,300

3. The Discount Rate Is 9% (15% × .6)
Discounted Cash Inflow

	Year 1	Year 2	Year 3
Cash Inflow	$38,000	$41,000	$44,300
Present Value@9%	.917431	.841680	.772183
Present Value	$34,862	$34,509	$34,208
	Total: $103,579		

Net Present Value:

Total Discounted Cash Inflow	$103,579
Initial Cost of the Project	60,000
Net Present Value	$43,579

CONCLUSIONS

Capital budgeting involves the appraisal of the desirability of capital projects. The conventional techniques covered in this chapter include (a) the discounted cash flow methods, (b) the accounting rate of return method, and (c) the payback method. The next chapter will expand these techniques to cover more complex issues that can be faced when evaluating a capital project.

NOTE

1. Under the general guidelines provided in the tax code, firms are permitted to switch from double declining balance to straight-line depreciation when it is to their advantage to do so. They switch at the point that minimizes the tax bill. From the seventh year in this case, straight-line depreciation charges are higher than double declining balance charges. This is because we are applying a constant rate to a declining balance, which will not carry to the end of the useful life.

Appendix 2.1: Alan Sangster, "Capital Investment Appraisal Techniques: A Survey of Current Usage," *Journal of Business Finance and Accounting* 20, 3 (1993), pp. 307–332.

INTRODUCTION

Organisational change, fuelled by the expansion of information technology, may have contributed to the erosion of the previously established relationship between company size and the quantitative investment appraisal criteria selected. This paper compares the results of a survey of the 500 largest Scottish companies with the findings of earlier UK studies and finds that companies are using more methods together, that usage of the more sophisticated discounted cash flow techniques is higher, and that usage of the less theoretically sound accounting rate of return technique is lower, than previous studies would have suggested for companies of the size involved. It concludes that a size/method selection relationship may only be identifiable when the companies involved are all part of one study, or the studies compared are contemporaneous.

The paper begins with a consideration of the process of organisational change: accounting is not a closed system. It exists within an environment (the organisation) and is subject to changes in that environment. It is also subject to changes in the wider environment outside the organisation. Thus, accounting change will result from events arising within the organisation in which it is operating, and from events arising in the organisation's external environment.

There is a natural resistance to organisational change: 'old habits die hard'. After an event occurs from which change may arise, it is often very difficult to foresee what changes may result. The reaction may be to ignore the event: 'what's it got to do with me?'; it may be to absorb it while leaving the ideologies of the organisation unchanged (for example, a change in the standard rate of VAT would probably be treated in this way); the organisation may absorb the change and adjust its ideologies; or, where the organisation as a whole has avoided any reaction, the event may be absorbed by a part of the organisation and then spread from within: the 'trojan horse' effect.[1]

Despite the accountant's image of being inflexible and old-fashioned, accounting has not stood still. As Hopwood et al. (1990, p. 102) state: 'accounting has not just evolved ... [it] has responded in a more positive way to external as well as internal pressures and circumstances, internalizing into itself residues of events and disruption in the contexts in which it operates'.

Carnall sees accounting change as being in five stages: denial (why change?); defence (stall for a while); discarding (adjusting to the change); adaption

* The author is from the Department of Accountancy, University of Aberdeen. (Paper received May 1990, accepted December 1990)

(implementation); and internalisation (acceptance that the new way is 'normal').[2] This would tend to be a somewhat slow and drawn out process: hard to detect initially, but ultimately obvious. The pace of accounting change was fairly slow up until the 1970s but, fuelled by the information technology explosion,[3] it is now occurring far more quickly than was previously the case.

More specifically, Hopwood (1990, pp. 12—13) states that computer-based technologies (i.e. information technology) have resulted in an amazing intensification of organisational changes; and that this has caused organisational trends (i.e. change) to be speeded up, rather than to be replaced by new ones. Further, 'the impact of new technologies on accounting is likely to be mediated and influenced by the organisational and cultural terrains into which the technologies are introduced'. Hopwood goes on to state (1990, p. 15) that: 'organisations are being changed in the name of [efficiency, value for money, cost effectiveness and the market] and ... new calls are being made for the extension of modes of economic calculation to objectify and operationalise the abstract concepts in the name of which change is occurring. Accounting and related bodies of techniques are important means for such operationalisation'.

Information technology has, therefore, been said to be responsible for speeding-up the rate of change within accounting. Changing external and internal pressures have resulted in a higher appearance of objectivity being required when change is being considered and decisions are being made. To these two factors can be added a third: the enormous growth in management education over the last few years, particularly through the provision of MBA courses on a full-time, part-time and, distance-learning basis. Such opportunities were few and far between, now they are available throughout the United Kingdom. As a result, managers are becoming more aware of the decision aids at their disposal, and are more equipped to apply the benefits of the information technology explosion in order to meet the higher requirement for apparent objectivity that now exists.

Yet, why should such environmental changes have led to any change in accounting practices? Could existing practices not just have been refined, rather than replaced by more sophisticated ones?

Scapens (1985) implies that replacement would arise when he refers to what he calls the 'costly truth' approach: 'truth' being the accounting system that ought to be used, given all the relevant costs and benefits of doing so. He states (Scapens, 1985, p. 121) that 'the necessary information may not be available within the constraints imposed by current information technology and the ability of existing management. Furthermore, even if such information could be provided, the costs of doing so may be extremely high ... the costs ... should not outweigh the benefits to be obtained therefrom.' Thus, when the costs of information are higher than the benfits of using it, it is irrational to seek that information. Scapens continues (1985, p. 121): 'Simple, and sometimes apparently "unrealistic", techniques are frequently observed in practice, despite an extensive literature which provides complex, and "more realistic" alternatives

...' (p. 128) 'The choice of a particular model will depend on the costs and benefits of that model, relative to the costs and benefits of alternative models. It would be quite reasonable for a decision maker to select a very simple model, if the costs of using the more complex alternatives exceed their benfits.'

The information technology explosion has served to reduce the costs of the provision of information. As a result, it is now rational to acquire information when previously it may not have been. That information may provide the opportunity to adopt methods and practices that were previously irrational. In addition, utilisation of increased education opportunities has had the effect of increasing the knowledge and skills of management. These two factors would suggest that the environmental changes referred to earlier could have led to changes in accounting practice. Such changes would have occurred first in those organisations which would have been the first to find that the benefits of obtaining the information deriving from such change exceeded its cost. Thus, when computers first appeared, it was only the largest companies, those who had the greatest economies of scale, who used them. Then, as costs fell in relation to computational power, more and more companies viewed them as being a cost-effective information source. Thus, information technology-led accounting change would tend to start in the largest companies and then trickle down to smaller and smaller ones until, ultimately, all companies had changed.

AREA OF INTEREST

One area where these changes may be having an effect upon accounting practice is quantitative capital investment appraisal. There have been a number of articles during the last decade concerning corporate practice in this area. Studies have been undertaken both in the UK and overseas and some attention has been given to comparisons between UK and US practice (see Mills, 1988a). In addition, attempts have been made to detect trends in the use of these techniques (see, for example, Kim et al., 1986).

In particular, much attention has been given to the use of discounted cash flow (DCF) in its principal forms of net present value (NPV) and internal rate of return (IRR). The case has often been made that companies should be using one or other of these techniques,[4] preferably NPV.[5] However, these are more time consuming and, therefore, more costly to use than the other principal techniques — payback and accounting rate of return (ARR). In the UK, studies have consistently shown that payback is used more often than either of the DCF techniques: a finding which is in keeping with the 'costly truth' hypothesis. The theorist's recommendation that NPV be used rather than IRR was generally found not to have been adopted (with the exception of the 1984 study by McIntyre and Coulthurst, which will be referred to later).

When Pike (1982) compared the usage of investment appraisal techniques in 1975 with that in 1980, he found that, despite evidence suggesting that the use of the DCF techniques was being depressed by managerial ignorance (see, Pike, 1982, pp. 53—54), there was a general rise in the number of methods used, and in the use of one method in particular, namely, IRR. He suggested that the level of sophistication of the methods used was related to company size but, as his 1975 and 1980 data were derived from a questionnaire which asked for details of historic (i.e. 1975) and current (i.e. 1980) usage, this would not satisfactorily explain the changes he identified. Some other factor had to be responsible and this he provided, by implication, when he stated that an expanding firm would require to use superior investment appraisal techniques in order to handle the increasing complexities that the expansion was generating (Pike, 1982, p. 80): he took the view that expansion-led organisational change was responsible for the shift in practice between the two dates which his study considered.

When Mills and Herbert (1987) compared their 1984 data with those from other studies, including Pike's, they also found that company size was a significant factor in the range and type of technique used. They did not consider the possibility that organisational change over time could have contributed to the differences they detected, preferring rather to treat all the data as contemporary. On the basis of Pike's findings, it may be that this was inappropriate: their analysis may have been affected by the undetected influence of organisational change upon the choice of techniques selected.

In response to ʼa question concerning future changes, Pike's survey respondents made reference to wider use being made of computers (see Pike, 1982, pp. 78—9). As those respondents had anticipated, information technology developed extensively during the 1980s. This had not been difficult to foresee in 1980/81 as these developments had been having a marked impact upon working practices since 1975.[6] In 1979, the first electronic spreadsheet (Visicalc) was introducedˮand many others followed. These have been regularly enhanced since they first appeared in order to make use of the vast increase in computing power that has arisen since the Apple microcomputer was introduced in 1977 and, given the benefits to be derived and the awareness that Pike identified, it is reasonable to suppose that corporate practice in the area of capital investment appraisal reacted accordingly. For example, it is likely that the use of the IRR technique, which is many times easier to apply using a computer than manually, will have risen during the five years or so since this was last examined. The impact of organisational change over time upon technique selection should be more apparent than ever before, and should be detectble where results contradict the earlier findings on size.

Thus, earlier studies had suggested three possible causes for differing organisational practices in this area: company size, managerial knowledge, and organisational change arising from expansion. As stated previously, organisational ideologies and mores will affect the impact of new technologies on accounting but, it could be argued, this will only hold in the short-term. In the longer-term, the 'trojan horse' effect referred to in the introduction will overcome these restraints and, ultimately, the new technologies will be fully utilised by all: ultimately, the only ones not using the more sophisticated techniques will be those who perceive that they have no need to do so. If that is the case, the impact of size upon the choice of appraisal criteria may be becoming far less apparent than previously. Also, if managerial knowledge is being improved through more education of managers, then this may lead to current criteria selection being more theoretically sound than in the past.

With this in mind, it was decided to conduct two surveys of current practice in companies operating in Scotland: one covered '*large*' companies, the other '*small*', their relative size being on the basis of turnover.[7] The survey sought to answer the following questions:

1.   What is the current usage[8] of the four most commonly cited quantitative methods of capital investment appraisal — payback, IRR, NPV and ARR?
2.   What changes have occurred in usage since the date of the last studies?
3.   Do larger companies make greater use of the more sophisticated DCF techniques than smaller companies?
4.   Is ARR maintaining its popularity despite its theoretical deficiencies?[9]

This paper considers the data derived from the '*large*' Scottish company study and relates them to the earlier larger company studies of Mills and Herbert, Pike, and the earlier smaller company study of McIntyre and Coulthurst. It seeks to show that earlier findings suggesting a relationship between size and the method of capital appraisal selected may now only be valid when the size difference is great, and should only be valid when the studies compared are contemporaneous. It suggests that information technology-led organisational change may have eroded this previously established relationship, and that it is likely to continue to do so. The '*small*' Scottish company study[10] comprised companies which were smaller than those studied by McIntyre and Coulthurst. Where appropriate, the data from it have been included in order to enhance the comparison between the (larger company-based) '*large*' Scottish company study and that of the (smaller company-based) study conducted by McIntyre and Coulthurst (1985).

SURVEY METHOD AND DISCUSSION OF THE RESULTS

The survey, carried out in Spring 1989, involved the largest companies (on the basis of turnover) registered and operating in Scotland: they were identified in the 1987 volume of Jordan's '*Scotland's Top 500 Companies*'. Turnover ranged from £5m to £2bn and the number of employees from 11 to over 41,000. As originally defined in the 1985 Companies Act (Section 248),[11] the majority were large firms, 14.8 per cent being medium-sized and 0.6 per cent small. Of the respondents, 42 per cent classified themselves as manufacturing

Table 1

Comparative Sizes of the Study Populations

Criterion:	Capital Expenditure	
	Mills & Herbert (1984) %	Pike (1980/1) %
Large	26	15
Medium	18	14
Small	56	71

Criterion:	Turnover	
	Mills & Herbert (1984) %	Current Study (1989) %
Large	27	1
Medium	27	2
Small	46	97

Criterion:	Companies Act Definition (indexed)[a]	
	Current Study (1989) %	McIntyre & Coulthurst (1984) %
Large	81	—
Medium	18	100
Small	1	—

Note:
[a] See note 11.

companies, with the next most common classifications being distribution (13 per cent) and engineering (11 per cent).

A total of 491 questionnaires were sent and 107 were returned completed, of which 94 were usable: this represents a response rate of 21.8 per cent which compares favourably with the 18.8 per cent achieved by McIntyre and Coulthurst (1985) in their 1984[12] survey of medium-sized British companies.

As has commonly been found with surveys in this field (see Mills, 1988b), the results are not directly comparable with others previously reported. The sample surveyed in each case comes from a different population. For example, 81 per cent of the companies included in the current study[13] were larger than those of McIntyre and Coulthurst who used a sample of 'medium-sized' companies as defined in the Companies Act 1981.[14]

The 1980/81 study of Pike (1982), which covered the change in practices between 1975 and 1980/81, was based on the top 300 UK companies measured by market capitalization. In the analysis of their 1984 study, Mills and Herbert (1987, pp. 14–15), in an attempt to enable greater comparisons to be made

Table 2

Significance Levels for Differences Between the Earlier Studies Usage of DCF Techniques (Based on a One-tailed Test of Proportions)[a]

	Mills/ Herbert (1984)	Pike (1980/1) (1975)	McIntyre/ Coulthurst (1984)
IRR	99% ——————————	99%[b]	
	99.9% ——————————	99.9%	
	99.9% ————————————————————————————————		99.9%
		95% —— 95%	
		99.9% ————————————————	99.9%
		99% ————————————————	99%
NPV	95% ——————————	95%	
	99.9% ——————————	99.9%	
	99% ————————————————————————————————		99%
DCF	n/a[c]		
		99.9% ————————————————	99.9%
		95% ————————————————	95%

Notes:
[a] H1: larger companies make greater use of IRR/NPV/DCF techniques in general.
[b] For IRR usage, there is a 99 per cent significance level of difference between these two studies.
[c] No data is available on this for the Mills and Herbert study.

between their survey results and others, used three different criteria to define company size: capital expenditure; turnover; and profit before interest and tax.[15] Table 1 shows how the various studies can be compared in terms of company size using the first two of these criteria and the Companies Act definition.[16]

On the basis of the data contained in Table 1, it appears that Mills and Herbert's companies were relatively larger than those of Pike; both Pike, and Mills and Herbert, were dealing with larger companies than those in the current survey, and McIntyre and Coulthurst with smaller ones. It has been suggested by Pike and by Scapens et al. (1982) that there is an association between company size and the use of DCF techniques. This was confirmed by Mills and Herbert (1987, pp. 74—77) and is supported by McIntyre and Coulthurst's results. Table 2 shows the significance levels for differences in the usage of DCF techniques between the earlier studies (based on a one-tailed test of proportions).[17] The percentages appearing at the ends of each horizontal line give the level of statistical significance found between the two study groups concerned for the method being reported. It confirms these earlier findings and seems to suggest that the relationship is stronger in respect of IRR, than with NPV.

Table 3

Usage of Quantitative Evaluation
Methods Found in the Current Scottish
Large Company Study

	%	Rank
IRR	58	2
NPV	48	3
Payback	78	1
ARR	31	4
DCF	73[a]	

Note:
[a] NPV but not IRR [15 per cent] + IRR but not NPV
[25 per cent] + both NPV and IRR [33 per cent] = 73
per cent.

If there had been no change through time in the choice of approaches adopted, it would be expected that use of DCF techniques, particularly IRR, would be lower, whether as a primary[18] or secondary method, in the current study than in the case of Pike and (more markedly) of Mills and Herbert, as the current study companies are smaller. On the same basis, as the current study companies are larger than those in the McIntyre and Coulthurst study, use of DCF techniques would be expected to be higher in the former than in the latter.

Analysis of the data from the earlier studies revealed a statistically significant difference in the application of NPV between the large company study of Mills and Herbert and two smaller company studies: Pike (both data sets) and McIntyre and Coulthurst.

A comparison of the results from the two current Scottish studies revealed no significant difference in the frequency of usage of NPV between the large and small companies. It could be argued that the Scottish studies findings show that size may no longer have the major impact upon organizational practice that the above analysis of the earlier study data revealed. More specifically, as the relative size of the companies in the McIntyre and Coulthurst's 1985 study lies between those of the two Scottish studies: it may be appropriate to suggest that the 'size factor' is not relevant to any comparison of the use of NPV between the findings of McIntyre and Coulthurst and the current study. If this is the case, it may be that any differences between the current study and the earlier ones could be due, in part at least, to the impact of organisational change over time upon the choice of techniques selected.

Table 3 shows the proportion of companies in the current study using the main quantitative methods of investment appraisal, and their ranking.

Usage of Quantitative Evaluation Methods: Comparison with Other Studies

	Current Study 1989 %	McIntyre/ Coulthurst 1984 %	Mills/ Herbert 1984 %	Pike 1980/1 %	Pike 1975 %
IRR	58	28	68	54	42
NPV	48	36	51	38	32
Payback	78	82	78	79	71
ARR	31	33	44	51	51
DCF	73	45	—	69	60
Other	2	4	—	7	5
None	8	0	—	0	4

As can be seen, the most popular of these four methods is payback with 78 per cent usage among the companies. It is used by 34 per cent[19] more companies than IRR, the second most popular method. However, payback is used by only seven per cent more companies than DCF techniques in general (NPV, or IRR, or both). Table 3 is expanded in Table 4 to include the findings of the three earlier studies.

Comparison of the current study with McIntyre and Coulthurst's results in Table 4 reveals a statistically significant difference (based on a one-tailed test of proportions, at the 99.9 per cent confidence level) in the usage of the more sophisticated IRR technique. Table 5 shows the data and levels of significance of difference in respect of the McIntyre and Coulthurst study and both the large and small current company studies.

As can be seen, a statistically significant difference (at the 99 per cent confidence level) was found in the frequency of usage of IRR among the companies in the current study and those drawn from a population of companies smaller than those in McIntyre and Coulthurst's study (i.e. those in the Scottish small company study). This would seem to confirm that size is a relevant factor. Yet it is interesting to note that usage in the Scottish small company study was higher than in that of McIntyre and Coulthurst, and the degree of significance was lower (99 per cent as opposed to 99.9 per cent) — despite the McIntyre and Coulthurst study comprising larger companies. In addition, no statistically significant difference was found in the usage of NPV between the Scottish small company study and either of the others, yet, there is evidence of a statistically significant difference between the Scottish large company study and that of McIntyre and Coulthurst. On the basis of that result, it can be suggested that size may be a less significant factor than was previously the case. The difference in the usage of these techniques between the Scottish small

Table 5

Evaluation Methods Used: Comparison Between the Two Scottish Studies and that of McIntyre and Coulthurst

	Current Large Company Study (1989) %	McIntyre/ Coulthurst (1984) %	Current Small Company Study (1989) %
IRR	58	28	39
significance:[a]	99.9%_____99.9%		
	99% _____ 99%		
NPV	48	36	42
significance:[a]	95%_____95%		
Payback	78	82	56
significance:[b]		99.9% _____ 99.9%	
	99% _____ 99%		
ARR[c]	31	33	26
DCF	73	45	54
significance:[a]	99.9%_____99.9%		
	99% _____ 99%		

Notes:
[a] One-tailed test, H1: larger companies make greater use of IRR/NPV/DCF techniques in general.
[b] Two-tailed test H0: there is no significant difference in proportionate usage of a method between the studies.
[c] A two-tailed test of proportions revealed no statistically significant difference between these three studies in the usage of ARR.

A one-tailed test was used for the tests on IRR, NPV, and DCF as previous study findings had suggested that there may be a relationship between company size and technique selection. A two-tailed test was used to test the other methods as no such evidence existed to justify use of a one-tailed test.

company study and that of McIntyre and Coulthurst, might be ascribed to the impact of organisational change over the five years between the two studies: any previous effect of size having been reduced (IRR) or eliminated (NPV), as usage is greater in the former than in the latter, larger company-based study.

Size could, therefore, be held to have less relevance than was previously the case. Table 6 shows the results of one-tailed significance tests upon the differences between the earlier studies and the current Scottish large company study in respect of their usage of the DCF techniques.

Consideration of the results contained in Table 6 suggests that the use of IRR is no longer related to company size for companies of relative sizes ranging from that of the current study to that of Mills and Herbert's study. Size may remain a significant factor between companies from within that range and those smaller than it, though the previous analysis of the data from the Scottish small

Table 6

Significance Levels for Differences Between the Current Study and Each of the Earlier Studies in Respect of Usage of DCF Techniques (Based on a One-tailed Test of Proportions)[a]

	Mills/ Herbert (1984)	Pike (1980/1) (1975)	Current Study (1989)	McIntyre/ Coulthurst (1984)
IRR			99.9%_____	99.9%
NPV			95%_____	95%
DCF	n/a[b]		99.9%_____	99.9%

Notes:
[a] H1: larger companies make greater use of IRR/NPV/DCF techniques in general.
[b] No data is available on this for the Mills and Herbert study.

company study has suggested that any remaining relationship is weaker than was previously the case.

The NPV result also suggests that size may no longer be relevant to its selection. As Table 2 showed, there was a statistically significant difference between the Mills and Herbert study and both the Pike data points, but only at the 95 per cent level for the Pike 1980/81 data, as opposed to the 99.9 per cent level for the 1975 data: clearly this suggests that, even then, the impact of size was diminishing. Table 2 also revealed a statistically significant difference between the Mills and Herbert and McIntyre and Coulthurst studies which were both conducted in 1984. The relative difference in company size was marked and the result suggests that, for relative size differences of that magnitude, size was relevant to the choice of method made at that time. No statistically significant difference in usage of NPV between the Scottish small company study and any of the others was identified. This seems to suggest that there is now a different relationship between the use of NPV and company size from that previously reported. It may be that no relationship exists or, more plausibly, that the level of usage in each of the company size groupings has changed. Whichever is the case, any differences detected between the current and previous studies in the use of NPV is due to factors other than size, most likely arising out of the impact of organisational change over time.

DCF usage is derived directly from the usage of IRR and NPV. As a result, Tables 2, 5, and 6 reveal a similar picture for DCF to that they portray for these techniques individually.

If DCF techniques have previously been found to be used more by larger companies, it may be that the other techniques have previously been used more by smaller ones. This is supported by consideration of the Pike study data in Table 4 regarding payback. In the case of ARR, when comparing their results

Table 7

Significance Levels for Differences Between the Studies' Usage of Payback and ARR (Based on a Two-tailed Test of Proportions)[a]

	Mills/ Herbert (1984)	Pike (1980/1) (1975)	Current Study (1989)	McIntyre/ Coulthurst (1984)
Payback		95% _____		_____ 95%[b]
ARR	95% _____		95%	
		99% _____	99%	
		99% _____		99%
		99% _____	99%	
		99% _____		99%

Notes:
[a] H0: there is no significant difference in proportionate usage of a method between the studies.
[b] For Payback usage, there is a 95 per cent significance level of difference between these two studies.

with those of Pike, Mills and Herbert found that smaller firms (Pike's) used ARR more than larger ones (Mills and Herbert's). In their 1980 survey, Scapens et al. found that ARR was ranked lower in large companies and, when Mills and Herbert (1987, p. 23) compared their study (which involved relatively larger companies) to that of Scapens et al., they found that ARR was more popular with companies in the latter study. In order to determine whether such a relationship can be supported by the data, a one-tailed test of proportions on the differences between the studies' usage of payback and ARR was conducted. It revealed no statistically significant differences in the usage of ARR, and only one in respect of payback: at the 95 per cent level between the Pike 1975 data and that of McIntyre and Coulthurst. Were size a factor in determining the usage of payback then it would surely have been evidenced by the existence of a statistically significant difference between the usage of payback reported by the contemporaneous McIntyre and Coulthurst and Mills and Herbert studies. That none was found suggests that, as with ARR, there is no inverse relationship between company size and the usage of payback.

Examination of the data in Table 4 does suggest, however, that there may be statistically significant differences between the usage of these techniques among the studies. A two-tailed test of proportions on the differences in usage of payback and ARR was carried out. Table 7 shows the result.

The previously held view that size and the use of ARR are inversely related, would suggest that the current study, which dealt with smaller companies than those of Pike and Mills and Herbert, would have found ARR to have been used more than in either of these studies. The fact that the opposite was found (see Table 4), and that the difference found is statistically significant between the current and Pike studies (see Table 7), would seem to suggest that there has been a marked decline in the popularity of ARR since 1980. It also suggests that some of the difference between the 1980/81 and 1984 studies could have been due to the impact of organisational change rather than merely to company size, as was suggested by Mills and Herbert.

Payback usage is only statistically significantly different in one case: between the Pike 1975 data and that of McIntyre and Coulthurst. As had been found using a one-tailed test of proportions, the result shows a 95 per cent level of significance. Consideration of the result from the Scottish small company study (given in Table 5) indicates that size is probably a factor, but in the opposite direction to that suggested by the Pike 1975 data. Payback is the most used method within the Scottish small company study, but, as with all the methods, it is less used by the companies in that study than by those in the Scottish large company study. It may be that previous analysis, which suggested the existence of a relationship between size and usage, may no longer be applicable to companies of size ranging from those in the McIntyre and Coulthurst study to those in the study by Mills and Herbert. It seems that size is a factor when considering difference in usage of payback between companies lying within that size range and smaller ones, but that it is a positive relationship, rather than the inverse one previously suggested.

Thus, analysis of the data in Table 4 leads to the conclusion that there appears to have been an erosion in the impact that company size has upon the selection of appraisal criteria: there may have been a 'trickle down' effect — the largest companies used the more sophisticated techniques first, then the next largest, then the next largest, etc. There is far greater usage of the DCF techniques evidenced by the current study than would have been the case had the size relationship been as before and nothing else changed. There is also far less usage of ARR than would have been suggested by the findings of previous studies relating size to usage. These results suggest that companies have been experiencing organisational change of a type which has led to a change in the selection of appraisal criteria. The hypothesis that this change may be derived from the information technology explosion of the last decade, along with an improvement in the general level of education of decision makers, matches these results and would account for the changes identified. These changes would apply to all companies and it is probable that usage has also changed in companies of the size studied by Mills and Herbert, and Pike. Indeed, this would need to have happened if size is still a relevant factor in the selection of appraisal criteria by the larger company. This analysis of the current study results suggests that size difference cannot explain differences in criteria selection between it and the earlier studies. A survey of companies of the size of those studied by Mills and Herbert will be required before this point can be determined.

While the selection of those appraisal methods which a company may apply appears to have changed since the earlier studies were undertaken, this will 'have had a major impact on the decisions being made only if the change is

Table 8

Comparisons of Primary Quantitative Method Usage (Using a Two-tailed Test of Proportions)[a]

	Current Study 1989 %	Mills/ Herbert 1984 %	Pike 1980/1 %
Payback	48(1)[b]	38(2)	32(2 =)
significance:	95%_____95%		
IRR	23(2)	43(1)	41(1)
significance	99%_____99%		
	99%_____99%		
NPV[c]	17(3)	21(3)	17(4)
ARR	14(4)	20(4)	32(2 =)
significance:	99.9%_____99.9%		
		95%_____95%	
	102[d]	122[d]	122[d]

Notes:

[a] HO: there is no significant difference in proportionate usage of a method between the studies.

[b] The number in brackets indicates the primary ranking of each method.

[c] No statistically significant difference was found between the ranking of NPV in these three studies.

[d] The totals exceed 100 because some companies ranked more than one method first.

reflected in the primary (i.e. most important) method applied. This is the method which has the greatest impact when vetting an investment proposal. It will often be the first whose results are consulted, leading to preliminary acceptance/rejection. It may be the only method used in many instances as the project which 'fails' according to the method's criteria may be discarded prior to its being reviewed in terms of other methods. Only those projects which are acceptable under the primary method may be subject to analysis by any other. Even where other methods are applied concurrently with, or before the primary method, it will be the latter which determines whether the project should be considered. The proportionate selection of primary method is shown in Table 8.

It can be seen that the choice in the current study is different from that in the others. Indeed, the difference between the current study and that of Pike is statistically significant, using a two-tailed test of proportions, at the 99 per cent level for IRR, 99.9 per cent for ARR and 95 per cent for payback. The IRR difference identified between the current and Mills and Herbert studies is statistically significant at 99 per cent. The current study found that more than twice as many companies ranked payback as the primary method as any other method. IRR, which was the most popular primary method in the other studies, was found to be in second place. It may be that this difference in ranking between payback and IRR is due, in part, to the difference in company size: the relatively smaller companies in the current study preferring to use the 'cheaper' payback technique rather than the more sophisticated IRR technique.

The analysis of the data in Table 4 suggested that IRR is being used more by companies than was previously the case. The data in Table 8 suggests that this change in usage may have involved IRR being used as a secondary method where previously it was not used at all.

The different primary usage of ARR shown in the Mills and Herbert and Pike surveys (20 and 32 per cent respectively) was attributed to different relative company size (see Mills and Herbert, 1987, pp. 26–27). When comparing their results with those of Pike, Mills and Herbert found that smaller firms (Pike's) gave ARR primary ranking more often than larger ones (Mills and Herbert's). These earlier findings suggested that size and the use of ARR as a primary method are inversely related. A one-tailed test of proportions supported this hypothesis at the 99 per cent confidence level for the difference between ARR ranking in the Pike, and Mills and Herbert studies. On that basis, the current survey, which dealt with smaller companies than the others in Table 8, would have found ARR to have been used more as a primary method than in either of the other two studies. The fact that the opposite was found, and that the difference was statistically significant, would suggest confirmation of the conclusion reached upon consideration of the results shown in Table 7: that there has been a marked decline in the popularity of ARR since 1980. Again, it may suggest that some of the difference between the 1980/81 and 1984 studies could have been due to the impact of organisational change rather than merely to company size, as was suggested by Mills and Herbert.

The Scottish small company study also found that payback had the highest primary ranking (42 per cent). McIntyre and Coulthurst's study involved the smallest companies of all the other studies. It does not include information on primary method selection. However, in those companies which use a single criterion only, they found that payback was most frequently used. Payback was the second most popular primary method identified by Mills and Herbert and Pike (though it was the most popular overall method in both these studies: see Table 4). This seems to suggests that payback is more likely to be the primary method in smaller companies, than in larger ones.

When decision makers claim to use more than one method, it is the primary method which is used to perform the initial vetting of the proposal. The other methods being applied, as appropriate, either to perform further vetting, or to provide further analysis which can be added to that resulting from the primary method analysis. For example, a decision maker whose primary and secondary methods were NPV and payback respectively, may vet the proposal using NPV and, if acceptable, then check that it was within his payback criterion of, for example, payback within three years. Were the importance of the two methods to be switched, for example, as a result of a change in company policy arising out of an increase in interest rates, then the sequence of application would be reversed. The lower the importance rating of a criterion, the less it would be applied in the appraisal process: only being used when circumstances required. For example, if ARR is ranked fourth it would probably only be used when the other criteria were unable to differentiate between mutually exclusive alternatives. Even where the primary method is not the first applied, by definition, it will always have precedence over the other methods in determining acceptance/rejection.

Thus, the key in any combinatorial application lies mainly in the selection of primary method. The lower the importance placed upon a criterion within a combination of criteria, the less its impact will be upon the appraisal process. Nevertheless, all criteria included in a combination will be applied when appropriate and their selection within that combination indicates that some faith is placed in their ability to assist in the appraisal process.[20] The use of more than one criterion is indicative of caution. Prudence would suggest that the more methods used in the appraisal process, the better, because the possibility of an inappropriate decision being taken is reduced as the number of checks implemented is increased. Organisations are changing: they are becoming more sophisticated, have available a vastly improved range of decision making aids, and their managers are becoming better educated. It is possible that, as a consequence of these organisational changes, criteria are now being applied, where previously they were not (see the previous discussion regarding primary method selection of IRR), and that greater care is now being taken to ensure that the most appropriate decisions are taken. The usage of the various combinations of the four main methods is shown in Table 9.

Analysis of this table revealed a statistically significant difference in the number of methods used by companies between the current study and that of McIntyre and Coulthurst (using a two-tailed test of proportions, at the 99 per cent level for two or more methods, and at the 99.9 per cent level for three or more methods). A similar result was found between the Pike 1980 data and the McIntyre and Coulthurst study, though the significance levels were switched to 99.9 per cent and 99 per cent respectively for the two-or-more and three-or-more method sets. No statistically significant difference was found between the current study and either of the Pike study dates. Nor was any found between the two Pike study dates.

In the current study, 23.5 per cent of the firms surveyed are shown to use a single evaluation method, the main method, as in Pike's 1980/81 study, being payback. The use of two methods at 25.5 per cent is considerably lower than that found by Pike (37 per cent) and, whereas he found that a combination of payback and ARR was as popular as one of payback and IRR, only the latter combination is found to be a popular choice in the current study. It is interesting to note that nothing was found in the current survey to substantiate

Table 9

Comparisons of the Frequency of the Use of Combinations of the Quantitative Evaluation Methods

	Current Study 1989 %	McIntyre/ Coulthurst 1984 %	Pike 1980/1 %	Pike 1975 %
No Method	8	0	0	4
Single Method				
Payback	14	37	11	12
ARR	2	4	8	14
IRR	4.5	2	4	6
NPV	3	4	3	1
	23.5	47	26	33
Two Methods				
Payback + ARR	3	12	12	10.5
Payback + IRR	13	5	12	10.5
Payback + NPV	6.5	10	6	5
ARR + IRR	2	—	3	1
ARR + NPV	1	2	1	2
IRR + NPV	—	2	3	3
	25.5	31	37	32
Three Methods				
Payback + ARR + IRR	5.5	2	10	7
Payback + ARR + NPV	4.5	2	6	6
Payback + IRR + NPV	20	5	10	8
ARR + IRR + NPV	1	—	1	1
	31	9	27	22
Four Methods				
Payback + ARR + IRR + NPV	12	13	10	9

McIntyre and Coulthurst's findings that NPV was more popular than IRR and that a combination of payback and NPV was a popular choice when two methods only were used. (Theirs was the only UK survey to have found this.)

The trend shown between Pike's two time points, whereby the use of two methods rose from 32 to 37 per cent, is clearly reversed and replaced by a shift towards the greater use of three and four methods. Analysis of the three-method use reveals a higher result in the current survey than in Pike's 80/81 data (31 per cent as against 27 per cent) and a clear change in emphasis with one combination, payback with IRR and NPV, being almost four times more common than any of the others. Pike had found this combination to be of equal

Table 10

Methods Adopted in Multiple Usage Companies: Comparison of Study Results

	Current Study 1989 %	McIntyre/ Coulthurst 1984 %	Pike 1980/1 %
Payback	94	94	89
ARR	42	57	57
IRR	78	51	66
NPV	66	64	51
DCF	95	77	85

frequency with that of payback with IRR and ARR. This again points to the reduction in the usage of ARR which was identified earlier.

One difference between the current survey and that of McIntyre and Coulthurst is striking. Their survey showed that 47 per cent of companies used a single method, compared to half that number (23.5 per cent) in the current study. (A two-tailed test of proportions found this to be statistically significant at the 99.9 per cent level, as was the difference in the levels of three method usage between these two studies.) This difference could be due to the different relative size of the companies in the two surveys but, as 18 per cent of the companies in the current survey were of the same relative size as the McIntyre and Coulthurst companies, this hypothesis would require that only 18.34 per cent of the other companiës in the current survey used a single method.[21] The Scottish small company study found 28 per cent usage of a single method and this would seem to confirm that, during the five years which have elapsed since the McIntyre and Coulthurst survey was undertaken, companies have increased the number of methods they apply — i.e. more data are now being generated to be used in the capital investment decision making process than was previously the case.

Table 9 also reveals that the position regarding ARR shown in Table 4, whereby the usage of ARR remained virtually unchanged between McIntyre and Coulthurst's study and the current one (33 and 31 per cent respectively), concealed the true picture. It is virtually unused by companies using a single method and only 25 per cent[22] of those using two methods are found to include it: this compares with 44 per cent of companies using two methods in the McIntyre and Coulthurst study and 42 per cent of those using two methods at both the Pike study dates. It is used now mainly in combination with two,

Table 11

Method Usage Comparison: Multiple Usage Companies (m) and Single Usage Companies (s)

	Current Study 1989		McIntyre/ Coulthurst 1984		Pike 1980/1	
	m%	s%	m%	s%	m%	s%
Payback	94	59	94	77	89	44
ARR	42	9	57	9	57	31
IRR	78	18	51	5	66	15
NPV	66	14	64	9	51	10
DCF	95	32	77	14	85	26

or all three of the others. Thus, while its overall usage is not statistically significantly different between the current and McIntyre and Coulthurst studies, the way in which it is used has changed.

The proportional usage of the four main methods by companies which apply more than one method is shown in Table 10.

It reveals that those companies using more than one of these methods — 69 per cent[23] (1989); 52 per cent (1984); and 74 per cent (1980/81) — appear to be making greater use of NPV (29 per cent increase since 1980/81), IRR (18 per cent), DCF in general (12 per cent) and payback (6 per cent), and less use of ARR (26 per cent decrease). Payback seems to have established itself as virtually a mandatory method whenever more than one method is to be used: this is a not unexpected situation given its historical popularity, its simplicity and the increasing awareness of the importance of cash flow management in business today.

Table 11 expands on the analysis of Table 10 to show the comparison between those companies that use more than one method, and those that use a single one.

All three studies show that companies which use more than one of these methods make far greater use of the DCF techniques than those that restrict themselves to one method only. (The current study shows, for the first time, that DCF among companies using multiple methods is more popular than payback, though only just and certainly not significantly so.) Such a result is only to be expected if it is assumed that lack of the use of multiple methods is partly due to an unwillingness to apply the more sophisticated methods; that is to say, the likelihood that more sophisticated methods will be used increases as more methods are used in combination. The increase in usage of these techniques is also not unexpected in the light of the growth in the availability and sophistication of computer spreadsheet packages, capable of easily performing whatever data analysis decision makers choose. Prior to 1979, such analysis was typically performed by hand. It was time consuming, repetitive, tedious to produce, and prone to error. There was considerable disincentive to apply DCF techniques and evidence exists that suggests that managers were also rejecting these techniques because of ignorance surrounding their application and suitability (see Pike, 1982, pp. 53–54). It is not surprising, now the psychological and educational barriers to their use have been removed and lifted, that the application of DCF techniques appears to be increasing.

Table 11 also suggests that even the companies using a single method might be moving towards the more sophisticated methods. A comparison between the current survey and that of McIntyre and Coulthurst reveals a difference in single method usage which cannot be entirely due to the difference in the relative sizes of the companies. The difference in single method usage between the current study and Pike's cannot be the result of company size difference as the change in the usage of DCF techniques is an increase, not a decrease on that shown by Pike.

SUMMARY OF FINDINGS

The current survey set out to examine the usage of quantitative techniques for capital investment appraisal in Scotland's largest companies and the results can be summarised as follows:

1. payback is the most popular method, then IRR, followed by NPV and, finally, ARR;
2. DCF techniques are almost as widely used as payback and, in companies using more than one of the four methods, the DCF approach may be more popular than payback;
3. IRR is more popular than NPV despite the theoretical superiority of the latter;
4. over 40 per cent of the companies surveyed use three or four methods;
5. ARR is mainly used with other methods: it is used by only nine per cent of those companies using a single method.

Comparisons with earlier studies suggest that:

(a) ARR is being used less than previously;
(b) DCF techniques are gaining in popularity;
(c) NPV is increasing in popularity at a faster rate than IRR;
(d) payback is consolidating its position as the most used of the four methods;
(e) individual companies are using more of the methods than previously;
(f) Mills and Herbert's findings that there is some association between size and the use of DCF techniques were not borne out by the current study: it appears that there has been an increase in usage among smaller

companies which has resulted in the erosion of this previously identified relationship;

(g) previous findings that suggested an inverse relationship existed between size and the use of ARR may no longer be valid.

So far as these findings are concerned: the reasons why payback remains popular despite its theoretical limitations have been covered elsewhere, both empirically (see, for example, Pike, 1982) and theoretically (see, for example, Van Horne, 1986, p. 130). The decline of ARR has been advocated for some time. The only surprise is that its demise has taken so long to come about. Although almost one third of the companies surveyed continue to use it, they do so more as an additional criterion measure rather than as the principal criterion. The move towards increased use of DCF techniques was expected. The fact that there is also evidence of a possible shift in emphasis towards NPV suggests that rather more than simply organisational change fuelled by the growth of information technology is the cause. A change in attitude towards the more theoretically sound of the DCF techniques would seem to indicate that managers are becoming more aware of the theoretical advantages of NPV, in relation to IRR. If one accepts that the theoreticians are correct, the quality of managerial decision making should be being enhanced as a result.[24]

CONCLUSIONS

As already stated, comparisons with other studies in this area are difficult. All the studies are different in terms of the method of analysis used, the population sampled, and, to a lesser extent, the questions asked.[25]

Mills and Herbert were at least partially successful in their attempt to overcome these difficulties through the alignment of their survey research to that of Pike and of Scapens and Sale (1981). While direct comparison between the survey results remained imprecise, they were able to adopt the size definitions applied to test for association between company size and the use of DCF techniques for their own survey data and thereby confirmed the previous studies' findings. However, it was not possible to eliminate overlap of size between the studies (see Mills and Herbert, 1987, p. 14) and it therefore proved impossible for them to state more than that one study concerned *proportionally* larger companies than another. In addition, they failed to undertake much of the analysis performed in the other studies (for example, the data contained in Table 9 above).

This analysis has attempted to overcome these difficulties by identifying where each study lies in a company size continuum ranging from the largest (Mills and Herbert) to the smallest (McIntyre and Coulthurst) — see Table 1 — and then repeating previously reported tests on the data from these past and the current studies. The relationship between size and technique selection previously identified was not disputed, except where evidence exists to challenge the hypothesis, as in the comparison between the current and McIntyre and

Coulthurst studies. Pike had suggested that organisational changes had occurred between 1975 and 1980/81. The later studies had ignored this factor, preferring to pursue the size hypothesis. This study reopens the question of the impact of organisational change upon the choice of technique selected. It has tested the accepted size hypothesis in order to demonstrate that technique selection has changed, and that such change could be the result of information technology led, and 'costly truth' motivated, organisational change. In doing so, it has shown that the situation has changed, for otherwise the size hypothesis could never have been valid: companies of the size examined in the current study are using more sophisticated techniques, more techniques overall, and are making less use of the less theoretically valid ARR technique than would have been expected from the results of earlier studies.

Conclusions drawn can only be directly related to companies of the size the current study examined and, until one of the studies is repeated using similar survey populations, questions *and* analysis methods, conclusions cannot be drawn regarding changing attitudes and practices of companies outwith the size covered in the current study. Nevertheless, it is illogical to suggest that such change will not have occurred. The inference from the current study results is that change has probably occurred in companies of all sizes. However, the exact nature of that change will remain unknown until further research is carried out.

It is plausible that these changes are the result of the expansion of facilities based on information technology (i.e. computers and computer packages), for this is an area of management decision making which ideally lends itself to these developments. It is also possible that the growth in management education in recent years has led to the more theoretically sound techniques being adopted to a greater degree than previously, particularly in response to the increased need to appear to objectify decisions of this type. Whatever the cause, it is clear that there has been a change and that there is a move towards greater use of the more sophisticated techniques. It also appears that the earlier work on the impact of size may have been subject to organisational change between the various survey dates. It would seem that further research in this area would be appropriate, particularly as the vastly reduced cost of hardware and software has, among other things, made the use of DCF techniques a relatively straightforward task for even the smallest of companies. A facility which may eventually contribute to the complete erosion of the relationship between size and the selection of quantitative appraisal techniques.

NOTES

1   For a fuller analysis, see Laughlin (1991).
2   For a fuller analysis see Carnall (1990, p. 141).
3   The information technolgy industry has been improving its fundamental technological cost performance at 30 to 40 per cent compound annually for the last thirty years — see Benjamin

and Scott Morton (1988). This has contributed to an enormous growth in the use of information technology over that period. This growth can be illustrated by findings such as those of Gurbaxani and Mendelson (1990) who found that data processing expenditure in the US (in 1972 dollars) rose from $30 billion in 1975 to $59 billion in 1987 — allowing for a 30 per cent compound cost performance growth factor, the 1987 figure bought the performance equivalent of $1,375 billion in 1975, i.e. a 45-fold purchased performance growth over the actual 1975 purchase. Of more direct relevance to the current study, Brancheau and Weatherbe's (1990) study of spreadsheet adoption among 500 professionals working in corporate finance and accounting departments showed a rise in usage of over 900 per cent, from a base of 35 users in 1981 to over 300 in 1987.

4   See, for example, Merrett and Sykes (1973, pp. 92–102).
5   See, for example, Levy and Sarnat (1986, p. 90).
6   See, for example, Hopwood et al. (1990, p. 69).
7   When the words 'large' and 'small' are used to differentiate the two Scottish studies, it is purely in the dictionary sense; there is no intention to suggest any more than that, on the basis of turnover, the companies in the 'large' study were larger than those in the 'small' study.
8   The aim was to determine overall usage, rather than specific usage in relation to, for example, types of investments, ranges of funding, or levels of risk.
9   See, for example, Ross and Westerfield (1988, pp. 282–84).
10 The companies in the Scottish 'small' company study were all drawn at random from a population comprising companies which would be defined as 'small' under the Companies Act definition (see note 11 for details of this definition). A total of 303 questionnaires were sent, of which 68 useable returns were received: a response rate of 22.4 per cent.
11 When a company satisfies two or more of the conditions relating to a size category then it is defined as coming within that category. The categories in May 19990 were:

	Small	Medium	Large
Turnover	≤£1.4m	≤£5.75m	>£5.75m
Gross Assets	≤£0.7m	≤£2.8m	>£2.8m
Employees	≤50	≤250	>250

12 The date given for each of the surveys mentioned in this article is the year during which it was conducted. This has been done in order to highlight the time interval between surveys rather than, as has been the practice, that between the date of publication of their results.
13 The terms 'current study' and 'Scottish large company study' are interchanged throughout, the latter being used, where appropriate, to differentiate between it and the Scottish 'small' company study.
14 There was no difference in the values used in the definitions of size between the 1981 and (original) 1985 Companies Acts. The McIntyre and Coulthurst study used 1982 data to determine company size, the current study used 1986 data. Between the two year ends, the Retail Price Index rose by 20.74 per cent (from 325.5 to 393). Applying this indexation factor to the 1985 Companies Act size bands given in note 11, in order that a truer comparison may be achieved with the earlier McIntyre and Coulthurst study, produces the following:

	Small	Medium	Large
Turnover	≤£1.69m	≤£6.94m	>£6.94m
Gross Assets	≤£0.85m	≤£3.38m	>£3.38m
Employees	≤50	≤250	>250

The indexed and non-indexed size groupings for the current study are therefore:

	Small	Medium	Large
Indexed	1.2%	17.7%	81.1%
Non-indexed	0.6%	14.8%	84.6%

All references to the comparative sizes of the companies in these two studies use the index-based definition.

15

	Small	Medium	Large
Capital Expenditure	<£ 20m	£ 20m– 50m	>£ 50m
Turnover	<£250m	£250m–750m	>£750m
Profit before Interest and Tax	<£ 25m	£ 25m– 75m	>£ 75m

16   The turnover levels used to determine company size used by Mills and Herbert (see note 15) are approximately 200 times greater than those of the Companies Act (see note 11). Almost all the companies in the current study which were classified as 'large' according to the Companies Act criterion were classified as 'medium' or 'small' under the Mills and Herbert turnover criterion.

17   A test of proportions was used for significance testing throughout. A Chi-square test was also conducted in each case, with broadly similar results.

18   The 'primary' method is that which the survey respondents indicated was the most important. (The current, Pike, and Mills and Herbert studies all specifically asked for this information — see note 25.)

19   78/58 = 1.34 ⇒ difference in usage of 34 per cent. This approach is adopted throughout whenever percentages are compared.

20   For examples of how companies use multiple methods in practice, see Pike (1982, pp. 86—95).

21   For every 100 companies in the current survey, 18 are of the same size as those in McIntyre and Coulthurst's survey; 47 per cent of 18 = 8.46. If nothing has changed between the two survey dates, 8.46 per cent of the current survey companies would be expected to use a single method because they are of the same size as those in the McIntyre and Coulthurst survey. That would mean that 18.34 per cent[(23.5 per cent−8.46 per cent)/82] of the other companies in the current survey used a single method.

22   Table 9 gives this to be 23.5 per cent and that for McIntyre and Coulthurst as 45.2 per cent: these differences are due to rounding.

23   Table 9 gives this to be 68.5 per cent and that for McIntyre and Coulthurst as 53 per cent: these differences are due to rounding.

24   No evidence exists to support the hypothesis that the adoption of the more sophisticated techniques brings about superior performance. Nevertheless, if these methods are more sound theoretically, all other things being equal, their use should provide the opportunity to achieve a superior performance. In addition, Moore and Reichert (1989) found that managerial sophistication, as reflected by the adoption of selected analytical practices and widespread encouragement of the use of microcomputers for financial analysis, positively affects the likelihood of better than average firm performance.

25   The current study questions were based upon those in the Pike study. All the studies used broadly similar questions though, as can be seen below, those of Mills and Herbert and McIntyre and Coulthurst went into more detail than the others in the principal question. Interestingly, McIntyre and Coulthurst did not include any request for ranking. The principal question in each survey was:

Current study
In evaluating capital investment proposals please indicate the method(s) used and rank the importance of each using 1 for the most important, 2 for the next, etc:
(a) Payback
(b) Internal rate of return
(c) Net present value
(d) Accounting rate of return
(e) Others (please list)

Pike
What investment appraisal criteria do you use? (Please indicate priorities by giving a 1 to the most important, 2 the the next etc.)
(a) Payback period
(b) Average rate of return
(c) Discounting — internal rate of return
(d) Discounting — net present value
(e) Other; please specify

Mills and Herbert
What financial analysis techniques are most often used in your organisation to appraise divisional capital projects?: (if more than one technique is used please indicate the importance of each by giving a 1 to the most important, 2 to the next, etc.)

(1) Net present value
(2) Internal rate of return
(3) Accounting rate of return
(4) Payback period
(5) Qualitative/non-financial
(6) Other, please specify

McIntyre and Coulthurst
Please indicate the evaluation formula/formulae which you usually use for evaluating the
prospective returns on your projects: *Few*   *Most*   *All*
                                          Projects   *Projects*   *Projects*

Payback
DCF: IRR
DCF:NPV
Accounting rate of return
Other: please specify

REFERENCES

Benjamin, R.I. and M.S. Scott Morton (1988), 'Information Technology, Integration, and Organizational Change', *Interfaces*, Vol. 18, No. 3 (1988), pp. 86–98.
Brancheau, J.C. and J.C. Wetherbe (1990), 'The Adoption of Spreadsheet Software: Testing Innovation Diffusion Theory in the Context of End-user Computing', *Information Systems Research*, Vol. 1, No. 1 (1990), pp. 115–143.
Carnall, C.A. (1990), *Managing Change in Organizations* (Hemel Hemptstead: Prentice Hall International (UK) Ltd., 1990).
Gurbaxani, V. and H. Mendelson (1990), 'An Integrative Model of Information Systems Spending Growth', *Information Systems Research*, Vol. 1, No. 2 (1990), pp. 23–46.
Hopwood, A. (1990), 'Accounting and Organisation Change', *Accounting, Auditing and Accountability*, Vol. 3, No. 1 (1990), pp. 7–17.
_____, M. Page and S. Turley (1990), *Understanding Accounting in a Changing Environment* (Hemel Hempstead: Prentice-Hall International (UK) Ltd., 1990).
Jordan & Sons (1987), *Scotland's Top 500 Companies, 1987* (Bristol: Jordan & Sons Ltd., 1987).
Kim, S.H., T. Crick and S.H. Kim (1986), 'Do Executives Practice What Academics Preach?', *Management Accounting* (USA), (November 1986), pp. 49–52.
Laughlin, R.C. (1991), 'Environmental Disturbances and Organisational Transitions and Transformations: Some Alternative Models', *Organizational Studies*, Vol. 12, No. 2 (1991), pp. 209–232.
Levy, H. and M. Sarnat (1986), *Capital Investment and Financial Decisions*, 3rd edition (London: Prentice-Hall International (UK) Ltd., 1986).
McIntyre, A.D. and N.J. Coulthurst (1985), 'Theory and Practice in Capital Budgeting', *British Accounting Review* (Autumn 1985), pp. 24–70.
Merrett A.J. and A. Sykes (1973), *Capital Budgeting and Company Finance*, 2nd edition (London: Longman Group Ltd., 1973).
Mills, R.W. (1988a). 'Capital Budgeting Techniques Used in the UK and the USA', *Management Accounting*, Vol. 61, No. 1 (1988), p. 26.
_____ (1988b), 'Capital Budgeting — the State of the Art', *Long Range Planning* (August 1988), pp. 76–81.
_____ and P.J.A. Herbert (1987), *Corporate and Divisional Influence in Capital Budgeting* (London: CIMA, 1987).
Moore, J.S. and A.K. Reichert (1989), 'A Multivariate Study of Firm Performance and the Use of Modern Analytical Tools and Financial Techniques', *Interfaces*, Vol. 19, No. 3 (1989), pp. 79–87.
Pike, R.H. (1982), *Capital Budgeting in the 1980s* London: CIMA, 1982).

Ross, S.A. and R.W. Westerfield (1988), *Corporate Finance* (St Louis: Times Mirror/Mosby Publishing, 1988).

Scapens R.W. (1985), *Management Accounting: A Review of Recent Developments* (London: MacMillan Publishers Ltd., 1985).

_____ and J.T. Sale (1981), 'Performance Measurement and Formal Capital Expenditure Controls in Divisionalised Companies', *Journal of Business Finance & Accounting* (Autumn 1981), pp. 389–419.

_____ _____ and P.A. Tikkas (1982), *Financial Control of Divisional Capital Investment* (London: CIMA, 1982).

Van Horne, J.C. (1986), *Financial Management and Policy*, 7th edition (London: Prentice-Hall International (UK) Ltd., 1986).

Chapter 3

Advanced Capital Budgeting

INTRODUCTION

This chapter expands the previous chapter, covering the principles of capital budgeting. It covers the advanced issues of replacement decisions, capital rationing, capital budgeting under uncertainty, and capital budgeting under inflation.

REPLACEMENT DECISIONS

The examples used to illustrate capital budgeting techniques were based on expansion projects. The analysis for replacement projects is slightly different. The following sections illustrate the replacement decision first where the lives of the projects are equal and, second, where the lives of the projects are unequal.

Replacement Decisions: Equal Lives

Assume that a machine purchased ten years ago by the Litton Company at a cost of $20,000 had an expected twenty-year useful life when purchased and zero salvage value. A straight-line depreciation charge of $2,000 makes the machine's present book value equal to $10,000. A new machine now being considered to replace the old one can be purchased for $30,000 and is expected to reduce operating costs from $10,000 to $4,000 for its ten-year useful life. The old machine can be sold for $4,000. The new machine is expected to have a $6,000 salvage value. Taxes are 48 percent, and an investment tax credit of

Exhibit 3.1
Replacement Decision Analysis

	Amount before tax	Effect, Net Of Taxes	Time Even Occurs	PV Factor at 12%
1 Cost of the New Machine	$30,000	$30,000	0	1.0
2 Salvage Value of Old Machine	($4,000)	($4,000)	0	1.0
3 Tax Effect of Sale of Old Machine[a]	($6,000)	($2,880)	0	1.0
4 Investment Tax Credit	($3,000)	($3,000)	0	1.0
5 Total Present Value of Outflows				

Net Inflows of the Life of the New Machine (t = 1 to 10)

6 Decrease in Operating Costs[b]	$6,000	$3,120 1 to 10		5.650
7 Depreciation on New Machine	$2,400 --------------	-----------	----------	
8 Depreciation on Old Machine	$1,000 --------------	-----------	----------	
9 Net Changes in Tax Savings from Depreciation	$1,400	$672 1 to 10		5.650
10 Salvage Value of New Machine	$6,000	$6,000 1 to 10		0.322
11 Total Present Value of Inflows				
12 NPV = $23,357 - $20,120 = $3,237				

[a]The tax effect of sale of old machine: Loss $\times t = [(\$10,000 - \$4,000) \times 0.48] = \$2,880$
[b]Cost reduction: Decrease in cost $\times (1 - t) = \$4,000(1 - 0.48) = \$2,080$

10 percent of the purchase price can be claimed on the purchase of the new machine. The cost of capital is 12 percent. Should the Litton Company replace the old machine?

The NPV of the replacement decision, computed in Exhibit 3.1 is $3,237. The new machine should be purchased to replace the old machine, given that it increases the value of the firm by $3,237.

Replacement Decisions: Unequal Lives

The procedure generally used to choose between two mutually exclusive replacement proposals with unequal lives is to convert the number of years of analysis to a common termination year through a series of *replacement chains*. For example, to choose between a four-year project X and a six-year project Y, it is necessary to compare a three-chain cycle for project X and a two-chain cycle for project Y, bringing the common termination year to 12.

Assume that the Shields Company is considering replacing a fully depreciated machine with one of two replacement machines. Machine X has a cost of $15,000, a five-year useful life, and will generate after-tax cash flow of $5,000 per year for five years. Machine Y has a cost of $18,000, a ten-year useful life, and will generate after-tax cash flows of $4,000 per year for ten years. The company's cost of capital is 12 percent.

To determine which machine should be chosen, the NPV of each machine can be computed:

NPV (X) = $5,000(3.605) − $15,000 = $3,025.
NPV (Y) = $4,000(5.650) − $18,000 = $4,600.

From these computations it appears that machine Y should be chosen. The analysis is incorrect, however, since a second investment can be made after five years if machine X is chosen, and the second investment may be profitable. A better analysis would be based on the common denominator of ten years. Therefore,

$$
\begin{array}{ccc}
& \text{Present value} & \text{Present value} \\
\text{NPV (X)} = & \text{of first investment} & + \quad \text{of second investment} \\
& \text{of machine X} & \text{of machine Y} \\
& = \$3,025 + \$3,025(0.567) & = \$4,740. \\
\text{NPV (Y)} = & & = \$4,600.
\end{array}
$$

The NPV of machine X is $4,740, which is higher than the NPV of machine Y.

CAPITAL RATIONING

Capital rationing exists when a firm faces limited supplies of funds, which precludes the acceptance of potentially profitable projects. Among the causes cited for capital rationing are (1) limits imposed on new borrowing, (2) a debt limit imposed by an outside agreement (for example, bond covenants), (3) limits on capital spending imposed on divisional management, and (4) management's desire to maintain a given dividend policy or a specific earnings-per-share or price/earnings ratio.

Conventional methods of evaluation with capital rationing consist of (1) ranking the projects under consideration from highest to lowest for whichever evaluation model is used, that is, IRR, NPV, or the profitability index (PI); and (2) selecting projects starting at the top of the ranking until funds are exhausted. Although these conventional methods based on either the IRR or the NPV techniques are simple, discontinuities or size disparities between projects prevent the choice of optimal projects. For example, a 20 percent return on $1,000 is considered better than a 15 percent return on $2,000, according to the conventional capital rationing method.

To correct the limitations of the conventional capital rationing methods, mathematical programming can be used to select the optimal combination of projects. In 1955, James H. Lorie and Leonard J. Savage were the first to suggest mathematical programming—in the form of a heuristic programming approach to deal with capital rationing. This attempt was followed by a more comprehensive treatment of the problem by H. Martin Weingartner, whose basic model follows:

Maximize

$$
\sum_{j=1}^{m} b_j X_j,
$$

Exhibit 3.2
Capital Rationing Example

Investment Proposal	Present Value of Outlay (Period 1)	Present Value of Outlay (Period 2)	NPV
1	$10	$5	$20
2	$20	$10	$30
3	$30	$10	$40
4	$40	$30	$50

subject to

$$\sum_{j=1}^{m} C_{tj}X_j \leq C_t \text{ for } t = 1, \ldots, n.$$

$$0 \leq X_j \leq 1.$$

X_j is an integer,
where

> b_j = Net present value of investment proposal j.
> X_j = 0 if the project is accepted, and 1 if the project is rejected.
> C_{tj} = Net cash need for proposal j in period t.
> C_t = Total budget for period t.

Because of the use of the last two constraints, this mathematical programming model is known as *integer programming*.

To illustrate the integer programming approach to capital budgeting, let us use the data shown in Exhibit 3.2. The present values of the two budget constraints are $90 in period 1 and $30 in period 2. The model will look like the following:
  Maximize

$$20x_1 + 20x_2 + 40x_3 + 50x_4$$

Subject to

$$10x_1 + 20x_2 + 30x_3 + 40x_4 \leq 90.$$
$$5x_1 + 10x_2 + 10x_3 + 30x_4 \leq 30.$$
$$0 \leq X_j \leq 1 \text{ for } j = 1, 2, 3, \text{ and } 4.$$

X_j is an integer.

CAPITAL BUDGETING UNDER UNCERTAINTY

Nature of Risk

Because the cash flows of a project often may be estimated on the basis of incomplete information, the capital budgeting evaluation must be performed in a climate of uncertainty. Although *uncertainty* and *risk* are sometimes used synonymously, they are different in the strict mathematical sense. *Risk* refers to the possible outcomes of a project to which probabilities can be assigned, whereas *uncertainty* refers to outcomes to which it is difficult to assign probabilities. Thus, the real interest lies with risk, because it is measurable.

Most decision makers are risk averse and perceive risk in different ways:

1. The *dollar price risk* is the risk associated with a decline in the number of dollars used to acquire a financial asset.
2. The *purchasing power risk* is the risk associated with a decline in the purchasing power of the monetary unit.
3. The *interest rate risk* is the risk associated with changes in the interest rate, which affect market values of many types of securities.
4. The *business risk* is the risk associated with the operational cash flows of a firm.
5. The *financial risk* is the risk associated with financial leverage.
6. The *systematic risk* or *market risk* is the risk associated with the common stocks of a particular industry.
7. The *unsystematic risk* is the risk associated with a particular company. Because the perception of risk by decision makers affects their decision, it should be taken into account in the decision-making process. Capital budgeting under uncertainty should incorporate risk in the evaluation process.

Risk-Adjusted Discount Rate Method

One of the techniques for incorporating risk in the evaluation process is the risk-adjusted discount rate, which consists of manipulating the discount rate applied to the cash flows to reflect the amount of risk inherent in a project. The higher the risk associated with a project, the higher the discount rate applied to the cash flows. If a given project is perceived to be twice as risky as most acceptable projects to the firm and the cost of capital is 12 percent, then the correct risk-adjusted discount rate is 24 percent. In spite of its simplicity, the risk-adjusted discount rate method is subject to the following limitations:

1. The determination of the exact risk-adjusted discount rate is subjective and, therefore, subject to error.
2. The method adjusts the discount rate rather than the future cash flows, which are subject to variability and risk.

Certainty Equivalent Method

Another technique for incorporating risk in the evaluation process is the certainty equivalent method, which involves adjusting the future cash flows so a project can be evaluated on a riskless basis. The adjustment is formulated as follows:

$$\text{NPV} = \sum_{t=1}^{n} [\alpha_t CF_t / (1 + R_F)] - I_0,$$

where

α_t = Risk coefficient applied to the cash flow of period $t(CF_t)$.
I_0 = Initial cost of the project.
R_F = Risk-free rate.

As this formula shows, the method proceeds by multiplying the future cash flows by certainty equivalents to obtain a riskless cash flow. Note also that the discount rate used is R_F, which is a risk-free rate of interest.

To illustrate the certainty equivalent method, assume an investment with the following characteristics:

I_0 = Initial cost = $30,000.
CF_1 = Cash flow, year 1 = $10,000.
CF_2 = Cash flow, year 2 = $20,000.
CF_3 = Cash flow, year 3 = $30,000.
α_1 = Certainty equivalent, year 1 = 0.9.
α_2 = Certainty equivalent, year 2 = 0.8.
α_3 = Certainty equivalent, year 3 = 0.6.

The NPV of the investment using a risk-free discount rate of 6 percent is computed as follows:

Period	Cash Flow $(CF_t)(\alpha_t)$	Risk Coefficent	Certainty Equivalent	Risk-Free Rate (R_F)	Present Value
1	$10,000	0.9	$9,000	0.943	$8,487
2	$20,000	0.8	$16,000	0.890	$14,240
3	$30,000	0.6	$18,000	0.840	$15,120
Present Value of Cash Flows					$37,847
Initial Investment					$30,000
Net Present Value					$7,847

Since the NPV is positive, the investment should be considered acceptable. The main advantage of the certainty equivalent method is that it allows the assignment of a different risk factor to each cash flow, given that risk can concentrate in one or more periods.

The certainty equivalent method and the risk-adjusted discount rate method are comparable methods of evaluating risk. To produce similar ranking, the following equation must hold:

$$\frac{(\alpha_t CF_t)}{(1 + R_F)^t} = \frac{CF_t}{(1 + R_A)^t},$$

where

α_t = Risk coefficient used in the certainty equivalent method.
R_F = Risk-free discount rate.
R_A = Risk-adjusted discount rate used in the risk-adjusted discount rate method.
CF_t = Future cash flow.

Solving for α_t, yields

$$\alpha_t = \frac{(1 + R_F)^t}{(1 + R_A)^t}.$$

Given that R_A and R_F are constant and $R_A > R_F$, then α_t, decreases over time, which means that risk increases over time. To illustrate, assume that in the previous example $R_A = 15\%$. Then

$$\alpha_1 = \frac{(1 + R_F)^1}{(1 + R_A)^1} = \frac{(1 + 0.06)^1}{(1 + 0.15)^1} = 0.921.$$

$$\alpha_2 = \frac{(1 + R_F)^2}{(1 + R_A)^2} = \frac{(1 + 0.06)^2}{(1 + 0.15)^2} = 0.848.$$

$$\alpha_3 = \frac{(1 + R_F)^3}{(1 + R_A)^3} = \frac{(1 + 0.06)^3}{(1 + 0.15)^3} = 0.783.$$

In many cases this assumption of increasing risk may not be realistic.

Probability Distribution

The probability distribution approach to the evaluation of risk assigns probabilities to each cash flow outcome. Various measures of risk can then be computed, giving information about the dispersion or tightness of the probability distribution. *Standard deviation* is a conventional measure of dispersion. For a single period, the standard deviation is computed as follows:

$$\sigma_t = \sqrt{\sum_{t=1}^{n} [X_{it} - E_t(X)]^2 \, P(X_i)_t},$$

where

    α_t = Standard deviation of period t's cash flows.
    X_{it} = Cash flow for the rth outcome in period t.
    $E_t(X)$ = Expected value of cash flows in period t.
    $P(X_i)_t$ = Probability of occurrence of cash flow X, in period t.

The expected cash flow $E_t(X)$ is computed as follows:

$$E_t(X) = \sum_{t=1}^{n} X_{it} P(X_i).$$

All things being equal, the higher the standard deviation, the greater the risk associated with the expected value.

Another measure of relative dispersion is the *coefficient of variation* (CV), a measure that compares the expected value and risk of a probability distribution. The coefficient of variation is computed as follows:

$$CV = \frac{\sigma}{E(X)}.$$

All things being equal, the smaller the coefficient of variation, the better the project. To illustrate these risk concepts, assume that projects A and B have the following discrete probability distributions of expected cash flows in each of the next three years:

Project A		Project B	
Probability	**Cash Flow**	**Probability**	**Cash Flow**
0.2	$1,000	0.3	$1,500
0.5	$2,000	0.3	$1,000
0.2	$3,000	0.2	$3,500
0.1	$4,000	0.2	$3,750

The expected value of cash flows of both projects can be computed as follows:

$E(A) = 0.2(\$1,000) + 0.5(\$2,000) + 0.2(\$3,000) + 0.1(\$4,000) = \$2,200.$
$E(B) = 0.3(\$1,500) + 0.3(\$1,000) + 0.2(\$3,500) + 0.2(\$3,750) = \$2,200.$

On the basis of the expected values as a measure of central tendency in the distribution, projects A and B are equivalent. To determine which project is riskier, the standard deviations for both projects can be computed as follows:

$$\alpha(A) = [0.2(\$1,000 - \$2,200)^2 + 0.5(\$2,000 - \$2,200)^2$$
$$+ 0.2(\$3,000 - \$2,200)^2 + 0.1(\$4,000 - \$2,200)^2]^{1/2} = \$871.77.$$
$$\sigma(B) = [0.3(\$1,500 - \$2,200)^2 + 0.3(\$1,000 - \$2,200)^2$$
$$+ 0.2(\$3,500 - \$2,200)^2 + 0.2(\$3,750 - \$2,200)^2]^{1/2} = \$1,182.15.$$

Thus, project B has a significantly higher standard deviation, indicating a greater dispersion of possible cash flows.

The standard deviation is an absolute measure of risk. For comparison, the projects also should be evaluated on the basis of their coefficient of variation, which measures the relative dispersion within the distribution. The coefficient of variation for both projects can be computed now:

$$= CV(A) \frac{\sigma_A}{E(A)} \times 100 = \frac{\$871.77}{\$2,200} = 39.6\%$$

$$= CV(B) \frac{\sigma_B}{E(B)} \times 100 = \frac{\$1,182.15}{\$2,200} = 53.7\%$$

The coefficient of variation for project B is significantly higher than for project A, which indicates again that project B presents a greater degree of risk.

The coefficient of variation is an especially useful measure when the comparison between projects leads to the acceptance of a given project based on a comparison between means, or when the comparison leads to the acceptance of a different project based on a comparison between standard deviations.

Multiperiod Projects

The computation of the measures of risk becomes more complicated when several periods are involved. Some assumptions must be made regarding the relationships between the period cash flows, namely, whether the cash flows are independent or dependent.

To illustrate, let us return to project A and assume (1) that the applicable discount rate (R) is 10 percent and (2) that the project calls for a $5,000 investment.

Independent of the nature of the relationship between cash flows in the three periods, the NPV of project A can be computed as follows:

$$NPV = \sum_{t=1}^{3} [\$2,000/(1 + 0.10)^t] - \$5,000 = \$471.$$

The standard deviation of the project will be computed differently according to whether we assume that the cash flows are dependent, independent, or mixed.

Independent Cash Flows

If we assume serial independence of the cash flows between the periods, the standard deviation of the entire project is

$$\sigma = \sqrt{\sum_{t=1}^{n} \sigma_t^2/(1 + r)^{2t}},$$

where

σ_t = standard deviation of the probability distribution
of the cash flows in period t.

Hence the standard deviation of project A, assuming serial independence, is

$$\sigma_A = \sqrt{(\$871^2/(1 + 0.10)^2) + (\$871^2/(1 + 0.10)^4) + (\$871^2/(1 + 0.10)^6)}$$
$$= \$358.04.$$

Dependent Cash Flows

In general, the cash flows of a given period are expected to influence the cash flows of subsequent periods. In the case of perfect correlation, the standard deviation of the entire project is

$$\sigma = \sum_{i=1}^{n} \sigma_t/(1 + r)^t$$

Therefore, the standard deviation of project A, assuming perfect correlation between interperiod cash flows, is

$$\sigma_A \sum_{t=1}^{3} \$871/(1 + 0.10)^i = \$2,166.17$$

Note that the standard deviation under the assumption of independence is $358.04, while under the assumption of perfect dependency it is considerably higher ($2,116.17). If the cash flows are perfectly correlated there is more risk inherent in the project than if the cash flows are independent.

Mixed Correlation

A project may include some independent and some dependent cash flows. Frederick Hillier proposed a model to deal with a mixed situation:

$$\sigma = \sum_{t=0}^{T} \sigma_{Y_t}^2 /(1 + r)^{2t} + \sum_{j=1}^{m} \left[\sum_{j=1}^{T} 6_{Z_{jt}} /(1 + r)^t \right]^2$$

Y_t = The independent component of the net cash flow in period t.

Z_{jt} = The jth perfectly correlated component of the net cash flow in period t.

To illustrate the computation of the standard deviation of a project with mixed correlation. Hillier assumed the following project data for a new product addition:

Year	Source	Expected Value of Net Cash Flows (In Thousands)	Standard Deviation
0	Initial Investment	($600)	$50
1	Production Cash Outflow	($250)	$20
2	Production Cash Outflow	($200)	$10
3	Production Cash Outflow	($200)	$10
4	Production Cash Outflow	($200)	$10
5	Production Outflow—Salvage Value	($100)	$10\sqrt{10}$
1	Marketing	$300	$50
2	Marketing	$600	$100
3	Marketing	$500	$100
4	Marketing	$400	$100
5	Marketing	$300	$100

Hillier also assumed that all the outflows were independent and that all marketing flow were perfectly correlated. If 10 percent is used as the risk-free rate, the expected value of the NPV for the proposal is

$$NPV = \sum_{t=1}^{S} \left[\overline{X} /(1 + 0.10)^t \right] - C_0$$

or

$$NPV = \frac{\$300 - 250}{(1.10)} + \frac{\$600 - \$200}{(1.10)^2} + \frac{\$500 - \$200}{(1.10)^3} + \frac{\$400 - \$200}{(1.10)^4}$$
$$+ \frac{\$400 - \$200}{(1.10)^4} - 600 = \$262.$$

The standard deviation is

$$\sigma = \sqrt{50^2 + \left(20^2 /(1.10)^2\right) + \left((10\sqrt{10^2} /(1.10)^{10}\right) + [50 /(1.10) + \ldots}$$
$$+ 100 /(1.10)_5]^2 = \$339.$$

Exhibit 3.3
Decision Tree Approach to Capital Budgeting

Period 1 Net Cash Flows A	Period 1 Initital Probability p(1)	Period 2 Net Cash Flows A	Period 2 Conditional Probability p(2/1)	Number of Cases	Joint Probability p	Total Net Cash Flows A	Expected Value of Total Net Cash Flows
	0.6	$20	0.3	1	0.18	$50	$9.00
$30	0.6	$30	0.4	2	0.24	$60	$14.40
	0.6	$40	0.3	3	0.18	$70	$12.60
	0.4	$30	0.2	4	0.08	$70	$5.60
$40	0.4	$40	0.5	5	0.2	$80	$16.00
	0.4	$50	0.3	6	0.12	$90	$10.80
Mean Value							$68.40

Moderate Correlation

In most cases, cash flows cannot be easily classified as either independent or perfectly correlated, and a decision tree approach can be used. In a capital budgeting context, this approach involves the multiplication of the conditional probabilities of correlated periods to obtain the joint probabilities that will specify the probabilities of multiple events. Exhibit 3.3 illustrates the decision tree approach to compute the joint probabilities and the expected value of a project.

Simulation

The preceding methods of dealing with uncertainty apply only when two probability distributions are considered. In most realistic capital budgeting situations, more than two variables are significant, and more than two variables are subject to uncertainty. The simulation technique takes into account the interacting variables and their corresponding probability distributions. David B. Hertz proposed a simulation model to obtain the dispersion about the expected rate of return for an investment proposal. He established nine separate probability distributions to determine the probability distribution of the average rate of return for the entire project. The following nine variables were considered.

Market Analysis
1. Market size.
2. Selling price.
3. Market growth rate.
4. Share of market.

Investment Cost Analysis

5. Investment required.
6. Residual value of investment.

Operating and Fixed Costs

7. Operating costs.
8. Fixed costs.
9. Useful life of facilities.

The computer simulates trial values of each of the nine variables and then computes the return on investment based on the simulated values obtained. These trials are repeated often enough to obtain a frequency distribution for the return on investment. This approach can also be used to determine the NPV or the IRR of a project.

CAPITAL BUDGETING UNDER INFLATION

Beginning with seminal work by Irving Fisher, economists have shown fairly conclusively that market rates of interest include an adjustment of expected inflation rate—the nonexistent "homogeneous expectation." This consensus forecast, therefore, is built into the discount rate used in capital budgeting. When rates of inflation were relatively low (say 2 to 3 percent) this did not lead to serious distortions in the IRR or NPV models, because any error in the rate estimation was immaterial in most cases. With the higher rates of inflation we are now experiencing, it is desirable to explicitly consider the rate of inflation in developing cash flow forecasts. The correct analysis can be done in either of two ways: (1) using a money discount rate to discount money cash flows, or (2) using a real discount rate to discount real cash flows.

Before illustrating either approach, let us explore the differences between money cash flows and real cash flows, and between real discount rate and money discount rate. Money cash flows are cash flows measured in dollars from various periods having different purchasing power. Real cash flows are cash flows measured in dollars having the same purchasing power. The real cash flow for a given year, expressed in terms of dollars of $year_0$ (the base year) is equal to the money cash flow for that year, multiplied by the following ratio:

Price level index in $year_0$
Price level index in $year_1$

For example, if an investment promises a money return of $100 for three years and the price index for years 0 through 3 is 100, 110, 121, and 133.1, respectively, then the real cash flows are as follows:

Year 1: $100 \times 100/110 = 90.90$.
Year 2: $100 \times 100/121 = 82.64$.
Year 3: $100 \times 100/133.1 = 75.13$.

The money discount rate, r, can also be computed. Assuming that f is the annual rate of inflation, I is the real discount rate, and the decision maker is in the zero tax bracket, then

$$r = (I + f)(1 + I) - 1,$$

or

$$r = I + f + if.$$

For example, if the real return before taxes is 3 percent, and the rate of inflation is 10 percent, then the nominal discount rate is

$$0.03 + 0.10 + 0.003 = 0.133.$$

To illustrate the correct analysis under inflation, assume the same data as in the previous example. The correct analysis can be either of two, as follows.

1. The first analysis discounts the money cash flows using a money discount rate. The present value of the investment will be computed as follows:

Period	Money Cash Flow	Nominal Present Value Factor at 13.3%	Present Value
1	100	0.8826	88.26
2	100	0.7792	77.92
3	100	0.6874	68.74
			234.92

2. The second analysis discounts the real cash flows using a real discount rate. The present value of the investment will give the same present value, as follows:

Period	Real Cash Flow	Real Present Value at 3%	Present Value
1	90.9	0.9709	88.254
2	82.64	0.9426	77.896
3	75.13	0.9151	68.751
			234.901

Assuming a marginal tax rate t on nominal income, the nominal discount rate will be computed as follows:

$$1 + (1 - t)r = (1 + f) + 1 + I(1 - t),$$

or

$$r = I + If + f/(1 - t).$$

Assuming the tax rate to be 30 percent, the nominal rate is then computed as follows:

$$r = 0.03 + (0.03 \times 0.10) + 0.10/(1 - 0.30)$$
$$= 0.1758.$$

In other words, a nominal rate of 17.58 percent is needed for an investor in a 30 percent tax bracket and facing an inflation of 10 percent to earn a real discount rate of 3 percent.

CAPITAL BUDGETING ILLUSTRATIONS

Problems

1. Certainty Equivalent Method. A project offers an initial cash outlay of $40,000, a annual expected cash inflow of $20,000 for three years, and no salvage value. The risk coefficients for the three periods are estimated to be 0.90, 0.80, and 0.75, respectively. The risk-free rate of interest is estimated to be 6 percent. Compute the NPV of the project.

2. Probability Distribution and Capital Budgeting. The Santini Company can invest in one of two mutually exclusive projects. The probability distribution of the two projects' NPVs is shown here:

Project A		Project B	
Net Present Value	Probability	Net Present Value	Probability
0.3	$2,000	0.4	$3,000
0.6	$4,000	0.4	$2,000
0.1	$6,000	0.2	$7,000

Required:

1. Compute the expected value, the standard deviation, and the coefficient of variation of each project.

2. Which of these two mutually exclusive projects should the Santini Company choose? Why?

3. *Capital Budgeting under Uncertainty.* Mr. Oliver is evaluating whether to invest $3,000,000 in a research project. If the research project is successful, the revenues net of operating costs (excluding the $3,000,000 outlay for the research and an initial investment in equipment) are estimated to be as follows:

Anticipated Net Revenue	Probability
$10,000,000	0.10
$20,000,000	0.25
$25,000,000	0.35
$30,000,000	0.20
$35,000,000	0.10

However, Oliver knows there is a 60 percent chance that the project will be unsuccessful.

Required: Assuming Oliver wishes to maximize the expected value of net cash flows, should the investment be made in the research project? Show all calculations.

4. *Capital Rationing.* The Francis Company is considering eight projects. The cost of capital is 12 percent, and the capital constraint is $500. Each project has a one-year life. The initial outlay and the cash flow at the end of year 1 for each project are as follows:

Project	Initial Outlay	Cash Inflow, End of Year 1
A	$100	$122
B	$100	$118
C	$100	$115
D	$200	$238
E	$200	$234
F	$300	$348
G	$400	$468

Required:

1. Compute the NPV and the IRR for each project.
2. Assuming the eight projects are not mutually exclusive, which combination of projects should the Francis Company choose? (Use NPV.)
3. Assuming projects A, B, E, and G are mutually exclusive, which combination of projects should the company choose? (Use NPV.)

5. *Mathematical Programming and Capital Budgeting.* The Pen-aids Company is considering the following investment proposals:

Projects 1 and 3 are mutually exclusive. The company has a budget constraint of $40,000 in year 1 and $30,000 in year 2.

Required:

1. Set up the selection process as a mathematical programming problem to maximize the NPV available from investment subject to the two budget constraints.

2. Set up the dual program assuming projects 1 and 3 are no longer mutually exclusive.

3. Explain the meaning of the dual values.

6. *Multiperiod Projects.* The Dickenson Company has determined the following discrete probability distributions for net cash flows generated by a contemplated project:

Period 1		Period 1	
Probability	**Cash Flow**	**Probability**	**Cash Flow**
0.10	$5,000	0.10	$6,000
0.20	$4,500	0.10	$2,000
0.10	$3,000	0.25	$5,000
0.20	$3,500	0.25	$3,000
0.40	$4,000	0.30	$4,000

The after-tax risk-free rate is 10 percent, and the project requires an initial outlay of $6,000.

Required:

1. Determine the expected value of the NPV.

2. Determine the standard deviation of the NPV, assuming that the probability distributions of cash flows for future periods are independent.

3. Determine the standard deviation of the NPV, assuming that that the probability distributions of cash flows for future periods are dependent.

7. *Replacement Decisions: Unequal Lives.* The Hass Company is considering replacing a fully depreciated lathe for trimming molded plastic with a new machine. Two replacement machines are available. Lathe X has a cost of $50,000, will last five years, and will produce after-tax cask flows of $15,000 per year for five years. Lathe Y has a cost of $60,000, will last ten years, and will produce net cash flows of $12,000 per year for ten years. The company's cost of capital is 10 percent. Should lathe X or Y be selected to replace the old machine?

8. *Replacement Decisions: Equal Lives.* The Davidson Company purchased a computer ten years ago with a cost of $20,000, a useful life of twenty years, and a zero salvage value at the end of its useful life. Straight-line depreciation is used. A new manager suggested that a new computer costing $30,000 be purchased. The new computer has a ten-year life and could reduce operating costs from $10,000 to $5,000. The old computer can be sold now at an estimated $4,000, and the new computer can be sold at the end of the ten years for $5,000.

Taxes are at 48 percent rate, and the company's cost of capital is 10 percent. An investment tax credit of 10 percent of purchase price can be used if the new machine is acquired. Should the Davidson Company buy the new computer?

9. *Real and Money Discount Rates.* Dr. Eric Magnum is considering a $900 investment that is expected to yield a return of $133 for the first two years and $1,133 in the third year. A rate of inflation of 10 percent and a real rate of 3 percent are expected. Magnum is in the zero tax bracket. Determine the net present value of the investment using: (1) a nominal discount rate, and (2) a real discount rate.

Solutions

1. Certainty Equivalent Method.

Period	Cash Flow	Risk Coefficient	Certainty Equivalent	Risk Free Rate	Present Value
1	$20,000	0.9	$18,000	0.943	$16,974
2	$20,000	0.8	$16,000	0.890	$14,240
3	$20,000	0.75	$15,000	0.840	$12,600
					$43,814
Investment					$40,000
NPV					$3,814

2. Probability Distribution and Capital Budgeting.

1. a. The expected value as follows:

$E(x) = \$2,000(0.3) + 4,000(0.6) + 6,000(0.1) = \$3,600$
$E(y) = \$3,000(0.4) + 2,000(0.4) + 7,000(0.2) = \$3,400$

b. The standard deviations of both projects may be computed as follows:

$\alpha(x) = [0.3(2,000-3,600)^2 + 0.6(4,000-3,600)^2 + 0.1(6,000-3,600)^2]^{1/2}$
$= \$1,200.$
$\alpha(y) = [0.4(3,000-3,400)^2 + 0.4(2,000-3,400)^2 + 0.2(7,000-3,400)^2]^{1/2}$
$= \$1,854.72.$

c. The coefficients of variation of both projects may be computed as follows:

$CV(x) = \$1,200/3,600 = 33.33\%$
$CV(y) = \$1,854.72/3,400 = \$54.557.$

2. Project A should be chosen. It has a higher NPV and both a lower standard deviation and coefficient of variation.

3. Capital Budgeting under Uncertainty. Generally, the students did well on this question. Many of my students failed to deduct the $3,000,000 cash outlay when computing the expected net cash flow if successful.

Anticipated Net

Revenues	Probability	Expected Value of Net Revenues
$10 million	0.10	$1,000,000
$20 million	0.25	$5,000,000
$25 million	0.35	$8,750,000
$30 million	0.20	$6,000,000
$35 million	0.10	$3,500,000
		$24,250,000

Payoff Table

		State	
		Success Prob. = .4	Unsuccessful Prob. = .6
Action	Invest	$21,250,000	−$3,000,000
	Don't Invest	$0	$0

$$E(\text{invest}) = P(\text{Success}) \times (\text{payoff/success}) + P(\text{unsuccessful}) \times$$
$$(\text{payoff/unsuccessful})$$
$$= .4(21,250,000) + .6(-3,000,000)$$
$$= 8,500,000 - 1,800,000$$
$$= 6,700,000$$

The decision is then to invest.

4. Capital Rationing.

1. NPV and IRR Results

Projects	Outlays	Cash Inflow	PV of Cash Inflow at 12%	NPV	IRR
A	$100	$122	$108.95	$8.95	92%
B	$100	$118	$105.37	$5.37	18%
C	$100	$115	$102.70	$2.70	15%
D	$200	$238	$212.53	$12.53	19%
E	$200	$234	$208.96	$8.96	17%
F	$300	$348	$310.76	$10.76	16%
G	$400	$468	$417.92	$17.92	17%

2. With NPV, we compute the NPVs for all combinations of projects whose outlays total $500.

A,B,C,D	$29.55	A,D,E	$30.44
A,B,C,E	$25.98	B,D,E	$26.86
A,B,F	$25.08	C,D,E	$24,19

A,C,F	$22.41	A,G	$26.87
B,C,F	$18.83	B,G	$23.29
D,F	$23.29	C,G	$20.62
E,F	$19.72		

The combination of projects with the highest NPV is A,D,E, with $30.44. The cost of the firm's shareholders of capital rationing is equal to the total NPV of all the projects, $67.19, minus the NPV of the chosen combination, $30.44, which is equal to $36.75.

3. The acceptable combinations are:

A,C,F	$22.41	C,G,	$20.62
B,C,F	$18.83	D,F,	$23.29
C,D,E,	$24.19	E,F,	$19.72

The combination of projects with the highest NPV is C,D,E. (Adapted with permission from James A. Hendricks, "Capital Budgeting, Decisions: NPV or IRR?" *Cost and Management*, March–April 1980, pp. 16–20.)

5. Mathematical Programming and Capital Budgeting.

    1. Primal Problem

        Max $30,000x_1 + 50,000x_2 + 24,000x_3 + 55,000x_4$

        Subject to

$$17,000x_1 + 22,000x_2 + 15,000x_3 + 25,000x_4 \leq 40,000$$
$$14,000x_1 + 26,000x_2 + 15,000x_3 + 16,000x_4 \leq 30,000$$
$$x_1 + x_3 \quad \leq 1$$
$$x_1, x_2, x_3, x_4 \geq 0$$

        All x's are integers.

    2. Dual Problem

        Min $40,000_{y1} + 30,000_{y2}$

        Subject to

$$17,000_{y1} + 14,000_{y2} \geq 30,000$$
$$22,000_{y1} + 26,000_{y2} \geq 50,000$$
$$15,000_{y1} + 15,000_{y2} \geq 24,000$$
$$25,000_{y1} + 16,000_{y2} \geq 55,000$$
$$y_1, y_2 \geq 0$$

    3. The dual values provide the shadow costs or opportunity costs of the resources, which are the rationed funds in years 1 and 2, respectively, so that the solution to the dual in this case will be the implicit interest rates, or maximum opportunity costs of money in years 1 and 2 to make the projects worthwhile. In other words, the solutions y_1, y_2 yield the effective "prices" of money in periods 1 and 2, respectively, expressed in terms of year 0.

6. Multiperiod Projects.

    1. Expected value of the NPV

        a. The expected value of cash flows for period 1 and 2 are:

EV(1) = 0.10(5,000) + 0.20(4,500) + 0.10(3,000) + 0.20(3,500) + 0.40(4,000) = $4,000
EV(2) = 0.10(6,000) + 0.10(2,000) + 0.25(5,000) + 0.25(3000) + 0.30(4,000) = $4,000

b. The expected Value of NPV is:

$$NPV = \sum_{i=1}^{2}(\$4,000/(1 + 0.10)^2) - \$6,000 = \$942.$$

2. Standard deviation: independent cash flows
   a. The standard deviation of cash flows for periods 1 and 2 are:
   $\sigma(1) = \{0.10(5,000 - 4,000)^2 + 0.2(4,500 - 4,000)^2 + 0.10(3,000 - 4,000)^2 + 0.20(3,500 - 4,000)^2 + 0.40(4,000 - 4,000)^2\}^{1/2} = \$548$
   $\sigma(2) = \{0.10(6,000 - 4,000)^2 + 0.10(2,000 - 4,000)^2 + 0.25(5,000 - 4,000)^2 + 0.25(3,000 - 4,000)^2 + 0.30(4,000 - 4,000)^2\}^{1/2} = \$1,140$
   b. The standard deviation of the project assuming serial dependence of the cash flows between the various periods:

   $$\sigma = \sqrt{(548)^2/(1 + 0.10)^2) + ((1,140)^2/(1 + 0.10)^4)} = \$580.26$$
   c. Dependent cash flows

   $$\sigma = ((548)/(1 + 0.10)^1) + ((1,140)/(1 + 0.10)^2) = \$1,440.33$$

7. Replacement Decisions: Unequal Lives.

NPV(x) = Present value of first investment in x + present value of
         second invesment in x.
       = {15,000(3.7908) - 50,000} + {6862(0.6209)} = $11.123
NPV(y) = {12,000(6.1446) - 60,000} = $13.735

Lathe Y should be chosen.
8. Replacement Decisions: Equal Lives.

Worksheet for Replacement Analysis
Net Outflow at the Time the Investment Is Made t = 0

	Amount Before Tax	Amount After Tax (net effect)	Year Event Occurs	PV at 10%	PV
1. Cost of the New Equipment	$30,000	$30,000	0	1.0	$30,000
2. Salvage Value of Old Equipment	($4,000)	($4,000)	0	1.0	($4,000)
3. Tax Effect of Sale of Old Equipment	($6,000)	($4,000)	0	1.0	($2,880)
4. Investment Tax Credit	($3,000)	($3,000)	0	1.0	($3,000)
5. Present Value of costs					$20,120

9. Real and Money Discount Rates.

1. At the nominal discount rate of 13.3 percent, the present value is computed as follows:

Period	Money Cash Flow	Nominal Present Value Factor	Present Value
1	$133	0.8826	$117.39
2	$133	0.7790	$103.61
3	$1,133	0.6876	$779.00
			$1,000.00

Net Present Value = $1,000 − $900 = $100

2. At the real discount rate, the present value is computed as follows:

Period	Money Cash Flow (1)	Price Level Relative (2)	Real Cash Flow (1)/(2)	Real Present Value Factor at 3%	Present Value
1	$133	1.100^A	$120.91	0.9709	$117.39
2	$133	1.210^B	$109.82	0.9426	$103.61
3	$1,133	1.331^C	$851.24	0.9151	$779.00
					$1,000.00

Net Present Value = $1,000 − $900 = $100
A = $1.00 × (1 + 0.10) = $1.10
B = $1.10 × (1 + 0.10) = $1.21
C = $1.21 × (1 + 0.10) = $1.331

CONCLUSION

Many capital budgeting techniques exist in the literature and in practice. The discounted cash flow methods take the time value of money into account to evaluate capital budgeting proposals. The two basic discounted cash flow methods are the internal rate of return and the net present value methods. Management should consider some of the conflicts between these two methods when choosing between them. Other problems in using capital budgeting techniques include problems with replacement decisions, problems with capital rationing, and problems with capital budgeting under certainty.

GLOSSARY

Accounting Rate of Return (ARR) Method. An evaluation process that uses the ratio of the average annual profit after taxes to the investment of a project.

Annuity. An arrangement for a series of cash flows payable at fixed intervals as the result of an investment.

Capital Budgeting. Long-term planning for proposed capital outlays and their financing.

Capital Rationing. The process of placing constraints upon the acquisition or use of capital resources in: capital budgeting decision.

Cash Flow. The amount of cash receipts and disbursements over a specific period of time for a given segment of a firm.

Discounted Cash Flow (DCF) Method. An evaluation process that uses present value concepts to measure the profitability of a project.

Internal Rate of Return (IRR) Method. An evaluation process that computes the interest rate equating the present value of an investment's cash flows and the cost of the investment.

Net Present Value (NPV) Method. An evaluation process that compares the cost of an investment with the present value of the future cash flows of the investment at a selected rate of return, or hurdle rate.

Payback Method. An evaluation process that computes the number of years before the initial cash outlay of a project is fully recovered by its future cash inflows.

Present Value. The amount that should be paid for the right to receive a payment (or a series of payments in the future [at an assumed interest rate] if the payment is to be received after a specific period of time).

Risk. A measure of the probability that unforeseen occurrences will cause estimates to vary from projections.

Time Value of Money. The ability of money to earn more money in the future.

SELECTED READINGS

Bailes, Jack C.; James F. Nielsen; and Steve Wendell. "Capital Budgeting in the Forest Products Industry." *Management Accounting* (July 1979), pp. 46–51, 57.

Bavishi, Vinod B. "Capital Budgeting Practices at Multinationals." *Management Accounting* (August 1981), pp. 32–35.

Bergeron, Pierre G. "The Other Dimensions of the Payback Period." *Cost and Management* (May 1978), pp. 35–39.

Doenges, R. Conrad. "The Reinvestment Problem in a Practical Perspective." *Financial Management* (Spring 1972), pp. 85–91.

Elliot, Grover S. "Analyzing the Cost of Capital." *Management Accounting* (December 1980), pp. 13–18.

Fremgen, James M. "Capital Budgeting Practices: A Survey." *Management Accounting* (May 1973), pp. 19–25.

Gaertner, James F., and Ken Milani. "The TRR Yardstick for Hospital Capital Expenditure Decisions." *Management Accounting* (December 1980), pp. 25–33.

Glahn, Gerald L.; Kent T. Fields; and Jerry E. Trapnell. "How to Evaluate Mixed Risk Capital Projects." *Management Accounting* (December 1980), pp. 34–38.

Hendricks, James A. "Capital Budgeting Decisions: NPV or IRR?" *Cost and Management* (March-April 1980), pp. 16–20.

Hertz, David B. "Investment Policies that Pay Off." *Harvard Business Review* (January-February 1968), pp. 96–108.

Hertz, David B. "Risk Analysis in Capital Investment." *Harvard Business Review* (January-February 1964), pp. 95–106,

Hespos, Richard F., and Paul A. Strassman. "Stochastic Decision Trees for the Analysis of Investment Decisions." *Management Science* (August 1965), pp. 244–259.

Hillier, Frederick. "The Deviation of Probabilistic Information for the Evaluation of Risky Investments." *Management Science* (April 1963), pp. 443–457.

Hing-Ling, Amy, and Hong-Shiang Lau. "Improving Present Value Analysis with a Programmable Calculator." *Management Accounting* (November 1979), pp. 52–57.

Johnson, Robert W. *Capital Budgeting* (Belmont. Calif.: Wadsworth Publishing, 1970).

Kim, Suk H., and Edward J., Parragher. "Current Capital Budgeting Practices." *Management Accounting* (June 1981), pp. 26–31.

Kirn, Suk H. "Making the Long-Term Investment Decision." *Management Accounting* (March 1979), pp. 41–49.

Lemer, Eugene M., and Alfred Rappaport. "Limit DCF in Capital Budgeting." *Harvard Business Review* (September-October 1968), pp. 133–139.

Norgaard, Corine T. "The Post-Completion Audit of Capital Projects." *Cost and Management* (January-February 1979), pp. 19–25.

Osteryoung, Jerome S. *Capital Budgeting: Long-term Asset Selection* (Columbus. Ohio: Grid, 1974).

Osteryoung, Jerome S.; Eiton Scott; and Gordon S. Roberts. "Selecting Capital Projects with the Coefficient of Variation." *Financial Management* (Summer 1977), pp. 65–70.

Pettway, Richard H. "Integer Programming in Capital Budgeting: A Note on Computational Experience." *Journal of Financial and Quantitative Analysis* (September 1973), pp. 665–672.

Puglisi, D. J., and L. W. Chadwick. "Capital Budgeting with Realized Terminal Values." *Cost and Management* (May-June 1977), pp. 13–17.

Raiborn, D. D., and Thomas A. Ratcliffe. "Are You Accounting for Inflation in Your Capital Budgeting Process?" *Management Accounting* (September 1979), pp. 19–22.

Roemmich, Roger A.; Gordon L. Duke; and William H. Gates. "Maximizing the Present Value of Tax Savings from Depreciation." *Management Accounting* (September 1978), pp. 55–57, 63.

Sangeladji, Mohammad A. "True Rate of Return for Evaluating Capital Investments." *Management Accounting* (February 1979), pp. 24–27.

Suver, James D., and Bruce R. Neumann. "Capital Budgeting for Hospitals." *Management Accounting* (December 1978), pp. 48–50, 53.

Truitt, Jack F. "A Solution to Capital Budgeting Problems Concerning Investments with Different Lives." *Cost and Management* (November-December 1978), pp. 44–45.

Uhl, Franklin S. "Automated Capital Investment Decisions." *Management Accounting* (April 1980), pp. 41–46.

Weingartner, H. Martin. "Capital Budgeting of Interrelated Projects: Surveys and Synthesis." *Management Science* (March 1966), pp. 485–516.

William, H. Jean, "On Multiple Rates of Return." *Journal of Finance* (March 1968), pp. 187–191.

Appendix 3.1: Arjun Chairath and Michael J. Seiler, "Capital Budgeting and the Stochastic Cost of Capital," *Managerial Finance* 23, 9 (1997), pp. 16–23.

Abstract

Despite its shortcomings, the IRR method continues to be a widely employed evaluation technique in capital budgeting. This paper demonstrates the reasons for its continued popularity. Specifically, the non-requirement of a discount rate is suggested to be an important factor in the choice of IRR over the NPV criterion. A major implication is that managers face a very elusive, or stochastic, discount rate for NPV analysis. Thus, the aversion to NPV may go beyond simple aesthetics.

I. Introduction

The internal rate of return (IRR) criterion in capital budgeting is often associated with two major problems. First, multiple IRRs may occur when dealing with a non-normal cashflow series. Second, the IRR technique assumes that the cashflows can be reinvested at the IRR instead of the more appropriate discount rate. The first problem makes the IRR criterion inappropriate for decision making under several conditions. The second problem is often associated with leading to a project-ranking problem between the IRR and the net present value (NPV) criteria. That is, the NPV and IRR will not always lead to the same accept-reject decision for mutually exclusive projects. An attempt to correct the flaws associated with the IRR has been made via the creation of a modified internal rate of return (MIRR) criterion. The MIRR computes the rate of return assuming that the cashflows will be reinvested at the discount rate. While the MIRR overcomes the problem of multiple rates of return, the ranking problem may persevere when initial investments are of unequal size.

Despite its shortcomings, the IRR method continues to be a widely employed evaluation technique. By some estimates, over 60 percent of U.S. and multinational firms employ IRR as the primary capital budgeting method (e.g., Moore and Reichert (1983) and Stanley and Block (1984)). In contrast, relatively few firms employ NPV as the the primary capital budgeting technique. It is often stated that IRR remains popular because it is easier to understand and interprete, as it provides a percentage rate of return rather than a dollar amount. However, it seems intuitively unlikely that these minor advantages alone would explain why managers are willing to use a criterion that leads them to make inaccurate capital budgeting decisions.

This paper offers an alternative, more theoretical reason for the continued popularity of the IRR technique in capital budgeting. Specifically, the non-requirement of a discount rate is suggested to be an important factor in the choice of IRR over the NPV criterion. The primary conclusion is that managers face a very elusive, or stochastic discount rate for NPV analysis thus rendering NPV analysis, in practice, less useful. Hence, the aversion to NPV may go far beyond simple aesthetics.

The next section discusses the theoretical underpinnings of the cost of capital process. Section III provides empirical evidence supporting the stochastic nature of the cost of capital. Implications for capital budgeting decisions are given in the final section.

II. The Theory Underlying the Cost of Capital

This section highlights the stochastic nature of the cost of capital. The emphasis is on the relationship between cost of capital and the corporations' internal characteristics, rather than on the general financing environment. The first part of this section is devoted to demonstrating that the weighted average cost of capital can theoretically be an unknown function of capital structure (as measured by debt to total capitalization). This would imply that managers would not have the knowledge as to whether new financing would be more or less expensive. The second part provides empirical evidence in support of this theme.

Consider a possibility in which a firm's current cost of debt and cost of equity are given by the linear forms:

$$k_b = \alpha_1 + \beta_b L \tag{1}$$

$$k_s = \alpha_2 + \beta_s L \qquad (\alpha_1, \alpha_2 > 0; \ \beta_b, \beta_s \geq 0) \tag{2}$$

where k_b, the cost of debt, and k_s, the cost of equity, are positive percentage rates, and L is the debt to total capitalization ratio of the firm. The positive constants, α_1 and α_2, represent the cost of debt and cost of equity if the firm carries no leverage, and β_b and β_s represent the bondholder and stockholder sensitivity to leverage.[1]

Since the after-tax weighted average cost of capital, W^τ, is given by

$$W^\tau = k_s(1-L) + k_b L(1-\tau_c), \tag{3}$$

where τ_c is the applicable corporate tax rate, substituting from (1), (2) to (3)[2]

$$W^\tau = (\alpha_2 + \beta_s L)(1 - L) + (\alpha_1 + \beta_b L)L(1 - \tau_c) = \dot{\alpha}_2 - \alpha_2 L + \beta_s L - \beta_s L^2 + \alpha_1 L$$

$$- \alpha_1 L \tau_c + \beta_b L^2 - \beta_b L^2 \tau_c = \alpha_2 + (\alpha_1 + \beta_s - \alpha_2 - \alpha_1 \tau_c)L + (\beta_b - \beta_b \tau_c - \beta_s)L^2. \tag{4}$$

Now consider the following possibilities:[3]

Possibility 1: $\beta_b = \beta_s = 0$ or k_b, k_s are not functions of L;

Possibility 2: $\beta_b > 0$, $\beta_s = 0$ or only k_b is a function of L;

Possibility 3: $\beta_s > 0$, $\beta_b = 0$ or only k_s is a function of L;

Possibility 4: β_b, $\beta_s > 0$ *or* k_b *and* k_s *are functions of L.*

If Possibility 1 describes the capital market environment, (4) simplifies to

$$W^\tau = \alpha_2 + (\alpha_1 - \alpha_2 - \alpha_1\tau_c)L. \tag{5}$$

Leverage has an impact on the *average* cost of capital as long as $\alpha_1/\alpha_2 >< (1-\tau_c)$. In the event that, $(\alpha_2/\alpha_1 > (1-\tau_c))$, the L coefficient is negative, and the well known Modigliani and Miller (1963) implication will hold wherein the average cost of capital is a linear declining function of leverage.[4] Any equilibrium with positive levels of equity and $[(\alpha_2/\alpha_1 > (1-\tau_c)]$ and $[\beta_b, \beta_s = 0]$ will violate the managerial principle of value maximization.

If Possibility 2 describes the capital market environment, from (4) we obtain

$$W^\tau = \alpha_2 + (\alpha_1 - \alpha_2 - \alpha_1\tau_c)L + \beta_b(1-\tau_c)L^2. \tag{6}$$

The sufficient conditions for a U-shaped W^τ function $(\delta W^\tau/\delta L < 0, \delta^2 W^\tau/\delta L^2 > 0)$ is $L < (\alpha_2 - \alpha_1(1-\tau_c))/2\beta_b(1-\tau_c)$. The second order condition is satisfied as long as $0 < \tau_c < 1$, since by definition, $\beta_b > 0$. A static tradeoff-consistent (convex) cost of capital function is thus feasible without the cost of equity being a function of L.

If Possibility 3 describes the capital market environment,

$$W^\tau = \alpha_2 + (\alpha_1 + \beta_s - \alpha_2 - \alpha_1\tau_c)L - \beta_s L^2. \tag{7}$$

The sufficient condition for a negatively sloped W^τ function is $L < [\beta_s - \alpha_2 - \alpha_1 (1-\tau_c)]/2\beta_s$.[5] The second order condition for a convex W^τ function is not met since $\delta^2 W^\tau/\delta L^2 = -2\beta_s$ (and since $\beta_s > 0$ by definition). Thus a convex W^τ function is not feasible if k_b is not a function of L.

Finally, if Possibility 4 describes the capital market environment,

$$W^\tau = \alpha_2 + (\alpha_1 + \beta_s - \alpha_2 - \alpha_1\tau_c)L + (\beta_b - \beta_b\tau_c - \beta_s)L^2. \tag{8}$$

A U-shaped W^τ function $(\delta W^\tau/\delta L < 0, \delta^2 W^\tau/\delta L^2 > 0)$, follows in the event that $L < [\alpha_2 - \alpha_1(1-\tau_c) - \beta_s]/[2(\beta_b(1-\tau_c) - \beta_s)$ and $\beta_b(1-\tau_c) > \beta_s$.[6]

The above illustrations of the cost of capital function under alternate sets of financing environments helps to highlight the importance of (i) understanding that a relationship between W^τ and L does not necessarily imply a relationship between L and the individual parts (k_s, k_b) in W^τ; and, (ii) understanding that the conditions for the convexity of the W^τ function may be far more complex than the simple argument that cost of equity and debt rise with the issuance of debt. For instance, it has been demonstrated that if possibility 4 describes the capital market environment, the necessary condition for convexity of the W^τ regression is that cost of debt is more sensitive to leverage than cost of equity.

III. Some Evidence on the Stability of the W^τ for US Firms

We now present some evidence relating to the temporal instability of the cost of capital function for a sample of 151 U.S. companies over the 1973 through 1990 period. The 151 companies represent NYSE firms for which monthly stock price information is continuously available on the tapes provided by the Center of Research in Security Prices (CRSP) over the 1971 through 1990 period.

Tests are conducted in the framework of the regression,

$$W^\tau = \alpha_0 + \beta_1 L_t + \beta_2 L_t^2 + \sum_{i=3}^{n} \beta_i C_t + \varepsilon_t, \tag{9}$$

where W^τ represents the cost of capital, L represents financial leverage, and C represents the set of firm-specific variables thought to impact the firms' cost of capital. The squared leverage term allows for the possibility of a nonlinear relationship between leverage and cost of capital, as implied by distress cost theories.

Cost of capital is defined as $W^\tau = k_s(S/(S+B)) + k_d(1-\tau)(B/(S+B))$, where k_s is the estimated cost of equity, k_d is the cost of debt (interest expense/debt), τ) is the marginal tax rate, S is the market value of equity, and B is total debt. Financial leverage is measured by $(B/(S+B))$. The variables B, k_d, and C, over the interval are obtained from the 1991 COMPUSTAT tapes. The time series on the cost of equity for each firm is estimated from monthly CRSP data by employing the Capital Asset Pricing Model, $k_{si} = RF + \beta_i(Rm-RF)$, where RF represents the yield on the one year t-bill, and R_m the return on the S&P 500 index (e.g., Lintner (1965)).[7]

Table 1 presents the results from the regression model for data that is aggregated within four intervals. The computed F-values from the Chow (1960) and Fisher (1970) tests for the equality of coefficients from contiguous regressions are provided alongside the results from each regression.

The coefficients for L are negative for all the interval regressions, consistent with the hypothesis of a cost savings from leverage. However, the notion of a convex relationship is not suggested. The L coefficient is insignificant for 3 of the 4 regressions, and is negative for the 1979-1981 regression. Several of the control variables are found to contain explanatory power. For instance, the size coefficient is significantly negative for 3 of the 4 regressions, and the growth coefficient is significantly positive in 2 regressions. However, it is notable that the coefficients for some of these variables are mixed. For instance, the uniqueness coefficient is alternately negative and positive.

Therefore, casual analysis of the t-statistics would indicate that the relationship between W^τ and L, and between W^τ and C are unstable over time. There is also considerable fluctuation in the adjusted-R^2 statistics, indicating that the system has temporally inconsistent explanatory power. The results from the Chow-Fisher tests further verify the instability of the systems estimated. The statistics that test the null hypothesis that all the coefficients from contiguous regressions are identical (Chow1), and the statistics that test the null that the L and L^2 coefficients from contiguous

Table 1
The Stability of the Cost of Capital: Interval OIS Estimates from Pooled Data

Dependent Variable is W^r a,b,c,d

	α	L	L^2	SIZ	GRO	DIV	IND	UNQ	LIQ	OR	F	R2	Chow1	Chow2
73-78	0.158φ	-0.092φ	0.026	-0.009φ	0.077φ	0.119	-0.003	-0.173*	0.002	0.068	11.05φ	.091	13.10φ	6.62φ
	(10.252)	(-2.576)	(0.500)	(-2.789)	(5.732)	(1.411)	(-0.914)	(-1.952)	(0.613)	(0.434)	(9.934)	(-2.585)		
	(9.934)	(-2.585)	(0.526)	(-2.795)	(5.000)	(1.538)	(-0.961)	(-1.923)	(0.602)	(0.601)				
79-81	0.181φ	-0.042*	-0.062*	0.002	-0.002	-0.464φ	0.002	-0.004	-0.002	0.087*	8.43f	.129	5.98φ	14.80φ
	(10.416)	(-1.181)	(-1.229)	(0.506)	(-1.054)	(-4.882)	(0.486)	(-0.044)	(-0.759)	(0.549)				
	(18.418)	(-1.660)	(-1.763)	(0.822)	(-0.972)	(-7.234)	(0.905)	(-0.087)	(-1.421)	(1.749)				
82-86	0.162φ	-0.049φ	0.004	-0.004*	0.026φ	0.003	0.003	0.150φ	-0.001	-0.012	22.19f	.202	7.95φ	7.33f
	(18.960)	(-3.984)	(0.345)	(-2.322)	(5.738)	(0.343)	(1.520)	(4.597)	(-0.321)	(-0.150)				
	(15.400)	(-3.611)	(0.400)	(-1.946)	(4.954)	(0.615)	(1.153)	(3.055)	(-0.245)	(-0.121)				
87-90	0.160φ	-0.060φ	0.009	-0.004**	0.001	0.002	-0.006φ	0.114φ	0.001	-0.017	22.65φ	.244		
	(15.807)	(-7.344)	(1.970)	(-1.950)	(0.030)	(0.539)	(-2.706)	(3.259)	(0.595)	(-0.171)				
	(12.958)	(-2.771)	(0.837)	(-2.204)	(0.032)	(-0.615)	(-2.887)	(3.498)	(0.511)	(-0.120)				

a. $W^r = k_s - (1-L) + k_b - (1 \tau_c) L$, where L is obtained using market value of equity.

b. Chow1: F-statistic from the Chow (1960) test of the hypothesis that all coefficients are identical over successive regressions; Chow2: F-statistic from the test of the hypothesis that the LEV coefficient is identical over successive regressions; F and R^2 are the F-value and adjusted R^2 statistics respectively.

c. t-statistics are in parentheses; t-statistics from the GLS estimation are given below those from the OLS estimation. The GLS coefficients are from the heteroscedasticity and autocorrelation-consistent matrix as in White and Domowitz (1984). The coefficients from the GLS estimation are identical to those from the OLS estimation.

d. SIZ is measured by log of Sales; GRO is measured by percentage change in total assets; DIV represents the dividend yield; IND is the industry classification dummy, 1 for manufacturing and 0 for nonmanufacturing; UNQ represents R&D expenses/sales, LIQ represents current assets/total assets; OR represents standard deviation of net operating income/total assets.

*, **, φ: significance levels of 10%, 5% and 1% respectively.

regressions are identical (Chow2), strongly reject the notion of stability in the system. The Chow1 and Chow2 F-statistics are computed to be significant at the 1 percent level of significance. Thus, there is strong evidence to indicate that both the determinants of W^{τ} and the relationship between W^{τ} and L are unstable over time.

The instability of the cost of capital function established in the present study does mean that even neutral leverage decisions that seem to serve no material purpose in one environment, may suddenly acquire or lose value in another environment. Given the generally episodic and costly nature of recapitalizations, the observation of an unstable W^{τ} function suggests that firms may not realistically be able to sustain value-neutral capital structures, as envisioned by the Static Tradeoff framework.

IV. Implications for Capital Budgeting Decisions

The cost of capital lies at the heart of most capital budgeting rules. Students in finance learn that cost of capital represents the discount rate to be employed in the NPV method, or the hurdle rate in the IRR method. Some students may also learn the caveats of blindly employing the NPV or IRR rules. Specifically, it is sometimes pointed out that a positive NPV project should be undertaken as long as doing so does not rule out a competing project of superior potential. However, it is text-book norm to avoid a detailed discussion on the nature of cost of capital as it applies to capital budgeting decisions. For instance, the stochastic nature of cost of capital and its relationship to the perceived risk of projects and financing decisions are generally relegated to secondary debate. Papers by Ingersoll and Ross (1992) and Ross (1995) indicate the importance of also considering the notion that some projects include a right or option on the investment, implying that the appropriate discount rate on these projects could be different from the quoted current cost of capital.

The arguments and evidence presented above highlight the stochastic nature of cost of capital and emphasize the importance of this characteristic in capital budgeting decisions. With a stochastic discounting variable, the decision to accept or reject a project becomes far more complex: the manager trades off the value of accepting a project today with the opportunity of undertaking the project at a later date when costs are lower; the manager faces the risk of accepting (rejecting) a yet-unfinanced investment when it should be rejected (accepted). It may be more practical, in a stochastic discount rate environment, to evaluate projects in terms of a *range* of viability, rather than base decisions on singular benchmarks. Under these circumstances, rates of return (rather than discounted cash flows) should be favored for budgeting and control decisions.

Chapter 4

Capital Budgeting for Multinational Firms

INTRODUCTION

Multinational companies rely on capital budgeting techniques for the evaluation of their direct foreign investment projects. The use of capital budgeting techniques is a direct consequence of their adoption of the stockholders' wealth maximization model as objective function.[1] Maximization of owners' wealth dictates the application of capital budgeting techniques in both the domestic and international contexts. There are specific problems, however, that may complicate capital budgeting for the multinational corporation. Accordingly this chapter examines the specific uses of capital budgeting techniques by multinational corporations in analyzing the financial benefits and costs of a potential investment. It also examines the problems associated with the management of political risks that can be faced when investing internationally.

FOREIGN DIRECT INVESTMENT

Multinational capital budgeting is a direct consequence of a foreign direct investment decision. Motives for direct foreign investment include: (1) strategic motives, (2) behavioral motives, (3) economic motives.[2]

Strategic Motives

Strategic motives for foreign investment include the five following categories.[3]

1. *Market seekers*, who produce in foreign markets either to satisfy local demand or to export to markets other than local market.

2. *Raw material seekers*, who extract raw materials wherever they can be formed, either for export or for further processing and sale in the host country.

3. *Production efficiency seekers*, who produce in countries where one or more of the factors of production are underpriced relative to their productivity.

4. *Knowledge seekers*, who invest in foreign countries to gain access to technology or managerial expertise.

5. *Political safety seekers*, who invest in countries that are considered unlikely to expropriate or interfere with their businesses.[4]

Behavioral Motives

Behavioral motives are those arising from estimates and some auxiliary motives.[5] The four arising are:

1. An outside proposal, provided it comes from a source that can not be easily ignored. The most frequent sources of such proposals are foreign governments, the distributors of the company's products, and its clients.

2. Fear of losing a market.

3. The "bandwagon" effect: very successful activities abroad of a competing firm in the same line of business, or a general belief that investment in some area is "a must."

4. Strong competition from abroad in the home market.[6]

The four motives are:

1. Creation of a market for component and other products.

2. Utilization of old machinery.

3. Capitalization of know-how; spreading of research and development and other fixed costs.

4. Indirect return to a lost market through investment in a country that has commercial agreements with these lost territories.[7]

Economic Motives

Economic motives for direct foreign investment are generally based on the theory of imperfection of individual natural markets for products, factors of production, and financial assets. As argued by Eiteman et al.:[8]

1. Product and factor market imperfections provide an opportunity for multinational firms to outcompete local firms, particularly in industries characterized by worldwide oligopolistic competition, because the multinational firms have superiority in econo-

mies of scale, managerial expertise, technology, differentiated products, and financial strength.

2. Oligopolistic competition also motivates firms to make defensive investments abroad to save both export and home markets from foreign competition.

3. The product theory suggests that new products are first developed in the most advanced countries by large firms that have the ability to undertake research and development. The new products are introduced into the home market and later exported. As the product matures and the production process becomes standardized, foreign competition reduces profits and threatens the home market. Part of the production process is then defensively relocated abroad to take advantage of lower unit costs of labor or other factors of production.

4. Defensive direct foreign investment may also motivated by "follow-the-leader" behavior; a desire to establish credibility with local customers; a "grow-to-survive" philosophy; a desire to gain knowledge by acquiring firms with valuable expertise; and a need to follow the customer in the case of service firms.

5. The theory of internationalization holds that firms having a competitive advantage because of their ability to generate valuable proprietary information can only capture the full benefits of innovation through direct foreign investment.

RISK ANALYSIS

Direct capital investment is not without specific risks that can affect the value and the feasibility of the project. The following list includes some of the risks that can be faced in the global economy.

1. A distortion of the value of the project may arise with the failure to distinguish between project and parent cash flows. A decision has to be made whether to analyze the capital budgeting decision from a project or a parent perspective.

2. Fluctuating exchange rates can also distort the value of the cash flows and the desirability of the project. Accurate forecasting of the exchange rates over the life of the project may be necessary for an accurate and reliable analysis of the capital budgeting decision.

3. Changes in the general price or specific price levels in the foreign country can also create a distortion in the capital budgeting decision if they are not accounted for. The inflation factor has to be incorporated in the analysis.

4. Various obstacles may be created by the foreign country to hinder the remittance of earnings to the parent firm. Examples of obstacles include fund blockages, exchange control appropriation, and various forms of foreign currency controls.

5. Other factors that can affect the remittance of funds to the parent company include tax laws and institutional factors as well as political factors.

Each of these risks needs to be accounted for in the analysis of a capital budgeting decision by multinational firms. The following questions need to be addressed:

- What level of confidence is present in the various elements of the cash flow forecast?
- For the elements involving the greatest degree of uncertainty, what will be the result of a large forecasting error?
- How sensitive is the value of the investment to the foreseeable risks?[9]

PROJECT VERSUS PARENT CASH FLOWS: THE ISSUES

Project cash flows and parent cash flows differ as a result of the various tax requirements and exchange controls that can affect the final amounts remitted to the parent company. Two schools of thought are instrumental in the choice of cash flows. One school of thought that discounts the effect of restriction on repatriation favors the use of the project cash flows in the capital budgeting analysis. Following this precept, the list of elements of projected return from an overseas industrial investment includes the following:

1. All income, operating and nonoperating, from the overseas operating unit, based on its demonstrated capacity to supply existing markets with its present management and excluding any impact of the merger of resources with those of the investing company.
2. Additional operating income of the overseas unit resulting from the merger of its own capabilities with those of the investing corporation.
3. Additional income from increased export sales resulting from the proposed investment action, including (a) additional export income at each U.S. operating unit that manufactures products related to those that will be produced overseas and (b) additional earnings from new export activity at the overseas operating unit resulting from its increased capabilities to sell beyond the boundaries of its traditional national markets.
4. Additional income from increased licensing opportunities shown both in the books of the affected U.S. units and the books of the overseas unit.
5. Additional income from importing technology, product design, or hardware from the overseas operating unit to U.S. operating units.
6. Income presently accruing from the investment but seriously and genuinely threatened by economic, political, or social change in an overseas region.[10]

A second position, derived from economic theory, is that the value of a project is determined by the net present value of future cash flows back to the investor. Therefore, the project cash flows that are or can be repatriated are included, since only accessible funds can be used to pay dividends and interest, amortize the firm's debt, and be reinvested.[11] In spite of the strong theoretical argument in favor of analyzing foreign projects from the viewpoint of the parent company, empirical evidence from survey of multinationals shows that firms are using project flows and rates of return as well as parent flows and rates of return.[12] In fact, a more recent survey shows that multinationals were almost evenly split among those that looked at cash flow solely from the parents' perspective, solely from the subsidiaries' perspective, and from both perspectives.[13] Those who viewed cash flow from the point of view of the subsidiary felt that the subsidiaries were separate businesses and should be viewed as such. Those who took the parent company's view argued that the investment was ultimately made from the parent company's stockholders. Finally, those who adopted both perspectives considered this the safest approach, providing two ways of making a final decision. One of the respondent treasures put it as follows:

The project must first be evaluated on its chances of success locally. It must be profitable from the subsidiary's point of view. Then you step back and look at it from the parents' point of view. What cash flows are available to be remitted or otherwise used in another country? What's going to come back to the parent is the real issue. The project has to meet both tests to be acceptable.[14]

What appears from the above discussion is that the use of the parent company's view is compatible with the traditional view of net present value in capital budgeting, whereas the use of the project's view leads to a closer approximation of the effect on consolidated earnings per share.[15]

An operational differentiation between project cash flows and present cash flows is as follows:

1. Cash flows generated by subsidiary
2. Corporate taxes paid to host government
3. After-tax cash flows to subsidiary
4. Retained earnings by subsidiary
5. Cash flows remitted by subsidiary
6. Withholding tax paid to host government
7. After-tax cash flows remitted by subsidiary
8. Exchange rate
9. Cash flows received by parent
10. Corporate taxes paid to local government
11. Cash flows receivable to parent

PROJECT VERSUS PARENT CASH FLOWS: AN EXAMPLE

To illustrate the differences between the subsidiary perspective and the parent company perspective in multinational budgeting, consider the example of a Jordanian subsidiary and a U.S.-based multinational corporation considering the decision to invest in new equipment on the basis of the following information:

• The cost of investment is JD 39,100. The exchange rate is $2/JD.
• The cash flows for an estimated useful life of six years are respectively, JD 20,000, JD 14,000, JD 10,000, JD 6,000, JD 5,000, and JD 4,000.

Exhibit 4.1
Subsidiary Views of Foreign Direct Investment

	Year 1	Year 2	Year3	Year 4	Year 5	Year 6
Cost of Investment JD 39,1000						
Cash Flows	JD 20,000	JD14,000	JD 10,000	JD 6,000	JD 5,000	JD 4,000
Discount Factor 10%	0.909	0.826	0.753	0.683	0.621.	0.564
PV of Cash Flows	JD18,J80	JD 11,564	JD 7,530	JD 4,098	JD 3,105	JD 2,256
Cumulative NPV	-JD 20,920	-JD 9,356	.-JD 1,826	-JD 2,272	-JD 5,377	-JD7,633

- The required rate of return is 10 percent.
- The Jordanian government does not tax the earnings of the subsidiary, but requires a withholding tax of 10 percent on funds remitted to the parent company.
- The U.S. tax rate on foreign earnings of the subsidiary is 25 percent.
- The exchange rate of the Jordanian dinar is estimated to be $2.00 at the end of years 1 and 2, $1.80 at the end of years 3 and 4, and $1.50 at the end of years 5 and 6.

The capital budgeting from the project or subsidiary perspective is shown in Exhibit 4.1. The cumulative net present value (NPV) is JD 7,633; therefore, the project is acceptable from the subsidiary's point of view. The capital budgeting from the parent's perspective is shown in Exhibit 4.2. The project appears profitable from the subsidiary's perspective, and unprofitable from the parent's perspective.

COST OF CAPITAL FOR THE MULTINATIONAL FIRM

In both the international rate-of-return method and the net present value method, a cost of "capital," or a "hurdle rate," is needed. The two rules of thumb are as follows:

1. The internal rate of return must be superior to the hurdle rate to be acceptable.
2. The present value, obtained by discounting cash flows at the hurdle rate, must be positive for a project to be acceptable.

For a multinational corporation, the overall cost of capital is the sum of the costs of each financing source, weighted by the proportion of that financing source in the firm's total capital structure. The weighted average cost of capital is therefore:

$$K = \frac{E}{V} \times K_e + \frac{D}{V}K_d(1 - t)$$

Exhibit 4.2
Capital Budgeting: Parent Company's Perspective

	Year 1	Year 2	Year3	Year 4	Year 5	Year 6
Cost of Investment	$78,200					
Cash Flows	JD 20,000	JD 14,000	JD 10,000	JD 6,000	JD5,000	JD 4,000
Withholding Tax (10%)	JD 2,000	JD 1,400	JD 1,000	JD 600	JD 500	JD 400
Funds Remitted	JD 18,000	JD 12,600	JD 9,000	JD 5,400	JD 4,500	JD 3,600
Exchange Rate	$2	$2	$1.80	$1.80	$1.50	$1.50
Funds to be Received	$36,000	$25,200	$16,200	$9,720	$6,750	$5,400
US Taxes Paid (25%)	$9,000	$6,300	$4,050	$2,430	$1,687.50	$1,350
After Tax Funds	$27,000	$18,900	$12,150	$7,290	$5,062.50	$4,050
Discounting Factor	0.909	0.826	0.753	0.683	0.621	0.564
PV of Cash Flows	$24,543	$15,611.40	$9,148.95	$4,979.07	$3,143.81	$2,284.20
Cumulative NPV	-$53,657	-$38,045.60	-$28,896.65	-$23,917.58	-$20,773.77	-$18,489.57

where

      K = weighted average cost of capital
      K_d = cost of debt
      K_e = test of equity
      t   = tax rate
      D = value of the firm's debt
      E = value of the firm's equity
      V = D + E = total value of the firm.

The cost of capital of a multinational corporation is assumed to be affected by a host of factors, including size of the firm, access to international capital markets, international diversification, tax concession, exchange risk, and country risk.[16] The larger the firm, the greater the access to international capital markets; the greater its international diversification, the more it capitalizes on tax concessions; the lower its exchange rate exposure, the lower the country risk and the lower the cost of capital to the multinational corporation (MNC).

A MULTINATIONAL CAPITAL BUDGETING EXAMPLE

Theoretically, the capital budgeting process for a MNC involves the following phases:

1. The identification of cash flows generated by the proposed project.
2. The identification of cash flows available for repatriation to the MNC.
3. The concession of cash flows by means of exchange rates.
4. The adjustments to compensate for financial risks, including sensitivity analysis.
5. The selection of a minimum rate of return.
6. The calculation of investment profitability, including sensitivity analysis.
7. The acceptance or rejection of the proposed investment.[17]

The input of multinational capital budgeting decisions are:

a. Initial investment
b. Consumer demand
c. Price
d. Variable cost
e. Fixed cost
f. Project lifetime
g. Salvage (liquidation) value
h. Fund-transfer restriction

i. Exchange rates

j. Required rate of return[18]

The net present value (NPV) method, is used, based on the following formulas:

$$\text{NPV} = -\text{IC} + \sum_{t=1}^{n} \frac{CF_t}{(1 + K)^t} + \frac{SV_n}{(1 + K)^n}$$

where

IC $\quad$ = Initial cost of the investment
CF_t $\quad$ = Cash low in period t
SV_n $\quad$ = Salvage value
K $\quad$ = Required rate of return on the project
N $\quad$ = Lifetime rate of return on the project

If the internal rate of return is used, the equation would be:

$$O = -\text{IC} + \sum_{t=1}^{n} \frac{CF_t}{(1 + r)^t} + \frac{SV_n}{(1 + r)^n}$$

where

r = internal rate of return

An illustration concerns the case of Computer Inc., a U.S.-based manufacturer that is considering exporting its PCs to Denmark. The decision was made to create a Danish subsidiary that will manufacture and sell the PCs in Europe.

1. *Revenue information*: The forecast price and sales of the PCs were as follows:

Year	Price per PC	Sales in Denmark and Europe
1	Krone 600	5,000,000 units
2	Krone 700	6,000,000 units
3	Krone 800	8,000,000 units

2. *Initial investment*: The parent company intends to invest a total of $200,000,000.

3. *Variable costs per units* are estimated as follows:

Year	Variable Cost per Unit
1	Krone 100
2	Krone 120
3	Krone 150

4. Fixed expenses are estimated to be KR 1,100,000,000 per year for the first three years.

5. Noncash expenses including depreciation expenses are estimated to be KR 200,000,000 per year.

6. Most government taxes include a 20 percent tax on earnings and a 10 percent tax on remittances to parent. The subsidiary intends to remit 50 percent of net cash flow to the parent company.

7. Exchange rates are estimated to be as follows:

Year	Exchange Rates of Krone
1	$0.15
2	$0.17
3	$0.20

8. Required rate of return for the project is 10 percent.

The capital budgeting analysis is shown in Exhibit 4.3. This shows that for the first three years considered, the project has a cumulative positive cash flow in year 3 of $219,010,514 The decision should be to accept the project.

CAPITAL BUDGETING ISSUES FOR MULTINATIONALS

Capital Budgeting under Inflation

Changes in the general price level can create a distortion in the capital budgeting analysis of multinationals. A specific consideration of the impact of inflation on the analysis is warranted. The correct approach includes either using a money discount rate to discount money cash flows, or using a real discount rate to discount real cash flows. Money cash flows are cash flows measured in dollars from various periods having different purchasing power. Real cash flows are cash flows measured in dollars having the same purchasing power. The real cash flow for a given year t expressed in terms of dollars of 0 (the base year) is equal to the money cash flow for that year t multiplied by the wing ratio:

$$\frac{\text{Price level index in year 0}}{\text{Price level index in year 1}}$$

For example, if an investment promised a money return of $100 for three years and the price index for years 0 through 3 is 100.0, 110.0, 121.0, and 133.1, respectively, the real cash flows are as follows:

Year 1: $100 \times 100/110 = 90.90$
Year 2: $100 \times 100/121 = 82.64$
Year 3: $100 \times 100/133.1 = 75.13$

Exhibit 4.3
Capital Budgeting Analysis: Computer Inc.

	Year 0	Year 1	Year 2	Year 3
1. Sales in Units		5,000,000	6,000,000	8,000,000
2. Price per Unit		KR600	KR700	KR800
3. Total Sale = (1) x (2)		KR3,000,000,000	KR4,200,000,000	KR6,400,000,000
4. Variable Cost		KR100	KR120	KR150
5. Total Variable Cost Per Unit		KR500,000,000	KR720,000,000	KR1,200,000,000
6. Fixed Cost		KR1,100,000,000	KR1,100,000,000	KR1,100,000,000
7. Noncash Expense		KR200,000,000	KR200,000,000	KR200,000,000
8. Total Expense = (5) + (6) + (7)		KR1,800,000,000	KR2,020,000,000	KR2,500,000,000
9. Before Tax Subsidiary Earnings = (3)-(8)		KR1,2000,000,000	KR2,180,000,000	KR3,900,000,000
10. Danish Government Tax (20%)		KR240,000,000	KR436,000,000	KR780,000,000
11. After Tax Subsidiary Earnings		KR960,000,000	KR1,744,000,000	KR3,120,000,000
12. Net Cash Flow to Subsidiary (11) + (7)		KR1,160,000,000	KR1,944,000,000	KR3,320,000,000
13. Remittance by Subsidiary		KR 580,000,000	KR972,000,000	KR1,660,000,000
14. Withholding Tax (10%)		KR58,000,000		KR166,000,000
15. Net Remittance by Subsidiary		KR522,000,000	KR874,800,000	KR1,494,000,000
16. Exchange Rate of Danish Krone		$0.15	$0.17	$0
17. Cash Flow to Parent		$78,300,000.00	$148,716,000.00	$298,800,000.00
18. PV of Parent Cash Flows at (1090)		$71,174,700.00	$122,839,416.00	$224,996,400
19. Initial Investment	$200,000,000			
20. Cumulative NPV of Cash Flows		($ 128,825,300.00)	($ 5,985,884.00)	$219,010,516.00

The money discount rate r can also be computed. Assuming that f is the annual rate of inflation, i is the real discount rate, and the decision maker is in the zero bracket, then

$$r = (1 + f)(1 + i) - 1$$
or
$$r = i + f + if$$

For example, if the real return before taxes is 3 percent, the rate of inflation is 10 percent, and the nominal discount rate is 10 percent, the nominal discount rate is:

$$0.03 + 0.10 + 0.003 = 0.133$$

To illustrate the correct analysis under inflation, assume the same data as in the previous example. The correct analysis can be either of two procedures. The first analysis discounts money cash flows using a money discount rate. The present value of the investment will be computed as follows:

Period	Money Cash Flow	Nominal Present Factor at 13.3%	Present Value
1	100	0.8826	88.26
2	100	0.7792	77.92
3	100	0.6874	68.74
			234.92

The second analysis discounts the real cash flows using a real discount rate. The present value of the investment will give the same present value as follows:

Period	Real Cash Flow	Present Value at 3%	Present Value
1	90.9	0.9709	88.254
2	82.64	39426	77.896
3	75.13	0.9151	68.751
			234.901

Assuming a marginal tax rate t on nominal income, the nominal discount rate will be computed as follows:

$$1 + (1 - t)r = (1 + f) + 1 + i(1 - t)$$
or
$$r = i + if + f/(1 - t)$$

Assuming the tax rate to be 30 percent, the nominal rate is then computed as follows:

$$r = 0.03 + (0.03 \times 0.10) + 0.10 / (1 - 0.30) = 0.1758$$

In other words, a nominal rate of 17.58 percent is needed for an investor in a 30 percent tax bracket and facing an inflation rate of 10 percent to earn a real discount rate of 3 percent.

Impact of Exchange Rate Changes

Capital budgeting for multinational corporations can lead to different results depending on the nature of the expectation of the levels of exchange rates. In general, three scenarios are possible:

(1) a stable exchange rate, (2) a strong exchange rate characterized by increasing values over the life of the project, and (3) a weak exchange rate by decreasing values over the life of the project. Exhibits 4.4 to 4.6 illustrate the impact of each of these three scenarios on the cumulative NPV of cash flows of a capital project by the Jordanian subsidiary of an American multinational corporation. The NPVs of the project are $43,610 under a strong rate scenario, $24,210 under a stable rate scenario, and $14,500 under a weak rate scenario. The large difference between these scenarios points to the importance of exchange rate fluctuations in multinational capital budgeting and also the importance of accurate exchange rate forecasting.

Foreign Tax Regulations

The tax regulations in the country where the project is planned are extremely important to the capital budgeting analysis. The first reason concerns the requirements of using tax cash flows for the capital budgeting decisions as well as a tax-adjusted project cost of capital. The second reason is that countries levy different income tax rates on the earnings of subsidiaries as well as remittance taxes when they are finally remitted to the parent company. The percentage of the profit that can be remitted can also be the subject of regulations that attempt to limit the amount of funds leaving the country, especially in case of the developing countries. Some countries, in fact, may require that a certain percentage of the profit be reinvested in specific areas of importance to the economic and social growth of the country.

Political and Economic Risk

Multinational companies face the risks created by political, exchange, and economic changes. This chapter covers some of the techniques used to manage

Exhibit 4.4
Capital Budgeting Analysis under a Strong Rate Scenario*

	Year 1	Year2	Year 3	Year 4	Year 5	Year 6
Funds Remitted After Withholding Taxes	JD 20,000	JD 20,000	JD 20,000	JD 20,000	JD 20,000	JD 20,000
Exchange Rate	$2.00	$2.10	$2.20	$2.30	$2.40	$2.50
Cash Flow to the Parent	$40,000	$42,000	$44,000	$46,000	$48,000	$50,000
Discount Rate	0.909	0.826	0.753	0.683	0.621	0.564
PV of Cash Flows	$36,360	$34,692	$33,132	$31,418	$29,808	$28,200
Cumulative NPV of Cash Flows	($ 113,640)	($ 78,948)	($ 45,816)	($ 14,398)	$ 15,410	$ 43,610

*Initial investment by the parent: $150,000.

Exhibit 4.5
Capital Budgeting Analysis under a Stable Rate Scenario*

	Year 1	Year2	Year 3	Year 4	Year 5	Year 6
Funds Remitted After Withholding Taxes	JD 20,000	JD 20,000	JD 20,000	JD 20,000	JD 20,000	JD 20,000
Exchange Rate	$2.00	$2.00	$2.00	$2.00	$2.00	$2.00
Cash Flow to the Parent	$40,000	$40,000	$40,000	$40,000	$40,000	$40,000
Discount Rate	0.909	0.826	0.753	0.683	0.621	0.564
PV of Cash Flows	$36,360	$33,040	$30,120	$27,320	$24,5401	$22,560
Cumulative NPV of Cash Flows	($ 113,640)	($ 80,600)	($ 50,480)	($ 23,160)	$1,680	$ 24,240

*Initial investment by the parent: $150,000.

Exhibit 4.6
Capital Budgeting Analysis under a Weak Rate Scenario*

	Year 1	Year 2	Year 3	Year 4	Year 5	Year 6
Funds Remitted After Withholding Taxes	JD 20,000	JD 20,000	JD 20,000	JD 20,000	JD 20,000	JD 20,000
Exchange Rate	$2.00	$1.80	$1.60	$1.40	$1.20	$1.00
Cash Flow to the Parent	$40,000	$36,000	$32,000	$28,000	$24,000	$20,000
Discount Rate	0.909	0.826	0.753	0.683	0.621	0.564
PV of Cash Flows	$36,360	$29,736	$24,096	$19,124	$14,904	$11,280
Cumulative NPV of Cash Flows	($113,640)	($83,904)	($59,808)	($40,684)	($25,780)	($14,500)

*Initial investment by the parent: $150,000.

113

political and economic risks. In a capital budgeting context, various ways may be used to account for political risks. One is to adjust each year's cash flows by the cost of an exchange risk adjustment. Other ways include shortening the minimum payback period, raising the discount rate or required rate of return without adjusting cash flows, and adjusting cash flows and raising the discount rate. A consensus seems to suggest that multinationals should use either the risk-adjusted discount rate or the certainty-equivalent approach to adjust proper estimates for political risk.[19]

Risk-Adjusted Discount Rate Method

One of the techniques for incorporating risk in the evaluation process is the risk-adjusted discount rate, which involves manipulating the discount rate applied to the cash flows to reflect the amount of risk inherent in a project. The higher the risk associated with a project, the higher the discount rate applied to cash flows. If a given project is perceived to be twice as risky as most projects acceptable to the firm and the cost of capital is 12 percent, the correct adjusted discount rate is 24 percent.

Certainty-Equivalent Method

Another technique for incorporating risk in the evaluation process is the certainty-equivalent method, which involves adjusting the future cash flows so that a project can be evaluated on a riskless basis. The adjustment is formulated as follows:

$$NPV = \sum_{t=0}^{n} \frac{\alpha_t CF_t}{(1 + R_F)^t} - I_0$$

where

α = Risk coefficient applied to the cash flow of period t (CF_t)
I_0 = Initial cost of the project
R_F = Risk-free rate.

As the formula shows, the method multiplies the future cash flows by certainty equivalents to obtain a riskless cash flow. Note also that the discount rate used is R_F is a risk-free rate of interest.

To illustrate the certainty:

I_0 = Initial cost = \$30,000
CF_1 = cash flow, year 1 = \$10,000
CF_2 = cash flow, year 2 = \$20,000
CF_3 = cash flow, year 3 = \$30,000

α_1 = certainty equivalent, year 1 = 0.9
α_2 = certainty equivalent, year 2 = 0.8
α_3 = certainty equivalent, year 3 = 0.6

The NPV of the investment using a risk-free discount rate of 6 percent is computed as in Exhibit 4.7.

Since the NPV is positive, the investment should be considered acceptable. The main advantage of the certainty-equivalent method is that it allows the assignment for a different risk factor to each cash flow, given that risk can be concentrated in one or more periods.

The certainty-equivalent method and the risk-adjusted discount rate method are comparable methods of evaluating risk. To produce similar ranking, the following equation must hold:

$$\frac{\alpha_t CF_t}{(1 + R_F)^t} = \frac{CF_t}{(1 + R_A)^t}$$

where

α_t = Risk coefficient used in the certainty-equivalent method
R_F = Risk-free discount rate
R_A = Discount rate used in the risk adjusted discount rate method
CF_t = Future cash flow.

Solving for t yields:

$$\alpha = \frac{(1 + R_F)^t}{(1 + R_A)^t}$$

Given that R_A and R_F are constant and $R_A < R_F$, then αt decreases over time, which means that risk increases over time. To illustrate, assume that in the previous example R_A = 15 percent. Then

$$\alpha_1 = \frac{(1 + R_F)^1}{(1 + R_A)^1} = \frac{(1 + 0.006)^1}{(1 + 0.15)^1} = 0.921$$

$$\alpha_2 = \frac{(1 + R_F)^2}{(1 + R_A)^2} = \frac{(1 + 0.006)^2}{(1 + 0.15)^2} = 0.848$$

$$\alpha_3 = \frac{(1 + R_F)^3}{(1 + R_A)^3} = \frac{(1 + 0.006)^3}{(1 + 0.15)^3} = 0.783$$

In many cases this assumption of increasing risk may not be realistic.

Exhibit 4.7
Using a Risk-Free Discount Rate

Period	Cash Flow (CF1)	Risk Coefficient (α)	Certainty Equivalent	Risk Free Rate (RF)	Present Value
1	$10,000	0.9	$9,000	0.943	$8,487
2	$20,000	0.8	$16,000	0.89	$14,420
3	$30,000	0.6	$18,000	0.84	$15,120
Present Value Cash Flows					$37,847
Initial Investment					$30,000
Net Present Value					$7,847

Expropriation

Multinational companies sometimes face the extreme outcome of political risk expropriation. One way to account for expropriation is to charge a premium for political risk insurance to each year's cash flow, whether or not such insurance is actually purchased. Another way, suggested by Shapiro, is to examine the impact of expropriation on the project's present value to the parent company. As a result, the old and new present values will be

$$\text{Old present value} = -C_0 + \sum_{t=1}^{n} \frac{X_t}{(1 + k)^t}$$

$$\text{New present value} = -C_0 + \sum_{t=1}^{h-1} \frac{X_t}{(1 + k)^t} + \frac{G_h}{(1 + k)^t}$$

where

C_0 = initial investment outlay
X_t = Parent's expected after-tax cash flow from the project in year t
n = Life of the project
k = Project cost of capital
h = Year in which expropriation takes place
G_h = Expected value of the net compensation provided.

The compensation (G_h) is supposed to come from one of the following sources:

1. Direct compensation paid to the firm by the local government.
2. Indirect compensation, such as other business contracts to the firm expropriated (an example would be the management contracts received by oil companies after the Venezuelan government nationalized their properties).
3. Payment received from political insurance.
4. Tax deductions received after the parent declares the expropriation as an extraordinary loss.
5. A reduction in the amount of capital that must be repaid by the project equal to the unamortized portion of any local borrowing.

Blocked Funds

Multinationals sometimes face the situation in which funds are blocked for various reasons, including forms of exchange control. Again, Shapiro suggested raising the present value expression to include the impact of blocked funds on the project's cash flows. As a result, the old and the new present values will be

Old present value $= -C_0 + \sum_{t=1}^{n} \dfrac{X_t}{(1 + k)^t}$

New present value

$$= -C_0 + \sum_{t=1}^{j=1} \dfrac{X_t}{(1 + k)^t} + \sum_{t=j}^{n} \dfrac{Y_t}{(1 + k)^t}$$
$$+ (1 - \alpha_j)\sum_{t=j}^{n} \dfrac{(X - Y_t)}{(1 + k)^t} + \alpha_j\sum_{t=j}^{n} \dfrac{(X - Y_t)}{(1 + r)^{n-t}}$$

where the symbols C_0, X_t, n, and k are as in the formulas used for expropriation. The new symbols are

j = Year in which funds become blocked
n = Year in which exchange controls are removed
α_j = Probability of exchange controls in year 1 and 0 in other years
Y_t = Units of currency that can be repatriated when exchange costs do exist.

Uncertain Salvage Value

When the salvage value may be uncertain, Madura suggested the estimation of a break-even salvage value or break-even terminal value, the salvage value for which NPV = 0. The break-even salvage value is estimated by setting the net present value equal to zero as follows:

$$\text{NPV} = -\text{OI} + \sum_{t=1}^{n} \dfrac{\text{CF}_t}{(1 + r)^t} + \dfrac{\text{SV}_n}{(1 + z)^n}$$

$$0 = -\text{OI} + \sum_{t=1}^{n} \dfrac{\text{CF}_t}{(1 + r)^t} + \dfrac{\text{SV}_n}{(1 + z)^n}$$

$$\text{SV}_n = \left[\text{OI} - \sum_{t=1}^{n} \dfrac{\text{CF}_t}{(1 + r)^t}\right](1 + z)^n$$

where

NPV = Net present value
0   = Zero
SV_n = Salvage value
OI   = Original investment
CF_t = Cash flow at time t
r = Desired rate of return.[20]

EVALUATION OF INTERNATIONAL ACQUISITIONS

Foreign mergers and acquisitions are on the increase, particularly in the United States, owing to the resulting wealth effects. The reasons for foreign investment in the United States include the following.[21]

1. Dollar devaluation effect expressed as a documented inverse relation between the exchange rate of the U.S. dollar and the level of foreign investment in the United States.[22]

2. Favorable tax treatment for foreign buyers because overseas firms that acquire American companies may have the ability to deduct interest on acquisition debt both in the United States and in their home countries, through, for example, the creation of a third-country subsidiary to finance the deal when this tax treatment of such units is favorable.[23] A description of a typical plan follows:

A typical plan would have the foreign acquirer borrow 100 percent of the acquisition cost and establish two subsidiaries, a US acquisition subsidiary and a finance subsidiary in a third country. The foreign acquirer injects a fraction of the borrowed funds as equity into its third-country finance subsidiary. The third-country finance subsidiary then would loan all of its funds to its brother/sister company, the US acquisition subsidiary. The foreign acquirer deducts interest expense on acquisition debt and receives an income tax benefit on its own operation from its home country. Meanwhile, the bulk of the borrowed funds are loaned by the third-country finance subsidiary, which deducts the interest expense on the debt against the income of the acquired operations and receives a US tax benefit. If the interest income that the third-country finance subsidiary receives from the US acquisition subsidiary does not trigger significant taxation in the form of US withholding tax, income taxation by the host country of the finance subsidiary or income taxation for the foreign parent, an extra tax benefit for the acquisition interest expense has been achieved.[24]

3. Goodwill accounting treatment because foreign companies create acquired goodwill through their choice of acquisition accounting:

In deciding how high to bid, foreign companies do not have to worry about penalizing future profits. They can write off goodwill immediately against their balance sheet reserves; this shrinks the balance sheet but profits are unaffected. If acquired goodwill is left on the balance sheet as is done in United States (and Canada), companies must then amortize it from profit over forty years; reported profits are reduced by the amortization charge each year for as many years as it takes to eliminate the acquired goodwill from the balance sheet altogether.[25]

The evaluation of international acquisition is similar to a capital budgeting problem. The decision is to determine if the net present value of a company from the acquiring firm's perspective (NPV_a) is positive. It may be computed as follows:

$$NPV_a = -(IO_f)SP_{-t} + \sum_{t=1}^{n} \frac{(CF_{f,t})(SP_t)}{(1 + r)^t} + \frac{SV_f SP_n}{(1 + r)^n}$$

where

NPV_n = Net present value of a foreign takeover prospect
IO_f = Acquisition price in foreign currency

SP   = Spot rate of the foreign currency
$CF_{f,t}$ = Foreign currency cash flows per period to be remitted
r = Required rate of return on the acquisition of the company
SV_f = Salvage value in foreign-currency units
n = Time at which the company will be sold.[26]

MANAGING POLITICAL RISK

Capital budgeting decisions as well as other operating, financing, and distribution decisions taken by multinational firms need to take into account the
impact of political risk on the potential outcomes of these decisions: There is
objective need for a definition of the nature of political risk, methods for forecasting it, and a role for management accounting in the management of this
political risk.

Nature of Political Risk

Political risk is a phenomenon that characterizes an unfriendly human climate
in both developed and developing countries. A high crime rate, or an upsurge
of violent unrest, even in highly developed countries qualifies such countries
for the dubious title of "political risk." Political risk essentially refers to the
potential economic losses arising as a result of governmental measures or special
situations that may either limit or prohibit the multinational activities of a firm.
Examples of these situations include those (1) when discontinuities occur in the
business environment, (2) when they are difficult to anticipate, and (3) when
they result from political change.

Political risk can affect all foreign firms; in such a case it is *macropolitical
risk*. It may, however, affect only selected foreign firms or industries, or foreign
firms with specific characteristics. In such a case it is *micropolitical risk*. In both
cases the risk refers to "that uncertainty stemming from unanticipated and unexpected acts of governments or other organizations which may cause a loss to
the business firm."[27] It is manifest through a climate of uncertainty dominated
by a probable loss to the business enterprise. It may arise from different sources.
Root noted that a wide spectrum of political risks may be generated "by the
attitudes, policies and overt behavior of those governments and other local
power renters such as rival political, parties, labor unions, and nationalistic
groups."[28] A study prepared for the Financial Executives Research Foundation
identified the following twelve political risk factors:

- radical change in government composition or policy;
- expropriation;
- nationalization;
- attitude of opposition groups;

- probability of opposition-group takeover,
- attitude toward foreign investment;
- quality of government management;
- ownership requirements;
- anti-private-sector influence;
- labor instability;
- relationship with the company's home government;
- relationship with neighboring countries.[29]

Political risk may lead to various outcomes, namely expropriation/nationalization, compulsory local equity participation, operational restrictions, discrimination, price controls, blockage of remittances, and breach of government contracts. Given the negative impacts of the outcomes of political risk on foreign operations, especially in the extreme case in which a government takes over a business activity through confiscation and expropriation, there is a strong need to be able to forecast political risk.

How to Forecast Political Risk

It would not be surprising to learn that various proposals have been made about how to forecast political risks; Robock and Simmonds suggested an evaluation of the vulnerability of a company to political risk by an analysis of its operations, with the following questions in mind:

- Are periodic external inputs of new technology required?
- Will the project be competing strongly with local nationals who are in, or trying to enter, the same field?
- Is the operation dependent on natural resources, particularly minerals or oil?
- Does the investment put pressure on the country's balance of payments?
- Does the enterprise have a strong monopoly position in the local market?
- Is the product socially essential and acceptable?[30]

Robert Stobaugh noticed that a number of U.S.-based multinational enterprises had developed scales with which to rate countries on the basis of their investment climates.[31] An *Argus Capital Market Report* offered for country risk analysis a laundry list of economic indicators to "educate the decision-maker and force him to think in terms of the relevant economic fundamental."[32] These indicators are monetary base, domestic base, foreign reserves, purchasing power parity index, currency/deposit ratio, consumer prices as a percentage change, balance of payments, goods and services as a percentage of foreign reserves, percentage change exports/percentage change imports, exports as a percentage of the GNP, imports as a percentage of the GNP, foreign factor income payments as a percentage of the GNP, average tax rate, government deficit as a percentage of the GNP, government expenditures, real GNP as a percentage change, and real per capita GNP as a percentage change.

Shapiro offered the following common characteristics of country risk:

1. A large government deficit relative to GDP.
2. A high rate of money expansion if it is combined with a relatively fixed exchange rate.
3. High leverage combined with highly variable terms of trade.
4. Substantial government expenditures yielding low rates of return.
5. Price controls, interest rate ceilings, trade restriction, and other government-imposed barriers to the smooth adjustment of the economy to changing relative price.
6. A citizenry that demands, and a political system that accepts, government responsibility for maintaining and expanding the nation's standard of living through public sector spending. The less stable the political system, the more important this factor is likely to be.[33]

More recently, Rummel and Heenan provided a four-way classification of attempts to forecast political interference: "grand tours," "old hands," Delphi techniques, and quantitative method.[34] A "grand tour" involves a visit of the potential host country by an executive or a team of people for an inspection tour and later to the home office. Superficiality and overdose of selective information have marred the grand tour technique.

The "old hands" technique involves acquiring area expertise from seasoned educators, diplomats, journalists, or businesspeople. Evidently, too much implicit faith is put in the judgment of these so-called experts.

The Delphi techniques may be used to survey a knowledgeable group. First, selective elements influencing the political climate are chosen. Next, experts are asked to rank these factors toward the development of an overall measure or index of political risk. Finally, countries are ranked on the basis of the index. As stated by Rummel and Heenan, the "strength of the Delphi technique rests on the posing of relevant questions. When they are defective, the entire structure crumbles."[35]

The quantitative methods technique involves developing elaborate models using multivariate analysis to either explain and describe underlying relationships affecting a station-state, or to predict future political events. Two such political risk models using this technique may be identified in the literature and are examined next.

The Knudsen "Ecological" Approach

Harald Knudsen's model involves gathering socioeconomic data depicting the "ecological structures" or investment climate of a particular foreign environment

Exhibit 4.8
The National Propensity to Expropriate Model

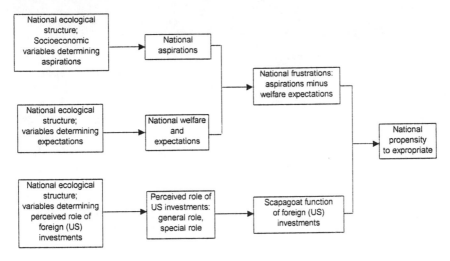

to be used to predict political behavior in general and the national propensity to expropriate in particular.[36] (The model is shown in Exhibit 4.8.) The model maintains that national propensity expropriate may be explained by "a national frustration" factor and "scapegoat of foreign investment." Basically, if the level of national frustration is high and at the time the level of foreign investment presence is also high, these foreign investments become a scapegoat, leading to a high propensity to expropriate. The level of frustration is envisaged as the difference between the level of aspirations and the level of welfare expectations. The scapegoat of foreign investment is determined by the perceived general and special role of foreign investment.

The variables are measured as follows. First, national aspirations may be measured by six proxy variables, namely degree of urbanization, literacy rate, number of newspapers, number of radios, degree of labor unionization, and the national endowment of national resources. Second, the welfare of people may be measured by proxy variables, namely infant survival rate, caloric consumption, number of doctors per population size, number of hospital beds per population size, percentage of housing with piped water supply, and per capita gross national product. Third, national expectations may be measured by the percentage change in per capita gross national product and the percentage of gross national product being invested. These are surrogate measures of the underlying factors in Knudsen's model. The model's reliability may be improved by a search for more relevant measures by subjecting a bigger selection of these surrogate measures to factors analysis. Such an analysis used in a confirmatory way may reduce their number to only the salient measure. But more research, especially in the management accounting field, may be needed to improve and test Knudsen's model or similar "components-based" models of predicting political risk.

The Haendel-West-Meadow "Political System Stability Index"

Another components approach to the forecasting of political risk was provided by Haendel, West, and Meadow in an empirical, indicator-based measure of political system stability, the Political System Stability Index (PSSI), in sixty-five developing countries.[37] It is composed of three equally weighted indices: the socioeconomic index, the governmental process index, and the societal conflict index, which is itself derived from three subindices on public unrest, internal violence, and coercion potential. All of these indices are derived from fifteen indirect measures of the political system: stability and adaptability. Basically, the higher the PSSI score, the greater the stability of the political system. The index was based on data from the 1961–66 period. There is a need to test the validity of the index with more recent data before using it as a forecasting tool. In any case, the model demonstrates again the feasibility of a components approach to the study of political risk. As stated by Haendel, the Political System Stability Index derives its importance from the role the political system plays in establishing power relationships and norms for resolving conflicts in society. It assumes that the degree of political stability in a country may indicate the society's capacity to cope with new demands.[38]

The Belkaoui and Belkaoui's Determinants of Political Risk Model

Belkaoui and Belkaoui developed a model for the specification and prediction of political risk (PR).[39] The dependent variable used is the political risk component of the ICRG (International Country Risk Guide). The independent variables are:

1. The United Nations Human Development Index (HDI).
2. The gross domestic saving as a percentage of gross domestic product.
3. The labor force as a percentage of total population (LFTP).
4. The terms of trade (TOT).
5. The total expenditures in educational and health as a percentage of gross domestic product (TEEHG).
6. The military expenditures as a percentage of gross national product (MEG).

The model is as follows:

$$PR = -10.281 + 63.103 \text{ HDI} + 0.561 \text{ GDSP} + 0.435 \text{ LETP} \\ - 0.154 \text{ TOT} + 1.105 \text{ TEEHG} - 1.120 \text{ MEG}$$

Basically, the higher the political risk, the lower the human development index, the lower the labor force as a percentage of the total population, the lower the gross domestic saving as a percentage of gross domestic product, and the lower the total expenditures in educational and health as a percentage of gross domestic product. Similarly, the higher the political risk, the higher the terms of trade, and the higher the military expenditures as a percentage of gross national product. This model is better explicated in the next chapter.

Coping with Political Risk

Forecasting political risk is not enough; the problem is how to cope and live with it or how to minimize it. Various techniques have been proposed for minimizing it. Eiteman and Stonehill suggested the following three categories of techniques for dealing with political risk:

1. Negotiating the environment before investment by concluding concession agreements, adaptation to host country goals, planned investment, and investment guarantees.

2. Implementing specific operating strategies after the investment decision in production, logistics, marketing, finance, organization, and personnel. For example, local zoning, a safe location of facilities, and control of transportation and of patents and processes are examples of operating strategies in production and logistics that may reduce the likelihood of political interference or expropriation.

3. Resorting to specific compensation strategies after expropriation, including rational negotiation, application of power tactics to bargaining legal remedies, use of the International Center for Settlement of Investment Disputes, and surrenders in the interest of seeking salvage.[40]

Another way of coping with political risk is to negotiate a tight investment agreement that spells out the specific rights and responsibilities of both the foreign firm and the host government. Eiteman and Stonehill suggested that the investment agreement spell out, among other things, the following policies on financial and managerial issues:

• The basis on which fund flows, such as dividends, management fees, and loan repayments, may be remitted.

• The basis for setting any applicable transfer prices.

• The right to export to third-country markets.

• Obligations to build, or fund, social and economic overhead projects, such as schools, hospitals, and retirement systems.

• Methods of taxation, including the rate, the type of taxation, and how the rate base is determined.

• Access to host country capital markets, particularly for long-term borrowing.

• Permission for 100 percent foreign ownership versus required local ownership (joint venture) participation.

- Price controls, if any, applicable to sales in the host country markets.
- Requirements for local sourcing versus import of raw materials and components.
- Permission to use expatriate managerial and technical personnel.
- Provision for arbitration of disputes.[41]

Haendel classified, appropriately, the traditional tools of risk management into five general categories:

1. Avoidance, whereby the risk manager may recommend not investing or diversifying or else impose a ceiling on the exposure a firm allows a country.
2. Transfer, whereby the risk manager may recommend including local individuals as either investors or managers.
3. Diversification and loss prevention, whereby the risk manager may recommend diversifying to reduce the reliance on a production facility of natural resource supply in any one country.
4. Insurance, whereby the risk manager may recommend that the firm secures insurance against political risk as a way of shielding the firm's assets from unexpected losses. This may even include self-insurance in the form of a separate fund.
5. Retention, whereby the risk manager may recommend that not all political risks can be avoided, transferred, diversified, or insured against. In such a case the firm should include political risk analysis in its decision-making process.[42]

The question remains to know what the multinationals actually do to cope with political risk. A study prepared for the Financial Executives Research Foundation found a number of techniques that could be used both before the investment and when operating overseas.[43] The techniques found to be most useful by participant firms in their preinvestment negotiations with local business, once investment had been made and the firms were committed, were maximizing the use of local debt and local funding, adapting to changing governmental priorities, sourcing locally to stimulate the economy and to reduce dependence on imports, and increasing exports. Besides using those techniques, the respondent firms admitted to insuring against the losses that might be caused by expropriation/confiscation, nationalization, foreign exchange inconvertibility, war, revolution or insurrection damages, kidnapping and ransom, long-term currency losses, and even inflation. The insurance was provided by the Overseas Private Investment Corporation (OPIC), a credit insurance program administered by the Export/Import Bank of the United States (Eximbank) jointly with Foreign Credit Insurance Association (FCIA), and private political risk insurance organizations like the American International Group (AIG) and Lloyd's of London.

Accounting for Political Risk

Accounting for political risk calls for a systematic approach to the assignment of a risk premium to a ROI budget. One approach consists of adjusting the corporate ROI by a numerical risk index developed for each country of operation. For example, assume that the Mantis company owns three affiliates in countries A, B, and C. For the first year, the actual divisional income and investment of each affiliate are as follows:

Division	Total Investment	Divisional Income
A	$1,000,000	$200,000
B	$5,000,000	$1,550,000
C	$2,200,000	$550,000

The Mantis Company requires an 8 percent return on its investments locally. In evaluating its foreign affiliates, the Mantis Company relied on a political risk instrument containing forty risk attributes. The scores for countries A, B, and C are as follows:

Country	Political Risk Index
A	$20
B	$10
C	$10

The adjusted ROI are computed as follows:

Division	Nominal ROI	Country Risk Coefficient	Risk Adjusted ROI	Actual ROI
A	$20	20/40 = 0.50	0.08/0.50 = 0.16	0.2
B	$10	10/40 = 0.5	0.08/0.25 = 0.32	0.31
C	$10	12/40 = 0.30	0.08/0.30 = 0.26	0.25

Other things being equal, the best performance is obtained by the affiliate in country B.

CONCLUSIONS

Capital budgeting for multinationals relies on the same evaluation techniques as for domestic operations. There are, however, many adjustments to be made to account for: project cash flows, the impact of inflation, the impact of changes in the exchange rate, foreign tax regulations, political and economic risk, expropriation, blocked funds, and uncertain salvage value. These issues and their corresponding solutions have been examined in this chapter. Political risk needs to be accounted for and managed when investing abroad.

NOTES

1. Ahmed Riahi-Belkaoui, *Accounting Theory* (London: International Thomson, 2000).

2. Thomas G. Evans, Martin E. Taylor, and Oscar J. Holzmann, *International Accounting and Reporting* (Cincinnati, Ohio: South-Western Publishing Co., 1994), pp. 322.

3. David K. Eiteman, Arthur I. Stonehill, and Michael H. Moffett, *Multinational Business Finance* (Reading, Mass., 1992).

4. Ibid.

5. Yani Abaromi, *The Foreign Investment Decision Process* (Boston: Harvard Braduate School of Business Administration, Division of Research, 1966).

6. Ibid., pp. 54–55.

7. Ibid., pp. 70–71.

8. Eiteman, Stonehill, and Moffett, *Multinational Process Finance*, pp. 32–33.

9. Michael R. Czinkota, Rietra Rivoli, and Illslea A. Ronkainen, *International Business* (Chicago: Dryden Press, 1989), p. 529.

10. Paul O. Graddis, "Analyzing Overseas Investments," *Harvard Business Review* (May–June 1966), p. 119.

11. A. C. Shapiro, "Capital Budgeting and Long-Term Financing," *Financial Management* (Spring 1978), p. 8.

12. V. B. Bavishi, "Capital Budgeting Practices of Multinationals," *Management Accounting* (August 1981), pp. 32–35.

13. Charles M. Newman II and I. James Czechowica, *International Risk Management* (Morristown, NJ: Financial Executives Research Foundation [FERF], 1983), p. 88.

14. Ibid., p. 89.

15. The weighted cost of capital concept can be extended to include debt denominated in foreign currencies, debt issued by foreign subsidiaries, and retained earnings of foreign subsidiaries.

16. Arthur Stonehill and Lessard Nathanson, "Capital Budgeting Techniques and the Multinational Corporation," *Journal of International Business Studies* (Spring 1975), p. 67.

17. John J. Clark, Thomas J. Hindelang, and Robert E. Pritchard, *Capital Budgeting: Planning and Control of Capital Expenditures*, 2nd ed. (Englewood Cliffs, N.J.: Prentice-Hall, 1984), pp. 419–426.

18. Jeff Madura, *International Financial Management* (St. Paul, Minn.: West, 1995), pp. 504.

19. Alan C. Shapiro, "Capital Budgeting for the Multinational Corporation," *Financial Management* (Spring 1978), p. 11.

20. Madura, *International Financial Management*, p. 457.

21. Nusret Calkici, Chris Hessel, and Kishore Tandon, "Foreign Acquisitions in the United States and the Effect on Shareholder's Wealth," *Journal of International Financial Management and Accounting* (March 1, 1991), pp. 38–60.

22. R. Caves, "Corporate Mergers in International Economic Integration," Working Paper (Center for Economic Policy Research, Harvard University, 1990).

23. R. Haas and J. Karls, "How Foreign Buyers Can Get Double Tax Deductions," *MergersAcquisitions* (July/August, 1989).

24. Ibid., p. 20.

25. Calkici, Hessel, and Tandon, "Foreign Acquisitions in the United States," p. 46.

26. Jeff Madura, *International Financial Management*, 3rd ed. (St Paul, Minn.: West, 1992), pp. 518.

27. Fred Greene, "Management of Political Risk," *Best's Review* (July 1974), p. 15.

28. Ibid., p. 73.

29. Newman and Czechowicz, *International Risk Management*, pp. 15–16.

30. S. H. Robock, and K. Simmonds, *International Business and Multinational Enterprises* (Howard, Ill.: Irwin, 1973), pp. 371.

31. Robert Stobaugh, Jr., "How to Analyze Foreign Investment Climates," *Harvard Business Review* (September-October 1969), pp. 101–102.

32. "A Primer on Country Risk," *Argus Capital Market Report* (June 4, 1975), pp. 15–25.

33. Alan C. Shapiro, "Currency Risk and country Risk in International Banking," *Journal of Finance* (July 1985), p. 891.

34. R. J. Rummel and David A. Heenan, "How Multinationals Analyze Political Risk," *Harvard Business Review* (January-February 1978), pp. 67–76.

35. Ibid., p. 70.

36. Harald Knudsen, "Explaining the National Propensity to Expropriate: An Ecological Approach," *Journal of International Business Studies* (Spring 1974), pp. 51–71.

37. Dan Haendel and Gerald T. West, with Robert G. Meadow, *Overseas Investment and Political Risk*, Monograph Series, no. 21 (Philadelphia: Foreign Policy Research Institute, 1957).

38. Dan Haendel *Foreign Investments and the Management of Political Risk* (Boulder, Colo.: Westview Press, 1979), pp. 106–107.

39. Janice Monti-Belkaoui and Ahmed Riahi-Belkaoui, *The Nature, Estimation, and Management of Political Risk* (Westport, Conn.: Greenwood Publishing, 1999).

40. D. K. Eiteman and A. I. Stonehill, *Multinational Business Finance* (Reading, Mass.: Addison-Wesley, 1989), pp. 203–223.

41. Ibid., p. 503.

42. Haendel, *Foreign Investments*, pp. 139–146.

43. Newman and Czechowicz, *International Risk Management*, p. 81.

SELECTED READINGS

Booth, Laurence D. "Capital Budgeting Frameworks for the Multinational Corporation." *Journal of International Business Studies* (Fall 1982), pp. 114–123.

Collins, J. Markham, and William S. Sekely. "The Relationship of Headquarters Country and Industry Classification to Financial Structure." *Financial Management* (Autumn 1983), pp. 45–51.

Doukas, John, and Nickolaos G. Travlos. "The Effect of Corporate Multinationality on Shareholders' Wealth: Evidence from International Acquisitions." *Journal of Finance* (December 1988), pp. 1161–1175.

Kester, W Carl. "Capital and Ownership Structure: A Comparison of United States and Japanese Manufacturing Corporations." *Financial Management* (Spring 1956), pp. 5–16.

Kim, Suk H., Edward J. Farragher, and Trevor Crick. "Foreign Capital Budgeting Practices Used by the U.S. and Non-U.S. Multinational Companies." *The Engineering Economist* (Spring 1984), pp. 207–215.

Monti-Belkaoui, Janice, and Ahmed Riahi-Belkaoui. *The Nature and Estimation and Management of Political Risk* (Westport, Conn.: Greenwood Publishing, 1999).

Oblak, David J., and Roy J. Helm, Jr. "Survey and Analysis of Capital Budgeting Methods Used by Multinationals." *Financial Management* (Winter 1981), pp. 34–41.

Riahi-Belkaoui, Ahmed. *Handbook of Cost Accounting: Theory and Techniques* (Westport, Conn.: Greenwood Publishing, 1991).

———. *The New Foundations of Management Accounting* (Westport, Conn.: Greenwood Publishing, 1991).

Shapiro, A. C. "Capital Budgeting and Long Term Financing." *Financial Management* (Spring 1978), pp. 5–25.

Srinivasan, Venkat, and Yong H. Kim. "Integrating Corporate Strategy and Multinational Capital Budgeting: An Analytical Framework." *Recent Developments in International Banking and Finance* (1988), pp. 381–397.

Stanley, Margorie T. "Capital Structure and Cost of Capital for the Multinational Firm." *Journal of International Business Studies* (Spring-Summer 1981), pp. 103–120.

Stanley, Marjorie T., and Stanley B. Block. "A Survey of Multinational Capital Budgeting." *Financial Review* (March 1984), pp. 36–54.

———, "An Empirical Study of Management and Financial Variables Influencing Capital Budgeting Decisions for Multinational Companies in the 1980s." *Management International Review* (November 1983), pp. 61–71.

Chapter 5

Estimating Political Risk for Capital Budgeting

INTRODUCTION

Political risk in general and political risk ratings in particular are of importance to managers of multinational firms eager to take political risk into account in their expansion capital budgeting, mergers, and other decisions. It would be much more practical and useful if these managers were able to not only rely on existing political risk ratings but also to replicate the same rating using an established political risk prediction model. Accordingly, it is the objective of this chapter to offer a political risk prediction model that replicates a known political risk index. The model, as suggested in the first three chapters, relies on economic and political variables that describe those aspects of the political and economic environment most linked to political risk.

POLITICAL RISK VARIABLES

The dependent variable is a political risk index. Various country risk ratings exist that pose choice problems. The measures include the following:

1. *Euromoney* issues a credit rating score that is a weighted average of three indicators: (a) market indicators that cover access to bond markets, sell-down performance, and access to trade financing (40 percent); (b) credit indicators that include payment record and rescheduling problems (20 percent); and (c) analytical indicators that cover political risk and economic performance and conditions (40 percent).

2. Institutional investors issue a country credit worthiness score based on ratings provided by leading international banks, which are asked to assign a grade to each country

on a scale of 0 (not creditworthy) to 100 (most creditworthy). The individual responses are then weighted according to an unpublished formula to produce a country credit-worthiness score.

3. The *International Country Risk Guide* (ICRG) of International Business Communi-cation Ltd. produces risk-rating scores that receive the most attention from foreign visitors. ICRG provides a composite risk rating as well as individual ratings for po-litical, financial, and economic risk. The political component, which makes up 50 percent of the composite score, includes factors such as government corruption and how economic expectations diverge from reality. The financial component includes such factors as the likelihood of losses from exchange controls and loan defaults. Finally, the economic component includes such factors as inflation and debt service costs. The maximum, or least risky, score is 100 for the political category and 50 each for the financial and economic risks. For the composite score, 85–100 is con-sidered very low risk; 70–84.5 is low risk; 60–69.5 is moderate risk; 50–59.5 is moderately high risk; and 0–49.5 is very high risk.

This brief description of the three risk measures indicates that the best can-didate for a dependent variable is the political risk component of the ICRG. It is used in this study.

EXPLANATORY VARIABLES

The set of explanatory variables is derived from descriptive and empirical studies of the political environment and economic environment, and of political risk. A description of these explanatory variables follows.

Human Development Index

Just as economic growth is necessary for a reduction of political risk, human development is also critical to lessening political risk. Human development is hampered by conditions of poverty, malnutrition, ill health, inadequate educa-tion, and gender disparities. When people face low human development condi-tions, they are less likely to be able to devote the resources and energy to create a politically stable environment. Obstacles to human development are also ob-stacles to a reduction in political risk. Human development is generally measured by the UN human development index (HDI), which is generally considered a more realistic measure of human development than mere GNP per head. The HDI is composed of three indicators: life expectancy, education, and income. The detailed computation of the index is shown in the Appendix 5.1. In the context of the prediction of political risk, the expected sign of the HDI is pos-itive. The higher the human development conditions, as measured by HDI, *the higher the political stability, as measured by the political risk index.*

Gross Domestic Savings as a Percentage of Gross Domestic Product

Economic theory holds that higher rates of savings and investment are crucial to the long-term growth of an economy.[1] Solov's framework[2] implies that a high investment on savings rate results in higher accumulated capital per worker and leads to an increase in the per capita output of the economy.

The linear stage of economic growth focuses on the importance to development of both the acquisition and use of capital and the historical development of the development countries. One example is Rostow's argument that the advanced countries have passed the stage of "takeoff into self-sustaining growth," while the underdeveloped countries are in a "preconditions" stage and in need of massive infusion of domestic and foreign savings before growth takes place.[3] A second example is the *Harrod-Domar growth model*, which simply states that the growth of national income will be directly, or positively, related to the savings ratio, and inversely, or negatively, related to the economy's capital/output ratio. None of these theories and models work effectively for the developing countries because more savings and investments are not sufficient for economic growth. Favorable institutional and attitudinal conditions need to be present before takeoff can take place. Gross domestic investment, as a percentage of gross domestic product, is positively associated with economic growth. This result is consistent with endogenous growth models, with an emphasis on broader concepts of capital, such as those of Rebelo[4] and Barro,[5] who argue that per capita growth and the investment ratio tend to move together. It can be easily argued that gross domestic savings or investment, as a percentage of gross domestic product, is a positive determinant of political stability. *Therefore, the higher the gross domestic savings, as a percentage of gross domestic product, the higher the political stability, measured by the political risk index.*

Labor Force as a Percentage of Total Population

A domestic problem that can affect political risk is unemployment. In the developing countries, not only is a very large section of the population unemployed, but unemployment seems to grow faster than employment, mainly due to the phenomenon of labor underutilization. Edgar Edwards distinguishes among the following forms of underutilization of labor: open unemployment; underemployment; the visible active but underutilized as disguised underemployment, hidden unemployment, and prematurely retired; the impaired; and the unproductive.[6] All major economic models of employment determination are advocated in the literature, namely, classical, Keynesian, the output/employment macromodel, the price-incentive micromodel, and the two-sector labor transfer model.

The classical model relies on the forces of supply and demand to set the wage rate and the level of employment. The Keynesian model relies on demand factors such as increases in government expenditures and encouragement of private investments to reduce unemployment. Both the classical and the Keynesian models are considered to be far from relevant to the developing countries. The output/employment macromodel argues that the rate of national output and employment depend on the rate of savings and investment, lending credence to the "big push" for industrialization in some developing countries. The price-incentive model maintains that the combination of labor and capital will be dictated by the relative factor prices. Cheap labor would lead to labor-intensive production processes. Finally, the two-sector labor transfer of rural urban migration focuses on the determinants of both demand and supply.

Two variations characterize the last model: the Lewis theory of development[7] and the Todaro model.[8] The Lewis model divides the economy into two sectors: (1) as a traditional, rural subsistence sector characterized by zero- or low-productivity surplus labor and (2) as a growing urban industrial sector characterized by an influx of labor from the subsistence sector. The Todaro model hypothesizes that migration is due to urban-rural differences in expected rather than actual earnings. All these approaches lead to a consensus position on employment strategy, which would include the following five elements: (1) creating an appropriate rural-urban economic balance; (2) expanding small-scale, labor-intensive industries; (3) eliminating factor-price distortions; (4) choosing appropriate labor-intensive technologies of production; and (5) noting the direct linkage between education and employment.[9]

The above analysis on the importance of unemployment posits the need to have a high labor price as a percentage of total population as a determinant of economic growth in general and political stability in particular. *Therefore, the higher the labor force, as a percentage of total population, the higher the political stability, measured by the political risk index.*

Terms of Trade

Developing countries suffer from two main limitations in their trading with developed countries. First, their exports are heavily composed of nonnumerical primary products, while their imports include everything from new materials to capital goods, intermediate-producer goods, and consumer products. Second, the commodity terms of trade, measured by the ratio between the price of a typical unit of exports and the price of a typical unit of imports, are deteriorating. The result shows up in a continuous deficit in the current and capital accounts of their balance of payments. To solve this problem a variety of options are used: export promotion or import substitution policies; encouragement of private foreign investment, or call for public and private foreign assistance; greater use of the Special Drawing Rights of the International Monetary Fund (IMF); foreign exchange controls or currency devaluation; economic integration with other developing countries in the form of customs unions, free-trade areas, or common markets.[10] But above all, the major option is the choice of a trade strategy for development. Should it be an outward- or inward-looking policy? An outward-looking policy results from the classical trade theory and comparative cost advantage arguments with the implication that free trade will maximize global output by allowing every country to specialize in what it does best. P. P. Streeten states that point as follows: "Outward-looking policies encourage not only free trade but also the free movement of capital, workers, enterprises and students, a welcome to the multinational enterprise, and open system of communications. If it does not imply laissez-faire, it certainly implies laissez-passer."[11]

An inward-looking policy results from the belief that the developing countries should be encouraged to engage in their own style of development and not be constrained by or dependent on foreign importation, and to learn by doing. Streeten explains this option as follows: Inward-looking policies emphasize the need for an indigenous technology, appropriate for the factors available in the country, and for an appropriate range of products. If you keep out the multinational enterprise, with its wrong technology, you will evolve your own style of development and you will be a stronger, more independent master of your own fate.[12]

In short, an outward-looking policy is identifiable with export promotion while an inward-looking policy is identifiable with import substitution. These two strategies, when added to the strategies of primary and secondary or manufacturing production, yield a fourfold division: primary outward-looking policies, secondary outward-looking policies, primary inward-looking policies, and secondary inward-looking policies.[13] The choice of any one of these options determines the nature of international trade of each developing country and of its impact on development.

Export promotion is good for economic growth, while trade restrictions can undermine the efficiency of the economy. The commodity or net barter terms of trade is the dimension most associated with higher exports and lower trade restrictions. Terms of trade is a positive determinant of economic growth. Countries in which terms of trade are greater were shown to experience greater economic growth. Given the association between economic growth and political stability, terms of trade may be hypothesized as a determinant of political risk. *Therefore, the lower the terms of trade, the higher the political risk.*

Total Expenditure on Health and Education as a Percentage of Gross Domestic Product

The expenditure on health and education, as a percentage of gross domestic product, leads to lower economic growth. The result was consistent with supply risk theorists who argue that the taxes required for financing government expenditures distort incentives and reduce efficient resource allocation and the level of output. However, the same expenditures on education and health are expected to generate a healthier political climate, resulting in a better political stability and lower political risk. *Therefore, the higher the total expenditures on health and education, as a percentage of gross domestic product, the higher the political stability, measured by the political risk index.*

Military Expenditures as a Percentage of Gross National Product

Military expenditures divest resources from projects benefiting economic growth, health, and education to name only a few public interest benefits. Military expenditures are generally motivated by a desire to be strong militarily to fend off imaginary or actual enemies, to attack rightly or wrongly other countries, and most of the time are used by the rulers of a nation to subjugate their own people. Needless to say, military expenditures are a deterrent to economic growth and a sure indication of an unstable or ruthless political regime. *Therefore, the higher the military expenditures, as a percentage of gross national product, the higher the political instability and the higher the political risk of a country.*

METHODOLOGY

The dependent variable used is the political risk component of the ICRG. The independent variables are (a) the human development index; (b) the gross domestic savings, as a percentage of gross domestic product; (c) the labor force, as a percentage of total population; (d) the terms of trade; (e) the total expenditures on education and health, as a percentage of gross domestic product; and (f) the military expenditure as a percentage of gross national product. The model is follows:

$$PR = \alpha_0 + \alpha_1 HDI + \alpha_2 GDSP + \alpha_3 LFTP + \alpha_4 TOT + \alpha_5 TEEHG + \alpha_6 MEG + \mu$$

where

PR	= Political risk index
HDI	= Human development index
GDSP	= Gross domestic savings, as a percentage of gross domestic product
LFTP	= Labor force, as a percentage of total population
TOT	= Terms of trade
TEEHG	= Total expenditures on education and health, as a percentage of gross domestic product
MEG	= Military expenditures, as a percentage of gross national product

Exhibit 5.1
Sample of Countries

1. Australia	13. India	25. South Korea
2. Austria	14. Japan	26. Spain
3. Brazil	15. Luxembourg	27. Sweden
4. Canada	16. Malaysia	28. Switzerland
5. Colombia	17. Mexico	29. Taiwan
6. Denmark	18. Netherlands	30. Thailand
7. Egypt	19. New Zealand	31. Turkey
8. Finland	20. Norway	32. United Kingdom
9. France	21. Pakistan	33. United States
10. Germany	22. Portugal	34. Venezuela
11. Greece	23. Singapore	
12. Hong Kong	24. South Africa	

The thirty-four countries chosen for analysis are shown in Exhibit 5.1. Because of data limitations, the sample was later reduced to twenty-two countries. The data used are shown in Exhibit 5.2.

RESULTS

Exhibits 5.3 and 5.4 show, respectively, the sample statistics and the Pearson correlation coefficients. The evidence, shown in Exhibit 5.5, reveals that political risk as measured by the ICRG political risk index is positively related to (a) the human development index; (b) the gross domestic savings, as a percentage of gross domestic product; (c) the labor force, as a percentage of total population; and (d) the total expenditures on education and health, as a percentage of gross domestic product and negatively related to (a) the terms of trade and (b) the military expenditures, as a percentage of gross national product. All the hypotheses in the study are verified. Basically, the higher the political risk, the lower the human development index, the lower the labor force as a percentage of total population, the lower the gross domestic savings as a percentage of gross domestic product, and the lower the total expenditures on education and health, as a percentage of gross domestic product. Similarly, the higher the political risk, the higher the terms of trade and the higher the military expenditure, as a percentage of gross national product. Exhibit 5.6 shows the actual and predicted political risk ratings for the twenty-two countries. Although the actual and predicted values, differ, the analysis does not result in aberrant predictions.

Exhibit 5.2
Data Used

OBS	PR	HDI	GDSP	LFTP	TOT	TEEHG	MEG
1	76	0.973	23	47.2	74	12.8	2.7
2	88	0.957	27	47.3	98	14.4	1.3
3		0.759	28	41.9	117	5.8	0.9
4	81	0.983	23	50.3	119	15.8	2.2
5	60	0.757	22	43.7	68	3.6	1
6	86	0.967	21	55.2	107	13.3	2.1
7		0.34	8	31.6	62	6.6	8.9
8	85	0.963	27	51.1	114	13.1	1.7
9	79	0.971	21	45	101	15.2	3.9
10	83.5	0.959	26	50.3	106	12.7	3.1
11		0.934	11	38.2	89	8.4	5.7
12	58	0.934	33	49.7	105		
13		0.308	21	37.9	119	4.3	3.5
14	65	0.955	23	40.4	108	10.8	2.3
15	80	0.993	33	50	157	13.3	1
16	63	0.884	38	42.1	108	3.4	5.2
17	93	0.954		42.8		10.3	0.8
18	71	0.802	36	43.8	74	9.7	6.1
19	71	0.838	23	38.4	67	4.5	0.6
20	85	0.976	23	41.2	91	15.3	3.1
21	78	0.959	26	45.9	110	11.8	2.2
22	87	0.978	28	50	67	14.2	3.2
23		0.311	13	28.8	106	2.4	3.3
24	69	0.879		45.6	107	10.5	6.7
25	79	0.879	41	48.6	101	6.3	5.5
26		0.766	25	36	73	5.2	3.9
27		0.951	22	36.3	103	9.2	2.3
28	81	0.982	21	51.4	95	16.5	2.9
29	93	0.981	31	49.2	103	12.9	1.9
30	71						
31	57	0.713	26	52.5	82	4.2	4
32		0.694	26	38.5	115	3.3	4.9
33	76	0.967	17	48.6	93	11.1	5
34	78	0.976	13	48.9	118	18	6.7
35	75	0.848	25	35.9	41	6.5	1.6

Exhibit 5.3
Sample Statistics

Variable	N	Mean	Std Dev	Sum	Minimum	Maximum
PR	27	76.6111	9.9984	2069	57	93
HDI	34	0.8572	0.1855	29.145	0.308	0.993
GDSP	32	24.4063	7.3347	781	8	41
LFTP	34	44.2441	6.3792	1504	28.8	55.2
TOT	33	96.9091	22.322	3198	41	157
TEEHG	33	9.8606	4.5303	325.4	2.4	18
MEG	33	3.3394	2.0228	110.2	0.6	8.9

Exhibit 5.4
Correlation Table

Pearson Correlation coefficients / Prob > $|R|$ under Ho : RHo = 0

	PR	HDI	GDSP	LFTP	TOT	TEEHG	MEG
PR	1	0.68148	-0.11946	0.22707	6.19903	0.67035	-0.30135
	0	0.0001	0.5782	0.2646	0.3402	0.0002	0.1432
	27	26	24	26	25	25	25
HDI		1	0.31939	0.65051	0.13673	0.70307	-0.29348
		0	0.0748	0.0001	0.448	0.0001	0.0974
		34	32	34	33	33	33
GDSP			1	0.38391	0.17925	-0.06811	-0.2553
			0	0.0301	0.3263	0.7158	0.1657
			32	32	32	31	31
LFIP				1	0.30843	0.62417	-0.18002
				0	0.0808	0.0001	0.3161
				34	33	33	33
TOT					1	0.25986	-0.12137
					0	0.1509	0.5082
					33	32	32
TEEHG						1	-0.09653
						0	0.5931
						33	33
MEG							1
							0
							33

Exhibit 5.5
The Determinants of Political Risk

Dependent Variable PR

Analysis of Variance

Source	DF	Sum of Squares	Mean Square	F Value	Prob>F
Model	6	1521.65988	253.60998	11.186	0.0001
Error	16	362.75316	22.67207	16	362.75316
C Total	22	1884.41304			

Root MSE	4.76152	R-Square	0.8075	
Dep Mean	77.28261	Adj R-sq	0.7353	
C.V.	6.16118			

Parameter Estimates

Variable	DF	Parameter Estimate	Standard Error	T for Ho: Parameter =0	Prob> |T|
INTERCEPT	1	-10.281884	23.85980313	-0.431	0.6723
HDI	1	63.103908	26.95574846	2.341	0.0325
GDSP	1	0.561722	0.18731334	2.999	0.0085
LFTP	1	0.435851	0.26252862	1.66	0.1163
TOT	1	-0.154276	0.05808353	-2.656	0.0173
TEEHG	1	1.105056	0.51673719	2.139	0.0482
MEG	1	-1.120916	0.62216954	-1.802	0.0905

CONCLUSION

The purpose of this chapter was to replicate the ICRG political risk index on the basis of economic and political variables proposed in the theoretical and empirical literature on the determinants of political risk. The evidence reveals that political risk measured by the ICRG political risk index responds to all the variables proposed with the exact sign. Basically the level of the United Nations human development index; the gross domestic savings, as a percentage of gross domestic product; the labor force, as a percentage of total population; and the total expenditures on health and education, as a percentage of gross domestic product negatively affect the political risk rating. In addition, the level of the terms of trade and the level of military expenditures, as a percentage of gross domestic product, positively affect the political risk rating. The model is not only explanatory but predictive of political risk.

Exhibit 5.6
Actual and Predicted Political Risk Ratings

OBS	Dep Var PR	Predicted Value	Residual
1	76	84.3118	-8.3118
2	88	85.2274	2.776
3		58.9546	
4	81	83.2272	-2.2272
5	60	61.2589	-1.2589
6	86	82.4305	3.5695
7		20.5998	
8	85	82.9089	2.0911
9	79	79.2449	-0.2449
10	83.5	80.969	2.531
11		60.9483	
12	58		
13		19.9388	
14	65	73.2051	-8.2051
15	80	82.0647	-2.0647
16	63	66.4634	-3.4634
17	93		
18	71	72.1048	-1.1048
19	71	66.2192	4.7808
20	85	81.5776	3.4224
21	78	78.4484	-0.4484
22	87	90.7229	-3.7229
23		11.7982	
24	69		
25	79	74.6144	4.7808
26		57.902	
27		69.6072	
28	81	86.2116	-5.2116
29	93	86.7154	6.2846
30	71		
31	57	59.7051	-2.7051
32		45.3098	
33	76	73.7851	2.2149
34	78	74.0994	3.9006
35	75	71.9844	3.0156

NOTES

1. C. I. Plossner, "The Search for Growth," in *Policies for Long Run Economics* (Kansas City: Federal Reserve Bank of Kansas, 1992), pp. 57–86.

2. R. Solov, "A Contribution to the Theory of Economic Growth," *Quarterly Journal of Economics* 3 (1956), p. 70.

3. W. W. Rostow, *The Stages of Economic Growth: A Noncommunist Manifesto* (London: Cambridge University Press, 1960).

4. S. Rebelo, "Long-Run Policy Analysis and Long-Term Growth," *Journal of Political Economy* 99 (1991), pp. 500–521.

5. R. J. Barro, "Economic Growth in a Cross Section of Countries," *Quarterly Journal of Economics* (May 1991), pp. 407–444.

6. Edgar O. Edwards, *Employment in Developing Countries: Report on a Ford Foundation Study* (New York: Columbia University Press, 1974), pp. 10–11.

7. Lewis [first name unknown], "Economic Development with Unlimited Supplies of Labor," 1961. The model was formalized and extended in J. C. H. Fei and G. Ramis, "A Theory of Economic Development," *American Economic Review* 51 (1961), pp. 326–352.

8. Michael P. Todaro, "A Model of Labor Migration and Urban Unemployment in Less Developed Countries," *American Economic Review* 59, 1 (1969), pp. 138–148.

9. Michael P. Todaro, *Economic Development in the Third World* (New York: Longman, 1985), pp. 244–245.

10. Felipe Pazos, "Regional Integration of Trade among Less Developed Countries: A Survey of Research," *Journal of Economic Literature* 8, 2 (1970), p. 374.

11. P. P. Streeten, "Trade Strategies for Development: Some Themes for the Seventies," *World Development* 1, 6 (June 1973), p. 1.

12. Ibid., p. 2.

13. Ibid.

SELECTED READINGS

Cosset, Jean-Claude, and Jean Roy. "The Determinants of Country Risk Ratings." *Journal of International Business Studies* 22, 1 (1991), pp. 135–142.

Riahi-Belkaoui, Ahmed. *Accounting in the Developing Countries* (Westport, Conn.: Quorum Books, 1994).

Todaro, Michael P. *Economic Development in the Third World* (New York: Longman, 1985).

Appendix 5.1: The Human Development Index

Beginning in 1990, the UN human development index is composed of the three indices of life expectancy, education, and income. Three steps are used to construct the HDI. First, a maximum and a minimum value of each of these basic variables—life expectancy (XI), literacy (X2), and (the log of) per capital GDP (X3)—are defined for each country. A deprivation indicator for the jth country with respect to the ith variable is defined:

$$Iij = \frac{(Max\ Xij - Xij)}{(Max\ Xij - minXij)}$$

Second, an average deprivation indicator (I_j), computed from the simple average of the three indicators, is

$$I_j = 1/3\ E\ I_{ij}$$

Third, the HDI is computed as one minus the average deprivation index:

$$(HDI)j = (1 - I_j)$$

The following example illustrates the computation of the HDI for the Bahamas:

Maximum country life expectancy	= 78.6
Minimum country life expectancy	= 42.0
Maximum country educational attainment	= 70.1
Minimum country educational attainment	= 9.1
Maximum country adjusted real GDP per capita	= 5,070
Minimum country adjusted real GDP per capita	= 350
Bahamas life expectancy	= 71.5
Bahamas educational attainment	= 68.1
Bahamas adjusted GDP per capita	= 4,997
Bahamas life expectancy deprivation	
= (78.6 − 71.5)/(78.6 − 42.0)	= 0.193
Bahamas educational attainment deprivation	
= (70.1 − 68.1)/(70.1 − 9.1)	= 0.032
Bahamas GDP deprivation	
= (5,070 − 4,997)/(5,070 − 350)	= 0.015
Bahamas average deprivation	
= (0.193 + 0.032 + 0.015) / 3	= 0.080
Bahamas human development index (HDI)	
= 1 − 0.080	= 0.920

Chapter 6

Leasing versus Purchasing

INTRODUCTION

Leasing has recently become an important source of financing for many types of assets. The lessee acquires the use of an asset while the title is retained by the lessor. More specifically, a lease is a contract between an owner (the lessor) and another party (the lessee) that grants the lessee the right to use the lessor's property under certain conditions and for a specified period of time. Because of the contractual nature of lease obligations, a lease should be considered a financing device and an alternative to debt financing. Both the lease rental payments and the payments of principal and interest on debt are fixed obligations. Any default in the payment of either obligation can create serious problems for a firm.

The decision to lease an asset is generally evaluated by comparing it with the borrowing decision necessary for an outright purchase of the same asset. Different valuation models have been proposed, and any choice can be challenged because of the controversial issues surrounding a given model and its corresponding variables and parameters. The main purpose of this chapter is to explain leasing arrangements and the main issues in financial leasing; and to provide a methodology for analysis.

The lease as a new form of financing undergoes constant change, as shown by the number and variations of the sources of leasing arrangements. Financial institutions involved in leasing differ mainly in their degree of specialization and include independent leasing companies, service leasing companies, lease brokers, commercial brokers, and insurance companies.

TYPES OF LEASING ARRANGEMENTS

Although it is possible to describe major forms of lease arrangements, the options, terms, and conditions may vary from contract to contract, giving a firm great flexibility in the adaptation of leasing as a financing method.

Operating versus Financial Leases

The first distinction to be made in leasing is between *operating* and *financial leases*. Under both contracts, the lessee agrees to make periodic rental payments. An operating lease is a short-term contract that is cancelable given proper notice at the option of the lessee, whereby the lessor gives the lessee the use of property in exchange for rental payments and at the same time retains the usual ownership risks (such as obsolescence) and rewards (such as a gain from appreciation in value at the end of the lease period). To compensate the lessor for assuming the ownership risks, the periodic rental payments of an operating lease will include a return on investment plus most ownership costs, such as maintenance, taxes, depreciation, obsolescence, casualty losses, and so forth. Examples of operating leases include car rentals, apartment rentals, telephone service, and space rental in shopping centers.

A financial lease is a comparatively long-term contract that is noncancelable by the lessor, who assumes little or no ownership costs. As a result, the periodic rental may include only a return on investment, and the lessee may be required to pay most of the ownership costs. At the termination of the lease, options may exist allowing the lessee to acquire the asset at either a nominal cost or no cost at all. The financial lease allows the lessor to recover the investment and even realize a profit through the lessee's continuous rental payments over the period specified by the contract. The financial lease gives the lessee continuous use of the asset at a certain cost and, consequently, is a means of financing the use (and not the ownership) of the asset. In other words, the difference between the operating and financial lease lies mainly in the cancellation and financing options. As opposed to an operating lease, a financial lease is noncancelable, and it can be perceived as a financing instrument.

Sales and Leaseback, Direct Leasing, and Leverage Leases

Another important distinction in lease financing is made between the sale and leaseback and direct lease arrangements. The difference lies in the nature of the prior ownership of the asset to be leased. Under the sale and leaseback arrangement, a firm sells an asset it owns to another party, which in turn leases it back to the previous owner. Under this popular arrangement, a company in need of liquidity receives cash from the sale of the asset while retaining the economic use of the asset during the lease period.

Under direct leasing, the lessee acquired the use of an asset it did not previously own. The lessee can enter into the leasing arrangement with a manufacturer, independent leasing company, or financial institution.

With the advent of direct leasing through commercial banks in 1963, a new lease arrangement appeared called a leverage lease. This is a tripartite arrangement whereby the lessor finances a portion of the acquisition of the asset (50 to 80 percent of the purchase price) from a lender (commercial bank), securing the loan by a mortgage of the leased property as well as by the assignment of the lease and lease payments. The leverage lease is a popular instrument for special-purpose leasing companies and partnerships of individuals in high tax brackets because of the tax benefits provided by the accelerated depreciation charges, the investment tax credit, and the interest on debt, and because of the favorable return on the equity participation by the lessor. From the point of view of the lessee, the leverage lease is similar to any other lease and, consequently, does not affect the method of valuation.[1]

Leverage leasing involves at least four parties: lessee, a manufacturer (or distributor), a lessor, and a lender. Arrangements are complex, and the parties enter into the agreement primarily for tax and financial cost savings rather than convenience. The lessee is able to obtain financial leasing from the lessor at a cost lower than the usual cost of capital; the lessor, being of a high income tax bracket, gains an investment tax credit (or capital cost allowance) benefit resulting in reduced taxes. The lessor passes on some of this benefit to the lessee through reduced lease costs.

Direct leasing, sale and leaseback, and leverage leasing are illustrated in Exhibit 6.1.

Maintenance, Nonmaintenance, and Net Leases

The assignment of responsibility for the maintenance of the asset during the life of a lease takes three forms: the *maintenance lease, nonmaintenance lease*, and *net lease*.

A maintenance lease assigns responsibility for the maintenance of a leased asset's good working order to the lessor. The lessor is required to incur the maintenance and repair expenses and the local and state taxes, and to provide insurance for the leased asset. The maintenance lease is preferable when the lessor is better equipped to provide low-cost repair than the lessee in terms of technology and skills. It is used mostly in rentals of automobiles, trucks, and specialized equipment, like computers, requiring a highly qualified maintenance staff.

A nonmaintenance lease assigns the responsibility for the maintenance of a leased asset to the lessee. The lessee is required to pay for all maintenance and repair costs and the local and state taxes, and to provide insurance. The nonmaintenance lease occurs principally in long-term leasing of land and buildings.

A net lease assigns total responsibility for an asset's maintenance to the lessee to the point that the lessee may be required to absorb all losses incurred by the

Exhibit 6.1
Leases according to Parties Involved

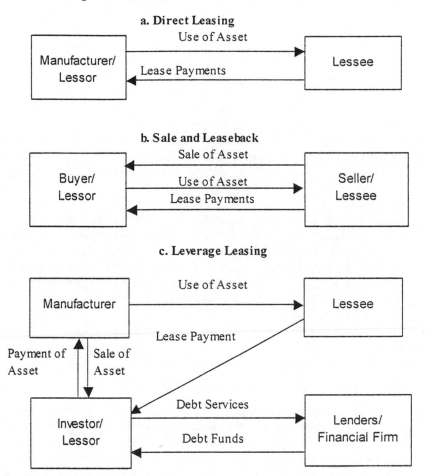

sale of the asset at the end of the life of the lease. This is typical in fleet leasing of vehicles. In car leasing the net lease is sometimes referred to as an open-end lease: In return for a slightly lower monthly lease fee, the lessee agrees to make up the price differential if the leased car sells for less than the prearranged price when the lease expires because of excess mileage, poor maintenance, or any other reason.

ADVANTAGES OF LEASING

When a firm wishes to have the use and services of an asset, it can either purchase the asset or lease it. The decision to purchase the asset entails first borrowing the funds and then buying the asset. Thus, when evaluating the advantages of the leasing alternative, a firm should keep in mind the fact that the other alternative is to borrow and buy, rather than just buy. The lease-or-buy decision rests on the comparison between two methods of financing, both requiring a fixed obligation redeemable over a future period. The leasing alternative, then, should be evaluated by comparing its advantages and effects on the lessee's cash flow with those of the borrowing alternative. Often-cited advantages of leasing as opposed to borrowing include (1) shifting the risks of ownership, (2) the avoidance of restrictions associated with debt, (3) the effect on cash and borrowing capacity, and (4) tax advantages.

Shifting the Risks of Ownership

A firm that purchases an asset is subject to the risk of obsolescence due to innovation in the field. Generally, in the decision to lease or buy an asset subject to a high rate of obsolescence, the leasing alternative will appear more appropriate. Through leasing rather than buying the asset, the lessee can shift the risk of obsolescence and of ownership to the lessor.

This argument in favor of leasing relies heavily on the assumption that the lessor is not aware of the rate of obsolescence and innovation in the field. In most cases, however, the lessor is very knowledgeable and is in a better position to anticipate the rate of obsolescence than the lessee. The lessor, well aware of the risks of ownership, will attempt to recover the investment plus interest over the lease period and will probably include an implicit charge for obsolescence in the computation of the rental payments. Only when the lessor inaccurately estimates the rate of obsolescence does the lessee benefit from shifting the risks of ownership. If the asset becomes obsolete more rapidly than the lessor anticipated, the leasing alternative will be beneficial to the lessee. The lessor can keep the rental payments low by spreading the risk of obsolescence over many lease contracts. The diversification in this case will benefit both the lessor and the lessee.

Avoidance of Restrictions Associated with Debt

Leasing is assumed to offer fewer restrictions than debt and, consequently, to provide more flexibility. Most loan agreements and bond indentures include protective covenant restrictions, but similar limitations are not as common in leasing. One usual restriction accompanying leasing is in the use of the leased property. For example, the use of the leased equipment may be limited in terms of the number of hours per day. Changes and adjustments in the leased equipment may also be prohibited unless authorized by the lessor.

The advantage of fewer restrictions with leasing than with debt financing will probably disappear in the near future. Most lenders impose restrictions on the amount to be leased for firms financed heavily by debt. Because leasing is becoming more and more accepted as a form of financing, protective covenants will probably be drafted for both leasing and bond indentures.

Effect on Cash and Borrowing Capacity

It is often said that leasing allows a firm to conserve cash and raise more funds than debt financing. This is based on the following claims—some supportable and some unsupportable—made on behalf of leasing.

People often argue that leasing allows the optimal use of cash leading to an improvement in a firm's total earning power. Thus, it is maintained, the capital intended for the purchase of fixed assets with low turnover is tied up for the acquisition of current assets with high turnover. Retailers most often are advised to rent their premises and allocate their capital to inventory and accounts receivable. Although seemingly attractive, this claim on behalf of leasing is the result of confusion about the relationship between the investment and financing decisions. It assumes that the financing method is a determinant of the mix of assets. A firm actually decides first on the optimal mix of assets necessary for its line of business and then decides on the proper way of financing this mix by comparing the costs of buying and leasing. The firm can decide either to borrow or to lease. In either case it decides to use the optimal mix of assets effectively and efficiently.

People also argue that leasing permits a firm not only to avoid buying an asset, but also to finance up to 100 percent of the cost of the asset. What is the impact on a firm's borrowing capacity? Does leasing provide more funds? The usual assumption is that leasing has no effect on a firm's borrowing power and a positive effect on its borrowing capacity. However, this line of reasoning is misleading. Given the fixed obligatory nature of the lease, it should be considered equivalent to an implicit loan of 100 percent of the funds needed. The borrowing capacity is definitely reduced, and the borrowing power must be compared with debt financing. The erroneous assumption that leasing provides more funds results from the conventional accounting treatment, whereby lease obligations are not shown by liabilities on the balance sheet. This situation has changed, and accounting treatments now tend to favor the capitalization of long-term leases.

Leasing permits the financing of capital additions on a piecemeal basis. To be practical, long-term debt financing must usually be arranged on a much larger scale than lease financing, which can be adjusted to each individual unit of property acquired. This can be a valid reason for using lease financing to make occasional asset acquisitions spaced over a period of time. However, this justification loses its validity when the total amount of capital additions over a given period is large enough to justify a debt issue. Long-term debt financing can be adapted to the timing of expenditures either through the use of interim bank borrowings with subsequent refunding or by a direct placement of securities with institutional investors, providing for a series of takedowns.[2]

Tax Advantages

A common argument to the lease-or-buy controversy is whether leasing offers tax advantages over ownership. Under present tax laws, rental payments are considered an operating expense and can be deducted from taxable income. This gives rise to two basic differences in the tax effects of leasing as compared with ownership:

1. Leasing makes it possible, in effect, to write off the depreciable portion of property over the basic term of a lease, which is generally shorter than the period that would be permitted for depreciation. The result is not a tax savings but a shift in the timing of deductions and tax payments similar to the effects of accelerated depreciation. To the extent that tax payments are deferred, the company benefits by having the use of these funds for the additional period.

2. Leasing makes it possible, in effect, to write off land values against taxable income, which is not allowed for depreciation purposes. The effect can be very significant where land represents a substantial portion of the total investment, as in urban department store properties. Although leasing provides a way of recovering part of the investment in land during the basic period of the lease, it also deprives the company of 100 percent of this value at the end of the period, which still leaves a net loss of 48 percent. Furthermore, if past trends in land value are any indication of the future trends, the loss could be considerably greater.[3]

Another cost implicitly packaged in the terms of any leasing contract is corrected with the federal income tax deduction. One of the frequently cited advantages of equipment leasing is that a leasing contract permits the lessee to enjoy a more advantageous stream of income tax expense deductions than would be possible with outright ownership of the equipment, where only depreciation and interest could be deducted. In fact, there may be some advantage if the lease payments are scheduled so they are higher in the earlier years of the lease than the sum of depreciation and interest and, conversely, lower in later years. Under these conditions, the present value of the tax deductions received under the lease plan is greater than the present value of the tax deductions under outright ownership. This advantage can be achieved in another way under financial leases. The agreement can be made for a relatively short initial term—say, five years. During this time the lessor recovers the entire cost of the equipment; if the lessee purchased the equipment directly, it would have to be depreciated over a longer time span—say, seven to ten years.[4]

The Economic Recovery Tax Act of 1981 allows companies to transfer the tax benefits of tax credits and of the Accelerated Cost Recovery System (ACRS) on new plants and equipment bought between January 1 and August 13, 1981, through what is called safe-harbor leasing. Such transactions are safe as long as the letter of the Internal Revenue Service regulations is followed. This is possible in two cases:

1. Under a reciprocal lease-sublease, the seller of the tax benefits (the

lessor-sublessee) acquires new equipment for its own use and, within three months of purchase, leases it to the buyer of the tax credits (the lessee-sublessor). The seller transfers tax credits to the buyer via the lease, and the buyer simultaneously subleases the property back to the seller (the user) without those credits. The rentals payable by the buyer exceed the rentals to be received by the buyer. This differential is effectively the purchase price of the tax credits transferred.

2. Under a sale leaseback, the seller of the tax benefits (the seller and lessee of the property) acquires new equipment for its own use and, within three months of purchase, sells it to the buyer of the tax benefits (the buyer and lessor of the property). This enables the seller to transfer to the buyer the tax benefits related to the equipment. The consideration is composed of a cash down payment of at least 10 percent of the original cost of the property and a note for the remainder. The buyer then leases the property back to the seller for a lease term that is equal to the term of the note. If the rentals under the lease are equal to the payments on the note (principal and interest), the buyer's initial investment (the down payment) is the purchase price of the tax benefits. The seller continues to be the user of the property. The seller may retain title to the property or reacquire title at the end of the lease term for a nominal amount, such as $1.[5]

The intent of the legislation is that tax leases will allow firms that do not owe taxes or are unable to realize certain tax benefits to realize those benefits by making them transferable. Instead of receiving the benefits directly as a reduction of income taxes payable, firms not owing taxes can realize them by selling the right to those benefits to other firms that can use them to reduce taxes payable.

Shortly after the passage of the act, the Ford Motor Company announced that it was selling to International Business Machines Corporation (IBM) its investment tax and depreciation deductions on "under $1 billion" worth of machinery, equipment, and tools acquired so far in 1981. Similarly, Bethlehem Steel Corp. and R. R. Donnelley & Sons Co. entered into a safe-harbor lease transaction that involves the exchange of tax credits. Donnelley will buy steel manufacturing equipment from Bethlehem and lease it back to the steelmaker.

A NORMATIVE MODEL FOR LEASE EVALUATION

Any model for lease evaluation is determined on a cash flow basis. The treatment of the variables in the model differs, depending on whether it is the lessee's or the lessor's model.

Lessor's Analysis

The lessor attempts to determine a rental payment amount that will insure that the present value of rental payments plus the present value of the salvage value of the asset equals or exceeds the original cost of the asset. The discount rate the lessor chooses will be adjusted for the recovery of both the cost of capital of the lessor and other ownership costs before taxes. The lessee may have the option of paying the rental payments at the beginning or the end of each year. Both cases will be examined using the following sample problem.

Assume a firm has decided to lease an asset under the following conditions:

Purchase price of the asset (A_0)	= $30,000
Expected salvage value of the asset (S)	= $10,000
Before-tax rate of return (K_L)	= $8%
Salvage value discount rate (K_S)	= 20%
Lease period (n)	= 5 years

To compute the rental payment, proceed as follows.
1. The present value of the salvage value (S_{PV}) is

$$S_{PV} = \frac{S}{(1 + K_S)^n} = \frac{\$10,000}{(1 + 0.20)^5} = \$4,018$$

$$= R_t + \sum_{j=2}^{5} \frac{R_j}{(1 + 0.08)^{j-1}}$$

2. The rental (R_j) if paid in advance is

$$A_0 - S_{PV} = R_t + \sum_{j=1}^{5} \frac{R_j}{(1 + K_L)^{j-1}}$$

$$\$30,000 - \$4,018 = R_j(1 + 3031213).$$
$$R_j = \$6,025.$$

3. The rental (R_j) if paid at the end of period is

$$A_0 - S_{PV} = \sum_{j=1}^{n} \frac{R_j}{(1 + K_L)^j}.$$

$$\$30,000 - \$4,018 = \sum_{j=1}^{5} \frac{R_j}{(1 + 0.08)^j}$$

$$= R_j(3.99271)$$
$$R_j = \$6,507.$$

Lessee's Analysis

The lessee's approach concentrates on how the asset is to be acquired, leaving to more conventional capital budgeting techniques the prior decision on whether the asset is to be acquired at all. Thus, the question the lessee examines is whether to borrow and buy or to lease. The answer is found by comparing the respective costs of both alternatives. The summary measure used for the comparison can be either the net present value advantage of leasing (NAL) or the pretax interest rate on the lease (X;). The NAL measure is expressed as follows:

$$NAL = A_0[1] - \sum_{j=1}^{n} \frac{R_j}{(1 + X_1)^j}[2] + \sum_{j=1}^{n} \frac{TR_j}{(1 + X_2)^j}[3] + \sum_{j=1}^{n} \frac{TD_j}{(1 + X_3)^j}[4]$$

$$+ \sum_{j=1}^{n} \frac{TI_j}{(1 + X_4)^j}[5] + \sum_{j=1}^{n} \frac{O_j(1 - T)}{(1 + X_5)^j}[6] - \frac{V_n}{(1 + K_S)^j}.$$

The variables included in the NAL equation are defined as follows:

A_0 = Purchase price of the asset.
R_j = Lease payment in period j.
D_j = Depreciation charge in period j.
V_j = Expected after-tax salvage value of the asset = S; − (S; − B;)Tr.
S_j = Salvage value in period j.
B_j = Book value in period j.
X_i = Discount rates to apply to the various cash flow streams of the equation.
T_S = Tax rate applicable to gains and losses on the disposal of fixed assets.
T = Corporate income tax rate.
n = Number of years covered by the lease agreement.
I_j = Interest component of the loan payment.
K_S = Salvage value discount rate.
O_j = Incremental operating costs of ownership in period t.

The interpretation of the NAL equation is influenced by the treatment of the key variables in the lease evaluation decision. The seven terms in the NAL equation can be interpreted as follows:

1. The purchase price of the asset is an unavoidable cost of purchasing.
2. The present value of the rental payments is a cost of leasing.
3. The present value of the tax shield provided by the rental payments is a benefit of leasing and, consequently, an opportunity cost of purchasing.
4. The present value of the tax shield provided by the depreciation expense is a benefit of purchasing.
5. The present value of the tax shield provided by the interest expense on a "loan equivalent" to a lease is another benefit of purchasing.
6. The present value of the after-tax operating cost is a burden of ownership.
7. The present value of the after-tax residual value is a benefit of ownership.

Summing the seven terms, the basic equation provides the net present value advantage of leasing. Setting NAL equal to zero and solving for X_i provides the pretax interest rate on the lease. The NAL equation can also be explained as follows.

1. The present value of the borrow-and-buy alternative is

$$A_0 - \sum_{j=1}^{n} \frac{TD_j}{(1 + X_3)^j} - \sum_{j=1}^{n} \frac{TI_j}{(1 + X_4)^j} + \sum_{j=1}^{n} \left[\frac{O_j(1 - T)}{(1 + X_5)^j} \right] - \frac{V_n}{(1 + K_s)^j}.$$

2. The present value of leasing is

$$\sum_{j=1}^{n} \frac{R_j}{(1 + X_1)^j} - \sum_{j=1}^{n} \frac{TR_j}{(1 + X_2)^j}.$$

3. NAL = Present value of borrowing and buying − Present value of leasing.

Two problems in the applicability of the NAL equation lie in the choice of the appropriate discount rates to be used and the computation of the loan equivalent to the lease.

The discount rates X_1, X_2, X_3, X_4, and X_5 are those applied by the market to evaluate the streams of distribution of R_j, TR_j, TD_j, TI_j, and $O_j(1 - T)$. Possible alternatives are a single discount rate or an appropriate rate for each stream. We will first use the after-tax cost of debt as a single discount rate for all streams; later in the chapter, the other alternatives proposed in the literature will be discussed. Thus, the after-tax cost of debt will be used for each cash flow stream except V_n, which will be discounted at its own rate ($K_S = 20$ percent) due to the uncertainty associated with this "estimated" value.

The loan equivalent decision also has generated a debate in the literature. This chapter will propose a first alternative and later present the other proposed alternatives. For the first alternative, it assumed that

$$P_0 = A_0,$$

$$= \sum_{j=1}^{n} \frac{L_j}{(1 + r)^j}$$

where

P_0 = Present value of the loan equivalent.
L_j = Loan payment at the end of each period j.
r = Pretax interest rate on term loans "comparable" to the lease.

To illustrate the lessee's analysis, the same problem presented in the lessor's analysis will be used. The data required are as follows:

$A_0 = \$30,000.$

$S = \$10,000.$

$R_j = \$6,025$ (at the beginning or each period).

$R_j = \$6,507$ (at the end of each period).

$D_j =$ Straight-line depreciation at period $j = \dfrac{A_0 - S}{n} = \$4,000.$

$O_j = \$2,000.$

$B = 0.$

$T_g = 10\%.$

$V_n = S - [(S - B)T_g] = \$9,000.$

$r = 6\%.$

$T = 50\%.$

$n = 5$ years.

$K_S = 20\%.$

The lessee's analysis proceeds as follows:

1. For the loan payment computation, it has been assumed in this analysis that $P_0 = A_0$, and

$$P_0 = \sum_{j=1}^{n} \frac{L_j}{(1 + r)^j}$$

Given the 6 percent pretax interest rate on loans, the amount of the annual loan payment at the end of each year is found by solving the following equation for L_j.

$$\$30,000 = \sum_{j=1}^{5} \frac{L_j}{(1 + 0.06)^j}$$

$$L_j = \$7,122.$$

2. When the rental payments are made in advance, the lease evaluation analysis proceeds by the computation of the NAL as follows:

$$\begin{aligned}
\text{NAL} = \$30,000 &- \left[\$6,025 + \sum_{j=1}^{4} \frac{\$6,025}{(1 + 0.03)^j} \right] + \sum_{j=1}^{5} \frac{(\$6,025)(0.5)}{(1 + 0.03)^j} \\
&- \sum_{j=1}^{5} \frac{(\$4,000)(0.5)}{(1 + 0.03)^j} - \left[\frac{\$800(0.5)}{(1 + 0.03)^1} + \frac{\$1,480(0.5)}{(1 + 0.03)^2} \right. \\
&\left. + \frac{\$1,142(0.5)}{(1 + 0.03)^3} + \frac{\$783(0.5)}{(1 + 0.03)^4} + \frac{\$403(0.5)}{(1 + 0.03)^5} \right] \\
&+ \sum_{j=1}^{5} \left[\frac{\$2,000(1 - 0.5)}{(1 + 0.03)^j} \right] - \frac{\$9,000}{(1 + 0.20)^5} \\
&= \$30,000 - (\$6,025 + \$22,396) + \$13,796 - \$9,159 - \$2,130 \\
&\quad + \$4,580 - \$3,617 \\
&= \$5,048 = \text{NAL when rental payments are made in advance.}
\end{aligned}$$

3. The lease evaluation analysis when the rental payments are made at the end of the period is as follows:

$$
\begin{aligned}
\text{NAL} = \$30,000 &- \sum_{j=1}^{4} \frac{\$6,507}{(1 + 0.03)^j} + \sum_{j=1}^{5} \frac{(\$6,507)(0.5)}{(1 + 0.03)^j} - \sum_{j=1}^{5} \frac{(\$4,000)(0.5)}{(1 + 0.03)^j} \\
&- \left[\frac{\$800(0.5)}{(1 + 0.03)^1} + \frac{\$1,480(0.5)}{(1 + 0.03)^2} + \frac{\$1,142(0.5)}{(1 + 0.03)^3} + \frac{\$783(0.5)}{(1 + 0.03)^4} \right. \\
&\left. + \frac{\$403(0.5)}{(1 + 0.03)^5} \right] + \sum_{j=1}^{5} \left[\frac{\$2,000(1 - 0.5)}{(1 + 0.03)^j} \right] - \frac{\$9,000}{(1 + 0.20)^5} \\
&= \$30,000 - \$29,800 + \$14,900 - \$9,159 - \$2,130 \\
&\quad + \$4,580 - \$3,617 \\
&= \$4,774 = \text{NAL when rental payments are made at the end of period.}
\end{aligned}
$$

These computations show the lease alternative to be preferable to the purchase alternative. Several points should be further emphasized:

1. Changing the depreciation method from straight-line to accelerated depreciation may change the outcome.
2. The timing of the rental payments has an impact on the NAL.
3. The analysis assumes that the acquisition price of the asset is equal to the principal of the loan.
4. All the cash flow streams except for the salvage value are discounted at the after-tax cost of debt.
5. It is assumed that the investment decision has been deemed acceptable. Only the financing decision remains to be evaluated in terms of a choice between borrowing and leasing.

ALTERNATIVE CALCULATIONS

The Johnson and Lewellen Approach

R. W. Johnson and W. G. Lewellen examined (1) whether the financing and investment decisions should be mixed in appraising lease possibilities and (2) which discount rate should be used.[6] Johnson and Lewellen pose the decision problem as a lease-or-buy rather than a lease-or-borrow decision, since a lease contract is simply an arrangement for the long-term acquisition of service, which does not differ in financing terms from the alternative acquisition-of-service arrangement called purchase. Hence the inclusion of a charge for interest as a "cost" of owning is viewed as a deficiency of current models for lease evaluation, and the concept of a loan equivalent is not necessary in the lease evaluation model.

The issue of the appropriate rate to use in discounting the cash flows relevant to the decision has been investigated by Johnson and Lewellen. They emphasize the following ideas:

1. The after-tax cash flows with predictability matching that associated with the firm's debt service obligations should be capitalized at the firm's after-tax borrowing rate (after-tax cost of debt). This will include the obligations incurred under the lease contract, such as lease payments and their respective tax savings.

2. The after-tax cash flows with uncertainty like the general risks faced by the firm in its line of business should be discounted at the firm's cost of capital. This will include the depreciation tax shield, the after-tax operating costs, and the salvage value.

The Johnson and Lewellen model now can be presented. It states:

$$\Delta NPV = NPV(P) - NPV(L)$$

$$= \sum_{j=1}^{n} \left[\frac{D_j T - O_j(1 - T)}{(1 + K)^j} \right] + \frac{V_n}{(1 + K)^j} - A_0 + \sum_{j=1}^{n} \frac{R_j(1 - T)}{[1 + r(1 - T)]^j}.$$

where

ANPV   = Change in the firm's net present value.
NPV(P) = The net present value of borrowing and buying.
NPV(L) = The net present value of leasing.
K   = Cost of capital at 12 percent.

A positive value of ONPV would imply that purchasing the asset is economically superior to leasing it. This would occur if the net salvage value exceeded after-tax operating costs or if the purchase price less depreciation tax savings were less than the burden of lease payments.

Using the data in the previous illustration, the Johnson and Lewellen model proceeds as follows:

1. If the rental payments are made at the beginning of the period:

$$\Delta NPV = \sum_{j=1}^{5} \left[\frac{\$2,000 - \$1,000}{(1 + 0.12)^j} \right] + \frac{\$9,000}{(1 + 0.12)^{-5}} - \$30,000$$

$$+ \left[\$6,025 + \sum_{j=1}^{4} \frac{\$6,025}{(1.03)^j} \right] - \sum_{j=1}^{5} \left[\frac{\$6,025(1 - 0.5)}{(1 + 0.03)^j} \right] = \$(6,664).$$

Thus, leasing is preferred.

2. If the rental payments are made at the end of the period:

$$\Delta NPV = \sum_{j=1}^{5} \left[\frac{\$2,000 - \$1,000}{(1 + 0.12)^j} \right] + \frac{\$9,000}{(1 + 0.12)^5} - \$30,000$$

$$+ \sum_{j=1}^{4} \frac{\$6,025}{(1.03)^j} - \sum_{j=1}^{5} \left[\frac{\$6,507(1 - 0.5)}{(1 + 0.03)^j} \right] = \$(6,388).$$

Leasing is preferred in this case as well.

As a result of discounting the costs of financing at $r(1 - T)$ and the ownership cash flows at K, the Johnson and Lewellen approach in this case creates a bias in favor of leasing. R. S. Bower contested the choice:

Johnson and Lewellen's selection of K as the discount rate is understandable but unappealing. It is understandable because K is the rate used in discounting depreciation shelters in conventional capital budgeting, where the shelter is part of the cash flow calculation. The selection of K is unappealing, though, because it involves discounting some of the tax shelter given up in leasing at a high rate, K, and discounting all of the tax shelter that comes with leasing at a low rate, $r(I - T)$. It is difficult to avoid the conclusion that a higher discount rate for the shelter element of lease cost does a great deal more to bias the analysis in favor of leasing than it does to recognize any real difference in risk.[7]

The Roenfeldt and Osteryoung Approach

The Roenfeldt and Osteryoung approach expanded on the Johnson and Lewellen approach by categorically separating the investment decision from the financing decision.[8] The methodology used consisted of (1) determining the desirability of the investment decision and (2) given that the investment decision was deemed desirable, evaluating the financing decision by comparing the after-tax cost of borrowing (r_b) with the after-tax cost of leasing (r_l).

Using the data from the illustration in the previous section, the Roenfeldt and Osteryoung approach proceeds as follows.

Step 1: The Investment Decision. The investment decision is made on the basis of a net present value or internal rate of return approach following traditional capital budgeting techniques. (See Chapter 2.) The computation of a net present value or internal rate of return involves estimating the annual sales generated by the asset and computing the resulting net cash flows, as follows:

	Year 1	2	3	4	5
1. Sales (Assumed)	$20,000	$20,000	$20,000	$20,000	$20,000
2. Depreciation	4,000	4,000	4,000	4,000	4,000
3. Cash Operating Costs	2,000	2,000	2,000	2,000	2,000
4. Taxable Income (Line 1 − Line 2 − Line 3)	14,000	14,000	14,000	14,000	14,000
5. Tax Liability (4 × T)	7,000	7,000	7,000	7,000	7,000
6. Net Cash Flow (Line 1 − Line 5 − Line 3)	11,000	11,000	11,000	11,000	11,000
7. Salvage Value (V)					9,000
8. Discount Factor (K = 12)					3.605
9. Discount Factor (Ks = 20)					0.402
10. Present Value of Cash Flow					39,655
11. Present Value of Vn					3,618
12. Total Present Value (Line 10 + Line 11)					$43,273

Thus, the net present value is equal to $13,273, or $43,273 − 30,000, and the investment is deemed desirable.

Step 2: The Financing Decision. The financing decision—to borrow or to lease—is made on the basis of a criterion of least cost by comparing the after-tax cost of borrowing (r_b) to the after-tax cost of leasing (r_l).

To compute r, the rate that equates the after-tax interest payments and amortization of the principal to the loan amount, the following formula is used:

$$A_0 = \sum_{j=1}^{n} \frac{L_j - I_j T}{(1 + r_b)^j},$$

or

$$\$30,000 = \sum_{j=1}^{5} \frac{\$7,122 - [0.5(I_j)]}{(1 + r_b)^j}.$$

The numerator (the net costs of borrowing) is computed as follows:

Year	Loan Payment	Interest	Shield (IjT)	Net Cost of Borrowing
1	$7,122	$1,800	$900.00	$6,222.00
2	7,122	1,480	740.00	6,382.00
3	7,122	1,142	571.00	6,551.00
4	7,122	783	391.50	6,730.50
5	7,122	403	201.50	6,950.50

Solving for r_b yields

$$r_b = 3\%$$

To compute r, the rate that equates the adjusted rental payments to the cost of the asset (A_0), Roenfeldt and Osteryoung make the following changes:

1. The rental payments are reduced by the amount of any operating costs assumed by the lessor.
2. The depreciation tax shield and after-tax salvage value are added to the cost of leasing.
3. Certainty equivalents are introduced into the operating and residual cash flows to adjust for risk.

The following formula is then used:

$$V_0 = \sum_{j=1}^{n} \left\{ \frac{[(L_j - \alpha_j O_j)(1 - T)] + D_j T}{(1 + r_l)^n} \right\} + \left[\frac{\alpha_n S_n - (\alpha_n S_n - B)T_g}{(1 + r_l)^n} \right].$$

where

α_j = Certainty equivalent for the operating costs.
α_n = Certainty equivalent for the salvage value.

Assuming $\alpha_j = 0.6$ and $\alpha_n = 0.99$, the cost of leasing (r_i) can be computed as follows:

1. If the rental payments are made at the end of the period,

$$\$30,000 = \left\{ \sum_{j=1}^{5} \frac{[\$6,507 - 0.6(\$2,000)](1 - 0.5) + [(4,000)(0.5)]}{(1 + r_i)^n} \right\}$$

$$+ \left\{ \frac{0.99(\$10,000) - [0.99(\$10,000) - 0](0.10)}{(1 + r_i)^n} \right\}$$

$$= \sum_{j=1}^{5} \left[\frac{\$4,653.5}{(1 + r_i)^n} \right] + \left[\frac{\$8,910}{(1 + r_i)^5} \right].$$

$r_i = 2\%$, and leasing is preferable to borrowing.

2. If the rental payments are made in advance,

$$\$30,000 = \left\{ \sum_{j=0}^{4} \frac{[\$6,025 - 0.6(\$2,000)](1 - 0.5) + [(\$4,000)(0.5)]}{(1 + r_i)^n} \right\}$$

$$+ \left[\frac{\$8,910}{(1 + r_i)^5} \right]$$

$r_i = 2.1\%$, and leasing is still preferable to borrowing.

Issues in Lease Financing

Bower summarized the following points of agreement and disagreement in the differing approaches to the lease-or-buy decision.[9] All the models require inputs that include the purchase price of the asset to be leased, (A_0), lease payments at the end or at the beginning of the period (R_j), a depreciation charge relevant for tax payments at the end of the period (D_j), a cash operating cost expected to occur in the period if the asset is purchased but not if it is leased (O_j), an expected after-tax salvage value of the asset at the end of the last period covered by the lease agreement (V_n), a pretax interest rate on the loan equivalent to the lease (r), an after-tax cost of capital for the corporation (k), a corporate income tax rate (T), and the number of periods covered by the lease agreement (n).

The points of disagreement relating to the lease-or-buy analysis include the following:

1. The choice of a summary measure, either the pretax interest rate on a lease (i) or the net advantage to a lease (NAL).

2. The inclusion or exclusion of some of the terms previously presented in the normative model.

3. The computation of the loan equivalent.

4. The choice of a discount rate for each of the cash flows included in the normative model.

The Bower Approach: A Decision Format

Bower has developed a decision format to reconcile the disagreements among the various approaches to the lease-or-buy analysis and still permit those interested to take advantage of the models' broad agreement on other points. The decision format examines the decision implications associated with different tax shelter discount rates.

The decision format uses the cost of capital (K) to calculate benefits that involve the purchase price, operating savings, and salvage value; it uses the appropriate interest rate (r) to calculate the present cost of the lease payments. The tax shelter effect is then calculated for rates of discount (X) from 0 through 14 percent.

The cost of purchasing (COP) depends on the purchase price, depreciation tax shelter, cash operating cost avoided by leasing, and salvage value:

$$COP = A_0 - \sum_{j=0}^{n} \left[\frac{TD_j}{(1 + X)^j} \right] + \sum_{j=0}^{n} \left[\frac{O_j(1 - T)}{(1 + K)^j} \right] - \frac{V_n}{(1 + K)^n}$$

The cost of leasing (COL) depends on the lease payment, the lease tax shelter, and the interest tax shelter lost by leasing:

$$COL = \sum_{j=0}^{n} \left[\frac{R_j}{(1 + r)^j} \right] - \sum_{j=0}^{n} \left[\frac{TR_j}{(1 + X)^j} \right] + \sum_{j=0}^{n} \frac{TI_j}{(1 + X)^j}$$

An illustrative example of Bower's decision format will be given using the data presented in the example in section 6.4.1. There is, however, one major change: The lease payment (R), as calculated in the lessor's analysis, will no longer be used. The equivalent loan is computed by Bower as follows:

$$\text{Loan equivalent } (P_0) = \sum_{j=0}^{n} \frac{R_j}{(1 + r)^j},$$

where

R_j = (Lease payment) = Loan payment (L_j)
r = Pretax interest rate on term loans "comparable" to the lease

Although most of the data supplied in the original example applies here, assume that as an alternative to purchasing, the asset can be leased for five years for a payment of $7,963 per annum.

In this case, the loan equivalent no longer equals the purchase price of the asset; instead, the following holds true:

$$\text{Loan equivalent } (P_0) = \sum_{j=1}^{n} \frac{\$7,962}{(1 + 0.06)^j} = \$33,538$$

The loan equivalent is

Year	Loan Payment	Loan Balances (Year Start)	Interest (6%)	Principal Repayment	Loan Balance (Year-End)
1	$7,962	$33,538	$2,012	$5,950	$27,588
2	7,962	27,588	1,655	6,307	21,281
3	7,962	21,281	1,277	6,685	14,596
4	7,962	14,596	876	7,086	7,541
5	7,962	7,510	452	7,511	0

The decision format is presented in Exhibit 6.2 and Exhibit 6.3. The column at the right in Exhibit 6.2 shows that when the tax shelter is discounted at $r(1-T)$ = 10 percent, the net advantage of purchasing is $49. At all discount rates above 9.65 percent, the lease has a net advantage. Therefore, if a decision maker analyzing a graph such as Exhibit 6.3 believes that the proper tax shelter discount rate lies well below the intersection point, the decision to lease rather than purchase would provide the greater financial benefit to the company.

In developing this decision format, Bower has devised a composite approach to the lease-or-buy decision that enables the executive to make a judgment on the principal disagreement among academicians and on how the proper tax shelter discount rate, $r(1 - T)$, may affect the ultimate cost of a decision.

LEASING ANALYSIS ILLUSTRATION

Problems

Analysis of the Lease-or-Buy Decision

The Holland Consulting Company is considering obtaining a piece of equipment having a five-year useful life and costing $15,000. As an alternative to purchasing, the company can lease the equipment for five years for a payment of $4,200 per annum. The equipment, which would be fully depreciated on a sum-of-the-years'-digits schedule, is expected to command a $1,500 cash salvage value at the end of year 5 and will require $1,000 more in annual (pretax) operating costs if it is owned rather than leased. The Holland Consulting Com-

Exhibit 6.2
Decision Format

Year t	Purchase Price A0	Lease Payment Rt = Lt	Tax Shelter Lease Payment TRt	Tax Shelter Depreciation TDt	Tax Shelter Loan interest TIt	After-Tax Operating Saving Ot (1-t)	After-Tax Salvage Vn
0	30,000						
1		7,962	3,981	2,000	1,006	1,000	
2		7,962	3,981	2,000	828	1,000	
3		7,962	3,981	2,000	638	1,000	
4		7,962	3,981	2,000	438	1,000	
5		7,962	3,981	2,000	226	1,000	9,000

Present Value at

	Purchase Price A0	Lease Payment Rt = Lt				Operating Saving Ot(1-t)	Salvage Vn
k=0.12	30,000	33,538				3,605	5,107
r=0.06							

	Lease Payment TRt	Depreciation TDt	Loan interest TIt	Cost of Purchasing	Cost of Leasing
0	19,905	10,000	3,136	18,498	16,769
0.02	18,764	9,427	2,993	19,071	17,767
0.04	17,223	8,904	2,868	19,594	19,183
0.06	17,769	8,425	2,737	20,073	19,506
0.08	15,895	7,985	2,624	20,513	20,267
0.10	15,091	7,985	2,518	20,916	20,965
0.12	14,351	7,210	2,419	21,288	21,606
0.14	13,667	6,866	2,327	21,632	22,198

Exhibit 6.3
Decision Format

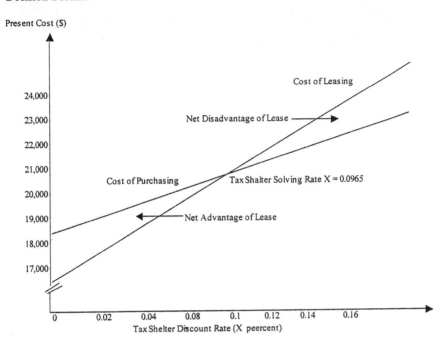

Present Cost ($)

pany is also assuming the corporate income tax rate to be 50 percent, the capital gains tax rate to be 30 percent, the cost of capital after taxes to be 12 percent, and the pretax effective interest rate to be 8 percent.

Required: Should Holland Consulting Company lease or buy the equipment? (Use the Johnson and Lewellen approach.)

Analysis of the Lease-or-Buy Decision

A decision format assumes the same data as in the previous analysis. This time, the Holland Consulting Company has decided to modify the Johnson and Lewellen approach as follows:

1. It will apply the cost of capital to the purchase price, after-tax operating savings, and after-tax salvage value.
2. It will apply the after-tax rate of interest to the lease payment, the lease payment tax shelter, and the depreciation tax shelter.
3. It will apply an after-tax rate of interest from 0 to 14 percent.

Required: Should the Holland Company lease or buy the equipment?

Analysis of the Lease-or-Buy Decision

Another decision format assumes the same data as in the previous analysis. This time, the Holland Consulting Company has decided to modify the Johnson and Lewellen approach as follows:

1. A loan equivalent is introduced in the evaluation. Findlay's loan equivalent formula is to be used.
2. The cost of purchasing depends on the purchase price, depreciation tax shelter, cash operating cost avoided by leasing, and salvage value.
3. The cost of leasing depends on the lease payment, lease tax shelter, and interest tax shelter lost by leasing.
4. The after-tax salvage and the after-tax operating savings are discounted at the cost of capital.
5. The lease payments are discounted at the pretax rate of interest.
6. The tax shelters are discounted at a rate of interest from 0 to 14 percent.

Required:

1. Determine the loan equivalent schedule using Findlay's equivalent loan.
2. Compute the costs of purchasing and costs of leasing, and determine if the Holland Consulting Company should lease or buy the equipment.

Lease and Inflation

Dr. Eric Nagnum is considering leasing an asset that is expected to provide a real cash flow of $1,000 per year for three years. A rate of inflation of 10 percent and a real rate of interest of 3 percent are expected.

Required:

1. Determine the nominal rate of interest.
2. Determine the present value of the lease.

Comparison of Lease Evaluation Models

The Richard Company is contemplating the addition of a truck to its commercial truck fleet. The truck costs $56,000, which does not include transportation costs of $4,000. The Richard Company has a policy of capitalizing freight in the determination of the acquisition cost. The truck has an estimated three-year useful life and a $2,000 residual value. Other relevant information for deciding whether to lease or buy the truck includes the following:

Borrowing rate: 6 percent.
Cost of capital before taxes: 20 percent.
Tax rate: 50 percent.

Depreciation method: sum-of-the-years'-digits method.

Rate of return on investment desired: 10 percent.

Salvage value discount rate: 20 percent.

Required:

1. From the lessor's perspective, determine the annual rental payment if paid in advance.

2. From the lessor's perspective, determine the annual rental payment if paid at the end of the period.

3. Present the normative model to be used by the lessee. What is required to express the model as an advantage to ownership?

4. Determine the loan payment on a loan equivalent to the lease.

5. From the lessee's perspective, should the Richard Company lease the equipment if the rental payment is made at the beginning of the period?

6. From the lessee's perspective, should the Richard Company lease the equipment if the rental payment is made at the end of the period?

7. Present the Johnson and Lewellen model that can be used by the lessee.

8. Repeat part 6 using the Johnson and Lewellen model.

Solutions

Analysis of the Lease-or-Buy Decisions: The Johnson & Lewellen Approach

To decide whether to Lease or buy, the Holland Consulting Company should proceed as follows:

	(1)	(2)	(3)	(4)		
Year	Tax Savings on Depreciation (t Dj)	After Tax Added Operating Costs Ot (1−T)	Salvage Value, Net of Taxes Vn	After Tax Lease Payment Lj (1−T)	Present Value of (1)−(2)+(3) at 12%	Present Value of (4) at 4%
1	(0.5) 5,000	(0.5) 1,000		(0.5) 4,200	$1,786	$2,019
2	(0.5) 4,000	(0.5) 1,000		(0.5) 4,200	1,196	1,942
3	(0.5) 3,000	(0.5) 1,000		(0.5) 4,200	712	1,867
4	(0.5) 2,000	(0.5) 1,000		(0.5) 4,200	318	1,795
5	(0.5) 1,000	(0.5) 1,000	(0.70) (1,500)	(0.5) 4,200	596	1,726
					$4,608	$9,349

Equipment purchase = $15,000

Therefore, ANPV = $4,608 − $15,000 + $9,439 = −$1,043

Conclusion = leasing is better than purchase.

Evaluating Capital Projects

Analysis of the Lease-or-Buy Decision: A Decision Format

To decide whether to lease or buy, the Holland Consulting Company should proceed as follows:

The purchase price net of salvage and the operating expenses that will now be covered by the lessor are the benefits associated with leasing. The lease payments, less any net additional tax shelter they provide, are the costs of leasing. The benefits, which are discounted at the cost of capital, are $16,206. The benefits in question appear and are graphed in the following table:

Tax Shelter

Year j	Purchase Price A0	Lease Payment Rj	Lease Payment tRj	Depreciation tDj	After Tax Operating Saving Oj (1−t)	After Salvage Vn
0	15,000					
1		4,200	2,100	2,500	500	
2		4,200	2,100	2,000	500	
3		4,200	2,100	1,500	500	
4		4,200	2,100	1,000	500	
5		4,200	2,100	500	500	1,050

Tax Shelter

Year j	Purchase Price A0	Lease Payment Rj	Lease Payment tRj	Depreciation tDj	After Tax Operating Saving Oj (1−t)	After Salvage Vn
PV						
K = 0.12	15,000				1,802	−596

	Lease	
	Benefit	Cost
	16,206	
	(@ 12%)	

0	15,000	−21,000	10.500	−7,500	18,000
0.02		−19,797	9,898	−7,164	17,063
0.04		−18,698	9,349	−6,852	16,201
0.06		−17,692	8,846	−6,654	15,410
0.08		−16,769	8,385	−6,296	14,680
0.1		−15,921	7,961	−6,046	14,006
0.12		−15,140	7,570	−5,813	13,383
0.14		−14,119	7,209	−5,596	12,806

t = 0.05 k = 0.12 r = 0.08

These two tables also show the costs of the lease discounted at various rates; therefore, they satisfy preferences for both present value and internal rate of return summary measures.

This lease has a net disadvantage at after-tax interest rates below .0399 and a net advantage at rates above this figure. At .04, the after-tax interest rate provided in the case, the net advantage is $5. The decision format indicates a borderline choice in favor of the lease or, more pragmatically, a choice that should make very little difference to the owners of the lessee corporation even if the executives are using 8 percent as the appropriate pretax borrowing rate when that rate is correctly 6 percent or 10 percent.

In conclusion, this format offers the executive a table and a graph that took the cost of capital as given in calculating the benefits of leasing and assumed that tax shelters should be discounted at the after-tax rate of interest and allows the executive to examine the decision implications associated with different interest rates.

Analysis of the Lease or Buy Decision: Another Decision Format

1. The loan is calculated as Findlay's loan equivalent. The loan schedule is:

Year	Loan Balance, Beginning of Year	Interest at 8%	Principal	Loan Balance, Year End
1	16,769	1,342	2,858	13,911
2	13,911	1,113	3,087	10,823
3	10,823	866	3,334	7,489
4	7,489	599	3,601	3,888
5	3,888	311	3,889	

2. The decision format applied to this problem appears in the following table:

Tax Shelter

Year j	Purchase Price A_o	Lease Payment R_j	Lease Payment tR_j	Depreciation tD_j	Loan Interest* tI_j	After-Tax Operating Saving $O_j(1-t)$	After-Tax Salvage V_n
0	15,000						
1		4,200	2,100	2,500	671	500	
2		4,200	2,100	2,000	556	500	
3		4,200	2,100	1,500	433	500	
4		4,200	2,100	1,000	300	500	
5		4,200	2,100	500	156	500	1,050

$t = 0.05$ $k = 0.12$ $r = 0.08$

PV*						Cost of	
						Purchasing	Leasing
K = 0.12	15,000						
r = 0.08		16,769					
0							
0.02			10,500	7,500	2,116	8,706	8,385
0.04			9,898	7,164	2,019	9,042	8,890
0.06			9,349	6,852	1,929	9,354	9,349
0.08			8,846	6,564	1,846	9,642	9,769
0.1			8,385	6,296	1,768	9,910	10,152
0.12			7,961	6,046	1,697	10,160	10,505
0.14			7,570	5,813	1,630	10,393	10,829
			7,209	5,596	1,567	10,610	11,127

*The loan is calculated as Findley's equivalent loan.

The loan schedule is:

Year	Beginning of Year	Interest at 8%	Principal	Year End
1	16,769	1,342	2,858	13,911
2	13,911	1,113	3,087	10,823
3	10,823	866	3,334	7,489
4	7,489	599	3,601	3,888
5	3,888	311	3,889	

PV of After-Tax Operating Savings = 1,802
PV of After-Tax Salvage Value = 596

When the tax shelter is discounted at $r(1 - t)$, 4 percent, the net advantage of leasing is $5, just as it was with the previous format. At all discount rates above 4.07 percent, the lease has a net disadvantage. If the estimates k and 4 are felt to be tightly bound, and if the executive making the decision holds the view that the proper tax shelter discount rate is well above $r(1 - t)$, then he will conclude from the decision format that a decision to sign this lease agreement could be of very little financial benefit to the company's owners and could do them damage.

Lease and Inflation

1. The nominal rate of return is: $r = 0.03 + 0.033 = 0.133$
2. The present value of the lease is as follows:

Period	Real Cash Flow	Price Relative	Money Cash Flow	Money Present Value Factor at 13.3%	Present Value
1	$1,000	1.1	1,100	0.8826	970.9
2	1,000	1.21	1,210	0.779	943
3	1,000	1.331	1,331	0.6876	915
					2,828.90

Normative Model for Lease Evaluation

1. The lessor determines first the present value of the residual as follows:

$$S_{PV} = \frac{S}{(1 + R)^{-t}} = \frac{2,000}{(1 + 0.2)^{-3}} = \$1,158$$

Then, the rental (X), if paid in advance,

$$C - S = X_1 + \sum_{t=2}^{3} \frac{X_t}{(1 + R)^{t-1}} = \$60,000 - 1,158 = X_1$$

$$+ \frac{X_2}{(1 + 0.1)} + \frac{X_3}{(1 + 0.1)^2}$$

$$X = \$21,056$$

2. The rental (X), if paid at the end of the period, may be computed as follows:

$$C - S = X_1 + \sum_{t=1}^{n} \frac{X_t}{(1 + R)^t} \text{ or } \$60,000 - \$1,158 = \$60,000$$

$$-1,158 = \sum_{t=1}^{n} \frac{X_t}{(1 + 0.1)^t}$$

$$X = \$23,660$$

3. The normative model to be used by the lessee is as follows:

$$NAL = \sum_{t=1}^{n} \frac{P - (I_t + D_t)T_c}{(1 + K_d)^t} + \frac{D_t(1 - T_c)}{(1 + K_d)^t} - \frac{S - (S - B)T_g}{(1 + K_s)} - \sum_{t=1}^{n} \frac{L_t(1 - T_c)}{(1 + K_d)^t}$$

where

   P = the loan payment: interest and amortization of principal
   L_t = the rental payment in period t
   I_t = the interest payment in period t
   D_t = depreciation in period t
   O_t = incremental operating costs of ownership in period t
   T_c = ordinary corporate tax rate
   T_g = tax rate applicable to gains and losses on the disposal of fixed assets
   S_n = expected cash value of asset in period N
   B = book value of asset is period N
   K_d = explicit after-tax cost of new debt capital
   K = weighted average cost of capital, after tax
   K_s = discount rate applied to residual values
   (Reversing the sign of NAL yields the advantage to ownership.)

4. Loan payment: The loan payment is found by:

$$\$60,000 = \sum_{t=1}^{3} \frac{L_t}{(1 + 0.06)^t}$$

$$L_t = \$22,447$$

Year	Payment (Lt)	Interest (It)	Principal	Balance
1	$22,447	$3,600	$18,847	$41,153
2	22,447	2,469	19,978	21,175
3	22,447	1,270	21,175	

5. Lessee's analysis when rental payments are made in advance.

Year	0	1	2	3	Explanation
1. Loan Payment		$22,447	$22,447	$22,447	
2. Interest		3,600	2,469	1,270	
3. Depreciation		29,000	19,140	9,860	
4. Tax Deduction (2 + 3)		32,600	21,609	11,130	
5. Tax Shield (4 × 0.50)		16,300	10,804	5,565	Salvage
6. Net Ownership Cost (1 − 5)		6,147	11,643	16,882	Value
7. After-Tax Lease Cost	10,753	10,753	10,753		
8. Advantage to Ownership	10,753	4,606	(910)	{(16,882)2,000} Value
9. Discount Factor (Kd = 3%)		0.971	0.943	{.915,.579}Ks = 20%
10. Present Value of Owner	10,753	4,472	(858)	{(15,447)1,158}
11. Advantage to Ownership				$78

6. Lessee's analysis when rental payments are made at the end of period.

Year	0	1	2	3	Explanations
Row 1 to 6 are similar to the previous lessee's analysis					
7. After-tax lease cost		$11,830	$11,830	$11,830	
8. Advantage to ownership		5,683	187	(5,052)	
8a. S				2,000	(Salvage Value)
9. Discount Factor (Kd = 3%)		0.971	941	0.915	
9a. (Ks = 20%)					
10. Present Value of Owning	$5,518	$5,518	176	(4,623)	
10a. S				1,158	
11. Advantage to Ownership				2,229	

7. Johnson and Lewellen's model states:

$$ANPV = NPV(P) - NPV(L) = \sum_{t=1}^{n} \frac{D_t T - O_t(1 - T)}{(1 + K)^t}$$

$$+ \frac{S - T_g(S - B)}{(1 + K)^n} - A_0 + \sum_{t=1}^{n} \frac{L_t(1 - T)}{(1 + K_d)^t}$$

where

ANPV = change in the firm's NPV
NPV (P) = the NPV of borrow and buy
NPV (L) = the NPV of leasing

8. The lessee's analysis using Johnson and Lewellen's model proceeds as follows:

Year	0	1	2	3	Total
1. Depreciation Tax Shield		$14,500	$9,570	$4,930	
2. Salvage				2,000	
3. After-Tax Lease Cost		11,830	11,830	11,830	
4. Discount Factor (K = 10x)		0.909	0.826	0.751	
5. Present Value of Ownership		13,180	7,904	3,702	$262,883
				1,502	(Salvage)
6. Discount Factor (Kd = 3%)		0.971	0.943	0.915	
7. Present Value of Leasing		11,487	11,156	10,824	33,467

Therefore, ANPV = $26,288 − $60,000 + $33,467 = ($245).
Leasing is preferred.

CONCLUSIONS

A firm enters into a leasing arrangement for many reasons. Some of the primary motivations follow:

1. Leasing enables a firm to take tax shelters.

2. A leasing arrangement conserves working capital.

3. Cash budgeting benefits, because leasing permits accurate predictions of cash needs.

4. Leasing allows a company to retain a degree of flexibility lost by debt financing (that is, bond indenture sometimes imposes restrictions on future financing).

5. A leasing arrangement provides convenience.

6. Leasing can provide an economical means of obtaining excellent servicing and maintenance of equipment if a maintenance lease is included.

7. An operating lease provides more flexibility than ownership if the asset becomes unprofitable; it avoids part or all of the risk of obsolescence; and it can provide for modern equipment from year to year.

Most of the significant methods of analyzing lease-or-buy alternatives use the same basic formula for calculation, but there is considerable disagreement in the calculation methods. The disagreement lies with both relevant alternatives and the choice of the best summary measure of comparison. The relevant alternatives include the outstanding principal of the loan equivalent; loan payments at the end of the period; the interest component of the loan payment; the principal component; the present value of the lease claim; and the discount rates to be applied to cash flows in each category, which are intended to reflect opportunity cost. Summary measures are either the increment in net present value of owners' wealth or the after-tax interest rate on the lease.

The disagreement is more significant in the treatment of the terms, including lease payments and the tax shelter acquired or given up if the lease is accepted. This is most obvious in the decision to include or exclude the tax deduction associated with interest on the equivalent loan.

Bower's decision format of lease analysis is the most appropriate method to use today. It is a composite of the factors agreed upon by other theorists, and it enables decision makers to choose the cost of capital and interest rate they feel is most appropriate during the relevant period for making their lease-or-buy decision. Bower's decision format also enables decision makers to see the effects of other costs and rates and make their decision in light of the uncertainty of these factors.

GLOSSARY

Direct Lease. A lessee acquires the use of an asset it did not previously own.

Financial Lease. A long-term contract that is noncancelable by the lessor, who assumes little or no ownership costs.

Leverage Lease. A tripartite arrangement whereby the lessor finances a part of the acquisition of an asset (50 to 80 percent of the purchase price) from a lender (commercial bank), securing the loan by a mortgage of the leased property as well as by the assignment of the lease and lease payments.

Maintenance Lease. Assigns responsibility for the maintenance of a leased asset's good working order to the lessor.

Net Lease. Assigns total responsibility for the maintenance of a leased asset to the lessee to the point that the lessee may be required to absorb all losses incurred by the sale of the asset at the end of the lease.

Nonmaintenance Lease. Assigns the responsibility for the maintenance of a leased asset to the lessee.

Operating Lease. A short-term contract that is cancelable given proper notice at the option of the lessee, whereby the lessor gives the lessee the use of property in exchange for rental payments and at the same time retains the usual risks and rewards of ownership.

Sale and Leaseback. A firm sells an asset it owns to another party, which in turn leases it back to the original owner.

NOTES

1. For a discussion of leverage leasing, see Robert C. Wiar, "Economic Implications of Multiple Rates of Return in the Leverage Lease Context," *Journal of Finance* (December 1973), pp. 1, 275–286; and E. Richard Packham, "An Analysis of the Risk of Leverage Leasing," *Journal of Commercial Bank Lending* (March 1975), pp. 2–29.

2. D. R. Grant, "Illusion in Lease Financing," *Harvard Business Review* (March-April 1959), p. 129.

3. Ibid., p. 126.

4. R. F. Vancil, "Lease or Borrow: New Method of Analysis," *Harvard Business Review* (September-October 1961), p. 127.

5. Financial Accounting Standards Board, *Accounting for the Sale or Purchase of Tax Benefits through Tax Leases*, Exposure Draft (Stamford, Conn.: FASB, November 30, 1981), p. 11.

6. R. W. Johnson and W. G. Lewellen, "Analysis of the Lease or Buy Decision," *Journal of Finance* (September 1972), pp. 815–823.

7. R. S. Bower, "Issues in Lease Financing," *Financial Management* (Winter 1973), p. 29.

8. R. L. Roenfeldt and J. S. Osteryoung, "Analysis of Financial Leases," *Financial Management* (Spring 1973), pp. 74–87.

9. Bower, "Issues in Lease Financing," p. 27.

SELECTED READINGS

Beechy, T. H. "The Cost of Leasing: Comment and Correction." *Accounting Review* (October 1970), pp. 769–773.

———. "Quasi-Debt Analysis of Financial Leases." *Accounting Review* (April 1969), pp. 375–381.

Billiam, Phillip L. "Lease versus Purchase: A Practical Problem." *Cost and Management* (September-October 1974), pp. 32–36.

Bower, R. S.; F. C. Herringer; and J. P. Williamson. "Lease Evaluation." *Accounting Review* (April 1966), pp. 257–265.

Burns, Jane O., and Kathleen Bindon. "Evaluating Leases with LP." *Management Accounting* (February 1980), pp. 48–53.

Doenges, E. C. "The Cost of Leasing." *Engineering Economist* (Winter 1971), pp. 31–44.

Duty, Glen L. "A Leasing Guide to Taxes." *Management Accounting* (August 1980), pp. 45–51.

Ferrara, William L.; James B. Thies; and Mark W. Dirsmith. "The Lease-Purchase Decision." *Management Accounting* (May 1980), pp. 57–59.

Findlay, M. Chapman, III. "Financial Lease Evaluation: Survey and Synthesis," mimeographed, abstracted in *Proceedings of the 1973 Annual Meeting of the Eastern Finance Association*, ed. Donald E. Fisher (Storrs, Conn.: April 12–14, 1973), p. 136.

———. "A Sensitivity Analysis of IRR Leasing Models." *Engineering Economist* (Summer 1975), pp. 231–242.

Franks, Julian R., and Stewart D. Hodges. "Valuation of Financial Lease Contracts: A Note." *Journal of Finance* (May 1978), pp. 657–669.

Johnson, R. W., and W. G. Lewellen. "Analysis of the Lease or Buy Decision." *Journal of Finance* (September 1972), pp. 815–823.

Levy, Haim, and Marshall Sarnat. "Leasing, Borrowing, and Financial Risk." *Financial Management* (Winter 1979), pp. 47–54.

Loretucci, Joseph A. "Financial Leasing: What's the Best Replacement Cycle?" *Management Accounting* (August 1979), pp. 45–48.

Millar, James A. "Hospital Equipment Leasing: The Breakeven Discount Rate." *Management Accounting* (July 1979), pp. 21–26.

Miller, M. H., and C. W. Upton. "Leasing, Buying and the Cost of Capital Services." *Journal of Finance* (June 1976), pp. 761–786.

Mitchell, G. B. "After-Tax Cost of Leasing." *Accounting Review* (April 1970), pp. 308–314.

Mokkelbost, Per B. "The Value of Leasing." Paper presented at the 1976 meeting of the Canadian Association of Administrative Sciences, University Laval, Quebec City, Quebec, May 31–June 2, 1976.

Myers, S. C.; D. A. Dill; and A. J. Bautista. "Valuation of Financial Lease Contracts." *Journal of Finance* (June 1976), pp. 799–819.

Roenfeldt, R. L., and J. S. Osteryoung. "Analysis of Financial Leases." *Financial Management* (Spring 1973), pp. 74–87.

School, Lawrence D. "The Lease-or-Buy and Asset Acquisition Decision." *Journal of Finance* (September 1974), pp. 1, 203–211, 214.

Vancil, R. R. "Lease or Borrow: New Method of Analysis." *Harvard Business Review* (September 1961), pp. 122–136.

Wyman, H. E. "Financial Lease Evaluation under Conditions of Uncertainty." *Accounting Review* (July 1973), pp. 489–493.

Chapter 7

Capital Budgeting for Social Projects

INTRODUCTION

Capital budgeting for social projects requires a consideration and measurement of environmental effects of the evolution and implications of the social projects. One way of contributing to a solution is to suggest ways of conceptualizing microsocial accounting and ways of measuring and evaluating the environmental effects of organizational behavior. The conceptualizing of microsocial accounting will provide a conceptual framework to justify and rationalize the new field and guide future developments. The techniques of measurement and evaluation will provide management with tools to incorporate consideration of the social consequences of its actions explicitly into a decision-making process and action and to provide both a corporation's particular constituencies and the general public with valid, pertinent data other than profit-and-loss statement information on which to base their evaluation of management's performance.[1] Accordingly, this chapter will present an "emerging" conceptual framework for microsocial accounting and ways of measuring and evaluating the environmental effects of organizational behavior.

TOWARD A CONCEPTUAL FRAMEWORK OF
MICROSOCIAL ACCOUNTING

A conceptual framework for microsocial accounting is equivalent to constitution; it should be a coherent system of interrelated objectives and fundamentals that can lead to consistent standards and that prescribes the nature, function, and limits of microsocial accounting. Such a framework would be useful for the development of a coherent set of standards and techniques, for the resolution of new and emerging practical problems, for increasing users' understanding of and confidence in social reporting, and for enhancing comparability among companies' social reports.

A conceptual framework for microsocial accounting does not exist for the moment in either the professional or academic literature. However, various attempts have been made in the accounting literature to outline some of the elements of the framework contributing to an "emerging" conceptual framework for microsocial accounting. These elements are the objectives, fundamental concepts, and operational guidelines.

Proposed Objectives

The objectives for microsocial economics are the first and essential steps to the formulation of a microsocial accounting framework. Then the socioeconomic accounting concepts will be true because they will be based on accepted objectives. In spite of the importance of these objectives, there has never been a formal attempt by the profession to accomplish such a task.

Several notable exceptions, which may serve as de facto objectives for microsocial accounting, were provided in an article by K. V. Ramanathan.[2] Three objectives are (1) to identify and measure the periodic net social contribution of an individual firm, including not only the costs and benefits internalized to the firm but also those arising from externalities affecting different social segments; (2) to help determine whether an individual firm's strategies and practices that directly affect the relative resource and power status of individuals, communities, social segments, and generations are consistent with widely shared social priorities on the one hand and individuals' legitimate aspirations on the other; (3) to make available in an optimal manner to all social constituents relevant information on a firm goals, policies, programs, performance, and contributions to social goals.[3]

The first two objectives are presented as measurement objectives of social accounting, while the third objective is a reporting objective. The first objective calls for the measurement of a firm's periodic net social contribution, which includes both private and social costs and benefits. The second objective calls for the measurement of the firm's contribution to social goals. The third objective calls for a reporting of the results of the first two objectives.

Proposed Concepts

Concepts based on the objectives of microsocial accounting would constitute the basic foundation for a microsocial accounting theory. In the article cited earlier, K. V. Ramanathan proposed six concepts of social accounting.[4]

1. A *social transaction* represents a firm's utilization or delivery of a socioenvironment resource that affects the absolute or relative interests of a firm's various social constituents and that is not processed through the marketplace.

2. *Social overheads (returns)* represent the sacrifice (benefit) to society from those resources consumed (added) by a firm as a result of its social transactions.

3. *Social income* represents the periodic net social contribution of a firm. It is computed as the algebraic sum of the firm's traditionally measured net income, its aggregate social overheads, and its aggregate social returns.

4. *Social constituents* are the different distinct social groups (implied in the second objective and expressed in the third objective of social accounting) with whom a firm is presumed to have a social contract.

5. *Social equity* is a measure of the aggregate changes in the claims that each social constituent is presumed to have in the firm.

6. *Net social asset* of a firm is a measure of its aggregate nonmarket contribution to the society's well-being less its nonmarket depletion of the society's resources during the life of the firm.[5]

The first concept, the social transaction, calls for recognition of all the "transactions" between the firm and society that are not handled presently through the marketplace. These nonmarket transactions are basically positive or negative externalities. The second concept is that of social overhead and social return. The nonmarket transactions resulting from the social transaction generate either a social overhead, which is a social cost imposed on society, or a social return, which is a social benefit. The third concept, social income, is a measure of the overall performance of the firm to include the traditional net income, the social overheads, and the social returns. The fourth concept is that of social constituents. To measure adequately, the social overheads, social returns, and the resulting social income, the different social groups likely to be affected by the firm's operational and other activities need to be identified. These groups are the social constituents of the firm, with whom the firm has an explicit or implicit social contract. The fifth concept is that of social equity, that is, the claims that each social constituent has in the firm. The sixth concept, social assets, constitutes the firm's nonmarket contribution to society, which are increased by positive externalities and decreased by negative externalities.

Proposed Qualitative Characteristics

To be useful, a microsocial accounting report must meet certain qualitative criteria. These criteria are intended to guide the social accountant to produce the "best," or most useful, information for managers. The Financial Accounting Standards Board, a standard-setting body for microsocial accounting, has proposed certain criteria for selecting and evaluating financial accounting and reporting policies.[6] These criteria, which also apply to microsocial accounting, include decision usefulness, benefits over costs, relevance, reliability, neutrality, verifiability, representational faithfulness, comparability, timeliness, understand-ability, completeness, and consistency. These criteria may be organized as a hierarchy of informational qualities.

Most microsocial accounting is concerned to some degree with decision making; thus, *decision usefulness* becomes the overriding criterion for choosing among microsocial accounting alternatives. The type of information chosen is the one that, subject to any cost considerations, appears the most useful for decision making.

Microsocial accounting information, like any other commodity, will be sought if the benefits to be derived from the information exceed its costs. Thus, before preparing and disseminating the cost accounting information, the benefits and costs of providing the information must be compared.

Relevance has been appropriately defined as follows: "For information to meet the standard of relevance, it must bear upon or be usefully associated with the action it is designed to facilitate or the result it is desired to produce. This requires that either the information or the act of communicating it exert influence . . . on the designated actions."[7] Relevance, therefore, refers to the information's ability to influence managers' decisions by changing or confirming their expectations about the results or consequences of actions or events. There can be degrees of relevance. The relevance of particular information will vary among users and will depend on their needs and the particular contexts in which the decisions are made.

Reliability refers to that "quality which permits users of data to depend upon it with confidence as representative of what it proposes to represent."[8] Thus, the reliability of information depends on its degree of faithfulness in the representation of an event. Reliability will differ among users depending on the extent of their knowledge of the rules used to prepare the information. Similarly, different users may seek information with different degrees of reliability.

The absence of bias in the presentation of accounting reports or information is neutrality. Thus, neutral information is free from bias toward attaining some desired result or inducing a particular mode of behavior. This is not to imply that the preparers of information do not have a purpose in mind when preparing the reports; it only means that the purpose should not influence a predetermined result. Notice that neutrality is in conflict with one of the concepts of social accounting, namely, the feedback concept. It may be argued that social accounting reports are intended to report on managerial performance and influence behavior and hence cannot be neutral.

Verifiability is "that attribute . . . which allows qualified individuals working independently of one another to develop essentially similar measures or conclusions from an examination of the same evidence, data, or records."[9] It implies consensus and absence of measurer bias. Verifiable information can be substantially reproduced by independent measures using the same measurement methods. Notice that verifiability refers only to the correctness of the resulting information, not to the appropriateness of the measurement method used.

Representational faithfulness and completeness refer to the correspondence between the accounting data and the events those data are supposed to represent. If the measure portrays what it is supposed to represent, it is considered free of measurement and measurer bias.

Comparability describes the use of the same methods by different firms, and consistency describes the use of the same method over time by a given firm. Both qualitative characteristics are more important for financial accounting information than for social accounting information.

Timeliness refers to the availability of data when they are needed or soon enough after the reported events. A trade-off is necessary between timeliness and precision.

The clarity of the information and ease of grasp by the users is its understandability. The preparer's level of understanding is generally different from the user's. Thus, efforts should be made by the preparer to increase the understandability of accounting information, in both form and content, to increase its usefulness to the user.

Proposed Conceptual Framework

A conceptual framework is a constitution, a coherent set of interrelated *objectives* and *fundamentals* that can lead to consistent standards and that prescribes the nature, function, and limits of financial accounting and financial statements. The objectives identify the goals and purposes of accounting. The *fundamentals* are the underlying concepts of accounting, concepts that guide the selection of events to be accounted for, the measurement of those events, and the means of summarizing and communicating them to interested parties. Concepts of that type are fundamental in the sense that other concepts flow from them and repeated reference to them will be necessary in establishing, interpreting, and applying accounting and reporting standards.[10]

Applied to microsocioeconomic accounting, the conceptual framework is intended to act as a constitution for the process of choosing techniques of measurement, evaluation, and communication of social information. The constitution specifies both objectives and fundamentals. The discussion in the previous sections centered on proposed objectives and fundamentals applicable to socioeconomic accounting. Therefore, an "emerging" conceptual framework for microsocial accounting seems to exist. Exhibit 7.1 provides an overview of the conceptual framework for microsocial accounting. At the first level, the proposed objectives identify the goals and purposes of microsocial accounting. At the second level are the proposed concepts and qualitative characteristics of microsocial accounting. Finally, at the third level, the operational guidelines specifies the techniques of measurement and evaluation for microsocial accounting. Examples of techniques of measurement and evaluation will be presented in the rest of the chapter. The conceptual framework for microsocial accounting pre-

Exhibit 7.1
A Conceptual Framework for Microsocial Accounting

	Objectives 1. Measurement 2. Reporting		First Level: Objectives
Qualitative Characteristics 1. Decision usefulness 2. Benefits over costs 3. Relevance 4. Reliability 5. Neutrality 6. Timeliness 7. Understanding 8. Verifiability 9. Representational faithfulness 10. Comparability 11. Cosistency 12. Completeness	Concepts 1. Social transaction 2. Social overhead 3. Social income 4. Social constituents 5. Social equity		Second Level Fundamental concept.
Techniques Measurement	Techniques of Evaluation	Techniques of Reporting	Third Level: Operational guidelines

sented in Exhibit 7.1 is only tentative, awaiting formalization by the accounting profession and other concerned groups.

MEASUREMENT AND EVALUATION IN MICROSOCIAL ACCOUNTING

The Concept of Environmental Damage

The environment is a resource that affects the ways things live and develop. It is above all a nonreproducible capital asset offering vital services to man. The most valuable of these services involves "the *dispersing, storing*, or *assimilating of residuals* which are generated as a byproduct of economic activity."[11] This service is generally portrayed in the materials balance model and its corollary, the principle of materials balance, which "portrays the flow of raw materials into consumer goods, then into wastes from production and residuals from consumption."[12] The other services provided by the environment involve a support of human life, amenity services, and a source of material inputs. Given these services the environmental quality is affected when the level and composition of these services are altered. The alteration or damage is generally caused by the wastes and residuals that the environment may fail to absorb or assimilate:

In economic terms, this damage is equal to the reduction in the value of environmental quality caused by the disposal of residuals. Hence, whenever residual disposal impairs life, reduces the value of property, or constrains the quality of natural recreation sites, the quality and quantity of nonresidual absorptive environment services is reduced and environmental damages exist. These damages are measured by the value of the non-waste-receptor environmental services forgone because the disposal or residuals. As such, environmental damage conforms to the classic economic notion of opportunity costs.[13]

Environmental damage is first a consequence of the overuse and abuse of what is in fact a free commodity. Second, it is aggravated by the widely held belief that the use of the residual absorptive services of the environment is limitless and costless. In fact, the damage itself results in reduction in the other environmental services in addition to a reduction in the residual absorptive services.

Optimal Level of Environmental Quality

The above discussion implies that environmental quality can be achieved by a reduction in environmental damage. There are two types of costs of damage associated with the use of the waste-absorptive services of the environment: the total damage costs created by the reduction in the nonresidual absorptive services of the environment due to residual discharges and the cost of abatement needed to reduce the residuals released to the environment. The optimal level of environmental quality will be the level that minimizes the sum of these two costs: damage costs and abatement costs. This strategy may be applied to any type of residual.

There are several studies attempting to estimate environmental damage in economic terms. These studies have attempted to measure *direct* damage in monetary terms and disamenities such as recreational and aesthetic losses. They are examined next.

Air Pollution

National estimates of air pollution damages exist for the United States, Canada, and Great Britain.[14] The damage caused by air pollution has also been examined in terms of its impact on human health, materials, vegetation, and property values.

With respect to human health, various studies have tried to assign economic values to the health effects of air pollution.[15] For example, Ridker defines four types of costs: those due to premature death, those associated with mobility, treatment costs, and prevention or avoidance costs. The costs of premature death due to disease are calculated as the sum of an individual's expected earnings discounted for each additional productive year of life had he not died prematurely. The following formula was used:

$$V_a = \sum_{n=a}^{\infty} \frac{Pa_1^n * Pa_2^n * Pa_3^n * Yn}{(1 + R)^{n-a}}$$

where

> V_a = present value of the future earnings of an individual at age n;
> Pa_1^n = probability that an individual of age a will live to age n;
> Pa_2^n = probability that an individual of age a will live to age n;
> Pa_3^n = probability that an individual of age a living at age n will be in the labor force at age n;
> Yn = earnings at age n;
> R = rate of interest.

Similarly, the burial costs associated with premature death are calculated as the difference between the present cost of burial and the present value of the future expected cost of burial. The following formula was used:

$$C_a = C_0\left[1 - \sum_{n=a}^{\infty} (Pa_1^n)/(1+R)^{n-a}\right]$$

where

> C_0 = cost of burial;
> C_a = present value of the net expected gain from delaying burial at age a;
> Pa_1^n and R as above.

Ridker computed the costs associated with various diseases and assumes that 20 percent of the costs may be attributed to air pollution. In fact, most other studies adopted the same approach, which is to estimate the costs of specific diseases and attribute a percentage of these costs to air pollution.

With respect to materials, the negative effects of air pollution include corrosion of metals, deterioration of rubber, discoloration of paint, and soiling. Various studies have tried to assign economic values to those consequences.[16] For example, the Midwest Research Institute (MRI) presents the results of a systematic study of all the physical and chemical interactions between materials, pollutants, and environmental parameters needed to assess the economic damage to materials from air pollution. The MRI study computes the economic value of the material and then applies the rate of deterioration to this value to estimate the economic loss from deterioration. The economic value of material exposed to air pollution Q is calculated as follows:

$$Q = P \times N \times F \times R$$

where

> P = product of the annual dollar production volume;
> N = economic life of the material based on usage;

F = weighted average factor for the percentage of material
    exposed to air pollution;
R = labor factor reflecting the in-place or as-used value of the material.

The rate of deterioration of interaction V is then calculated by estimating the difference between the deterioration rates in polluted and unpolluted environments divided by the average thickness of the material. The MRI study also computes the costs due to soiling by assigning an economic value to aesthetic loss suffered by a material through soiling.[17] The formula used is

$$L = Q \times V$$

where

$$Q \qquad = \text{value of the exposed material as defined earlier}$$
$$V \qquad = \text{soiling interaction value per year}$$
$$V_{fibers} \quad = 0.10 \; \Delta f/RW$$
$$V_{nonfibers} = 0.10 \; \Delta f/RWpt$$

where

W = material price per pound;
R = labor force;
p = density;
t = average thickness;
Δf = increased frequency of cleaning due to pollution.

With respect to vegetation, several studies attempted to estimate damage to vegetation from air pollution.[18] These studies were, however, criticized for the limitations of their methodologies.[19]

With respect to property values, several studies attempted to estimate the effects of air pollution on residential property values. The estimates were based on linear regression models using either a cross-sectional or a time series approach. The units show negative, although not significant, effects of pollution on property value, rent, and land use intensity.

Noise

The effects of noise are generally assembled through its effects on property values, with property values as dependent variables and noise parameters as one of the independent variables.[20] Other studies relied on a survey in which people were asked how much less a certain house in a noise-defined environment would have to be than an ordinary house before one could consider buying it.[21] These studies are far from being conclusive in the damage produced by noise. To that effect Wyzga states:

Theoretically from surveys, litigation, etc., it appears as if there is damage involved, which includes a decrease in property value, but the studies to date have been largely unsuccessful in uncovering any relationship between noise levels and property values. It could be that most of these studies have not properly adjusted for housing supply or the fact that some individuals are more sensitive to noise than others. These and other potential influences need to be investigated, and more realistic models need to be developed if we are to obtain reasonable estimates of the relationship between noise and property values.[22]

Water Pollution

Various studies investigating the damages caused by water pollution focused on the disamenities due to pollution. Most studies concerned themselves with measuring the recreational benefits arising from the use of unpolluted water. Various measurement methods used for estimating recreational benefits are given by Clawson and Knetsch.[23] These are as follows:

1. *Maximum price method*: estimates the total benefit of a recreational resource to be the sum of the maximum prices that various users would pay for the employment of the resource.
2. *Gross expenditure method*: estimates the total amount spent on recreation by the user as a surrogate measure of recreational benefits.
3. *Market value of fish method*: estimates the market value of fish caught by the user as a surrogate measure of recreational benefits.
4. *Cost method*: equates the benefits to the costs used to generate them.
5. *Market value method*: uses the prices charged at privately owned recreational areas as a surrogate measure of recreational benefits.
6. *Direct interview method*: assesses directly how much the users are willing to pay for using the resource.

Estimating Social Costs

Having identified the nature of the environmental damage and the resulting environmental damage functions, the next step is the economic measurement of the environmental damage. The idea is to attach a monetary value to each type of damage. In general, two types of damages are considered: financial losses and amenity losses.[24] Financial losses may be defined as the change in the level of outlays following a change in environmental quality. Examples of financial losses include productivity losses resulting from the environmental damage and increased costs of health care. Amenity losses may be defined as the psychic costs resulting from the suffering, bereavement, and limitation imposed on individuals, families, and society.

The estimation of financial losses generally relies on direct determination of the monetary value of changes in the demand for marketable goods and services due to environmental changes. Four problems may be identified with this approach:

1. the specification of effects, or the problem of identifying the marketable goods and services that are affected by a change in the environment;
2. the relating of effects to a specific level of environmental deterioration;
3. the problem of finding the proper prices, including the interest rate, that should be used in a monetary evaluation;
4. the problem of interpreting the calculated financial values and relating them to the monetary damage in the context of the problem under study.[25]

The estimation of amenity losses differs because of their intangible nature. The methods used tend to be indirect. One method may be to use questionnaires in which the affected individuals are asked to specify the amount of money necessary to compensate them for environmental deterioration. A second method is to use the relationship between the loss of a specific amenity and the demand for private goods to estimate the amenity loss. A third method is to use the market reactions in terms of changes in prices. A comparison of land values, for example, may indicate a loss of amenity. Finally, litigation results may be used to estimate amenity losses.

Estimating Social Benefits

Social benefits are the gains associated with a reduction of the externality or nuisance. In the case of pollution, for example, the benefits are measured by a comparison of the existing level of pollution and "acceptable" level of pollution. Thus, benefits result from a "willingness to pay" to reduce the nuisance. It implies the existence of a demand curve for the effects of improvement of environmental quality. Benefit estimation is then reduced to a determination of the demand curve for environmental quality.[26] Three techniques have been used to estimate the demand in connection with air and water pollution: measuring benefits from market data; measuring benefits from nonmarket data; and measuring benefits on the basis of property values.

Measuring benefits from market data uses the relationships between private marketed goods and public goods to draw inferences on the demand of public goods. The demand for the public good is inferred from market transactions on the related private good. The level of environmental quality as a public good, however, enters the individual utility functions in the broad categories. First, it is an input in the production of market goods and services. Its demand can be estimated by examining changes in factor incomes such as land units, costs savings in production, and changes in consumer associated with the private good outputs.[27] Second, if it enters directly in the utility function as a consumption good, its demand can be estimated in terms of shifts in the demand curve for a private complementary good, or in terms of the demand for a perfect substitute.

Measuring benefits from nonmarket data relies on nonmarket means such as surveys, questionnaires, bidding games, and voting. The idea is to induce people to reveal directly or indirectly their preferences for the provision of public goods. Basically, three approaches may be used. The first approach is to ask people about their willingness to pay to obtain a given level of public good.[28] The second approach is to ask individuals how much of the public good they would demand at a given price or under given conditions of taxation.[29] The third approach uses a voting mechanism in which two parties or candidates compete for votes after adopting different positions on the provision of a public good.[30]

Ronald Ridker was the first to use property values as a basis for benefit estimation. He argues as follows:

If the land market were to work perfectly, the price of a plot of land would equal the sum of the present discounted streams of benefits and costs derivable from it. If some of its costs rise (e.g., if additional maintenance and cleaning costs are required), or if some of its benefits fall (e.g., if one cannot see the mountains from the terrace) the property will be discounted in the market to reflect people's evaluation of these changes. Since air pollution is specific to locations and the supply of locations is fixed, there is less likelihood that the negative effects of air pollution can be significantly shifted on to other markets. We would therefore expect to find the majority of effects reflected in this market, and we can measure them by observing associated changes in property values.[31]

Following Ridker's example, the approach adopted was to derive benefit measures from property value differences at a point in time.

Various social programs may be necessary to connect some of the social ills imposed by the environmental effects of organizational behavior. A choice has to be made for the program most suitable and most feasible given the state of the technology and the funds available. This section of the chapter presents two widely accepted techniques for the evaluation programs: cost-benefit analysis and cost-effectiveness analysis.

Cost-Benefit Analysis

Cost-benefit analysis is a method used to assess the desirability of projects when it is necessary to take both a long and a wide view of the impact of the proposed project on the general welfare of a society.[32] It calls for an enumeration and evaluation of all the relevant costs and benefits the project may generate and for choosing the alternatives that maximize the present value of all benefits less costs, subject to specified constraints and given specified objectives. Cost-benefit analysis is very useful when all the economic impacts of a project, indirect as well as direct effects, have to be considered. It is a favorite method of analysis by governmental agencies for assessing the desirability of particular program expenditures and/or policy changes. In fact, it has been formally adopted into U.S. federal government budgetary procedures under the Planning-

Programming-Budgeting System (PPBS).[33] It acts as a structure for a general theory of government resource allocation. Above all, it is a decision technique whose aims are first to take all effects into consideration and second to maximize the present value of all benefits less that of all costs, subject to specified constraints. This brings into focus the major considerations of cost-benefit analysis:

1. What are the objectives and constraints to be considered?
2. Which costs and benefits are to be included?
3. How are the costs and benefits to be valued?
4. What are the investment criteria to be used?
5. Which discount rate should be used?

Objectives and Relevant Constraints

The main objective of cost-benefit analysis is to determine whether or not a particular expenditure is economically and socially justifiable. The basic criteria used in cost-benefit analysis is an efficiency criterion. One such efficiency criterion is Pareto optimality. A program is said to be Pareto efficient if at least one person is made better off and no one is made worse off. This criterion is too strong and too impractical for cost-benefit analysis, however, given that few programs are likely to leave some individuals better off and no one worse off. A weaker notion of efficiency, known as the Kaldor-Hides criterion, is generally used for cost-benefit analysis. Under this criterion, also known as the potential Pareto improvement criterion, a program is acceptable if it is Pareto optimal or if it could redistribute the net benefits to everyone in the community so that everyone is at least as well off as they were before the initiation of the program.[34] Basically, a program is efficient and should be undertaken if its total discounted societal benefits exceed the total discounted costs.

Besides the objectives of cost-benefit analysis, which are basically intended to maximize society's wealth, it is important to recognize some of the constraints. Eckstein provided a helpful classification of constraints.[35] These include:

1. *Physical constraints*: The program alternatives considered may be constrained by the state of technology and more generally by the production function, which relates the physical inputs and outputs of a project.
2. *Legal constraints*: The program alternatives considered must be done within the framework of the law. Examples of legal constraints include property rights, time needed for public inquiries, regulated pricing, the right of eminent domain, and limits to the activities of public agencies.
3. *Administrative constraints*: Each of the alternative programs requires the availability and the hiring of individuals with the right administrative skills.
4. *Distributional constraints*: Any program is bound to generate gainers and losers. The unfavorable effects on income distribution may be alleviated by expressing the ob-

jective of cost-benefit analysis as either maximizing the excess of total benefits over total costs subject to constraints on the benefits less costs of particular groups or maximizing the net gain (or minimizing the net loss) to a particular group subject to a constraint relating to total benefits and costs.

5. *Political constraints*: Political considerations may act as constraints, shifting the decision from what is *best* to what is *possible*. Regional differences and presence of various competing interest groups are examples of actors bound to create political constraints on the choice of the best program.

6. *Budgetary constraints*: Capital rationing and evaluating may act as constraints, shifting the objective function from maximizing to suboptimizing of net benefit given a target budget.

7. *Social and religious constraints*: Social and religious taboos are bound to act as constraints, shifting the decision from what is *best* to what is *acceptable*.

Enumeration of Costs and Benefits

Enumeration of costs and benefits is important in determining which of the costs and benefits of a particular project should be included in a cost-benefit analysis.

Benefits of a project are either direct or indirect. Primary or direct benefits of a project "are those benefits which accrue directly to the users of the service provided by the project." They consist of "the value of goods or services that result from conditions with the project as compared to conditions without the project."[36] Indirect or secondary benefits of a project are those benefits accruing to others that the users of the service provided by the project. They are of two types: real or technological benefits or pecuniary benefits.[37] Real or technological benefits are those benefits resulting from changes in total production possibilities and consumption opportunities. For example, if a dam creates a reduction in flooding and more pleasant scenery, these benefits are real benefits. Pecuniary benefits are those benefits that alter the distribution of total income without changing its volume. They generally take the form of lower input costs, increased volumes of business, or changes in the land values. *Only direct real benefits should be included; pecuniary benefits should be excluded in the enumeration of the benefits of a project.* Other benefits that are of an intangible nature and difficult to identify should be considered also. Costs of a project are also either direct or indirect. Direct or primary costs of a project are costs incurred directly by the users of the service provided by the project. They include the capital costs, operating and maintenance costs, and personnel expenses required by the project. Indirect or secondary costs are incurred by others than the users of the service provided by the project. They may also be of two types: real or technological and pecuniary costs. *Again, only the real secondary cost should be counted in a cost-benefit analysis.*

Briefly, in enumerating the costs and benefits of a project, the analyst must be careful to distinguish their allocative effects from their pecuniary or distributional effects. In fact, the confusion of pecuniary and allocative effects constitutes a primary defect in many analyses of the efficiency of public projects. The only effects that should be taken into account in enumerating the costs and benefits of a public project are the real or technological externalities, that is, those that affect total opportunities for production and consumption, as opposed to pecuniary externalities, which do not affect total production or consumption.

Valuation of Costs and Benefits

In general, benefits should measure the value of the additional goods or services produced or the value of cost savings in the production of goods or services, while costs should measure the value of real resources displaced from other uses.

Assuming a competitive economy, benefits and costs will be valued on the basis of the observable market prices of the outputs and inputs of the program. More precisely, the benefits will be valued in either the market price of the output of the program or on the amounts users are willing to pay if charged (i.e., the consumers' surplus, which is the difference between the aggregate willingness to pay and the costs of the projects).

Where market prices do not accurately reflect the value of the market transactions to society as a result of externalities, the shadow prices, as adjusted or input prices, may be used. The general principle for estimating shadow prices for the output of public projects is to simulate what users would be willing to pay if they were charged as if the goods were sold in perfectly competitive markets.

Investment Criteria

Cost-benefit analysis is a method used to evaluate long-term projects. As such, the benefits and costs of each project have to be discounted to be comparable at time 0 when evaluation and decision on the projects have to be made. There is a need to rely on some form of discounting in the choice of investment criteria. There are exactly three possible investment or decision criteria: net present value; benefit-cost ratio; and internal rate of return.

Under the net present value, the present value of a project is obtained by discounting the net excess of benefits (B_t) over costs (C_t) for each year during the life of the project back to the present time using a social discount rate. More explicitly,

$$V = \sum_{t=1}^{\alpha} (B_t - C_t)/(1 + r)^t$$

where

   V = value of the project;
   B_t = benefit in year t;
   C_t = cost in year t;
   r = social discount rate;
   α = life of the project.

Basically a project is found acceptable if the present value V is positive. If there are binding constraints on a project (for example, budget appropriation, foreign exchange, private investment opportunity forgone), then the following model proposed by Steiner[38] would be more appropriate:

$$V = \sum_{t=1}^{\alpha} (B_t - C_t)/(1 + r)^t - \sum_{j=1}^{n} p_j k_j,$$

where

   p_j = shadow price of a binding constraint;
   k_j = number of units of a constrained resource.

Under benefit-cost ratio, the decision criterion is expressed in terms of the ratio of the present value of benefits to the present value of costs (both discounted at the social discount rate). More explicitly, the benefit-cost ratio is:

$$\frac{\sum_{t=1}^{\alpha} b_t/(1 + r)^t}{\sum_{t=1}^{\alpha} c_t(1 + r)^t}$$

Basically all projects that are not mutually exclusive with a benefit-cost ratio in excess of 1 are acceptable.

Under internal rate or return, the decision criterion is expressed in terms of the internal rate of return; that is to say, the discount rate will equate the net benefits over the life of the project with the original cost. In other words, 2 is the rate of interest for which

$$\sum_{t=1}^{\alpha} b_t/(1 + r)^t - \sum_{t=1}^{\alpha} c_t(1 + r)^t = 0$$

Basically all projects where the internal rate of return exceeds the closer social discount rate are deemed acceptable.

Choice of a Discount Rate

The choice of a discount rate is important for at least two reasons. A high rate will lead the firm or the government away from the undertaking of the project, while a low rate may make the project more acceptable from a return point of view. Furthermore, a low discount rate tends to favor projects yielding net benefits further into the future relative to projects yielding more current net benefits. Choosing the appropriate interest rate therefore becomes an important policy question. There are several possible alternative rates.

Given that the discount rate allows the allocation of resources between the public and private sectors, it should be chosen so that it indicates when resources should be transferred from one sector to another. This means that the discount rate should represent the opportunity cost of funds withdrawn from the private sector to be used in the public sector. As Baumol states, "The correct discount rate for the evaluation of a government project is the percentage rate of return that the resources utilized would otherwise provide in the private sector."[39]

These considerations enter in the choice of the *marginal productivity of capital as a discount rate in private investment*: "(1) an effort to minimize governmental activity; (2) a concern for efficiency; and (3) a belief that the source of funds for government investment in the private sector or that government investment will displace private investment that would otherwise be made."[40]

Social time preference expresses a concern for future generations in the sense that the welfare of the future generations will be increased if investments are made now. It follows that the discount rate should be the *social rate of time preference*, that is to say, the compensation required to induce consumers to refrain from consumption and save. One study committee argued that the federal government should use the "administration's social rate of time discount" to be established by the president in consultation with his advisors, such as the Council of Economic Advisors.[41] The strongest argument for the social rate of time preference was made by Pigou, who suggested that individuals were short-sighted about the future ("defective telescopic faculty") and the welfare of future generations would require governmental intervention.[42]

Advantages and Limitations

There are thousands of cost-benefit analyses of government projects. The popularity of the method is a witness to some of its advantages. There are also some limitations well recognized in the literature. Let's examine some of the advantages and limitations of both. Among the advantages of cost-benefit analysis we may cite the following:

1. It is most effective in dealing with cases of intermediate social goods.[43]
2. It establishes a framework for a reasonably consistent evaluation of alternative pro-

jects, especially where the choice set is narrow in the sense that the projects are not only similar but generate the same volume of externalities.

3. It allows one to ascertain the decisions most advantageous in terms of the objectives accepted.

Among its limitations we may cite the following:

1. There are limits within which social objectives can be measured in money terms. An example of nonefficiency objectives that are not measurable in dollar terms is an equitable distribution of income.

2. Cost-benefit analysis falls under what is known as partial equilibrium analysis. It is useful in evaluating only projects that have negligible impact outside the immediately affected areas of the economy.

3. There are obvious problems of enumeration and evaluation of the costs and benefits of particular projects.[44] A committee of the House of Representatives, pointing to the difficulty inherent in estimating the direct effects of a policy and assigning dollar terms to them, argued that such estimates are seldom accurate.[45] Similarly, Baram argued that "monetization of environmental and health amenities constitutes an inappropriate treatment of factors that transcend economies."[46]

COST-EFFECTIVENESS ANALYSIS

The difference between cost-effectiveness analysis and cost-benefit analysis is merely a difference of degree and not in kind. While cost-benefit analysis is concerned with quantifying both benefits and costs in money terms and determining the most efficient way to conduct a given program, cost-effectiveness assumes that the outputs of a given program are useful and valuable without attempting to measure their values. Thus, cost-effectiveness analysis may be merely defined as "a technique for choosing among *given* alternative courses of action in terms of their cost and effectiveness in the attainment of *specified* objectives."[47] This definition assumes that the objectives are known and well specified and the only concern in with cost-effectiveness considerations. Consider, however, another definition where cost-effectiveness is "a technique for evaluating broad management and economic implications of alternative choices of action with the objective of assisting in the identification of the preferred choice."[48] This last definition implies less well-defined objectives, solutions, and criteria of effectiveness. In any case, the methodology will be the same under both approaches.

Methodology

Before introducing the methodology, we should keep in mind that cost-effectiveness analysis is used generally for projects where the aim is to minimize the costs associated with the attainment of any given objective or objectives. As such it may be outlined as a sequence of general steps:[49]

1. *Definition of objectives*: The basic requirement for cost-effectiveness analyses is that the objectives be *specifiable*.

2. *Identification of alternatives*: Devising various feasible options for accomplishing objectives.

3. *Selection of effectiveness measures*: This step is considered the most difficult in cost-effectiveness analysis since the desirability of a given program may change depending on the type of effectiveness measure used.[50]

4. *Cost estimates*: The estimation of costs for each alternative, precisely as in cost-benefit analysis.

5. *Selection of a decision criterion*: Two major types of criteria are used in cost-effectiveness analysis: a constant cost criterion, or a least-cost criterion. The constant cost criterion allows one to determine the output that may be achieved from a number of alternative systems, all of which require the same outlay of funds. In short, the constant cost criterion specifies what the analyst can get for his or her money and how to maximize effectiveness at a given cost. The least cost criterion allows one to identify the least expensive option for achieving a certain level of output. In other words, it attempts to minimize cost while attaining a given level of effectiveness. N. M. Singer illustrated adequately the differences between the constant cost and least-cost criteria: "The differences among the various types of systems analysis can be seen by comparing the operations research problem, to collect refuse with a given fleet of trucks, to studies that would be made under the other methodologies. At least cost study would determine the collection system of minimum cost for the given pick-up locations: that is, the capital and labor inputs would be permitted to vary. A constant cost study would examine the various outputs that could be produced for the cost of the garbage truck fleet: commuter transit if the money were spent on buses, highway safety if the money were spent on roadgrading equipment, education if the funds were spent on schools, and so forth. Finally, a benefit-cost study would estimate the value that consumers place on the garbage pick-up and would then recommend whether or not to undertake the program."[51]

6. *Creation of models*: The next step is to formulate analytical relationships among costs, effectiveness, and environmental factors. Given these relationships, the next step is to choose either the alternative that maximizes effectiveness with given cost or the alternative that minimizes costs given a desired level of effectiveness.

Limitations

Three limitations of cost-effectiveness analysis are generally considered.[52] First, judgment may be necessary to delineate factors and interrelationships and to interpret the results. Second, it may be difficult to select measures of effectiveness. Third, imperfect information and insufficient input information may distort the analysis. Finally, the analysis is too deterministic and does not account for uncertainty.

CONCLUSIONS

This chapter suggested ways of conceptualizing microsocial accounting and ways of measuring and evaluating the environmental effects of organizational behavior. A tentative conceptual framework is presented as a way of conceptualizing microsocial accounting. This framework rests on proposed objectives, concepts, and qualitative characteristics of microsocial accounting. The measurement of the environmental effects of organizational behavior rests on measurement of social costs and social benefits. Various ways of measuring social costs and benefits are presented. The evaluation of social programs rests on two established techniques, namely, cost-benefit analysis and cost-effectiveness.

What is conveyed in this chapter is, first, that a conceptual framework for socioeconomic accounting is feasible and, second, that techniques of measurement evaluation of the environmental effects of organizational behavior are available. What remains to be accomplished by corporate firms and interest groups is a trial implementation and "legitimization" of microsocial accounting.

NOTES

1. Meinoff Dierkes and Raymond A. Bauer, *Corporate Social Accounting* (New York: Praeger 1973), p. xi.

2. Kavassen V. Ramanathan, "Toward a Theory of Corporate Social Accounting," *Accounting Review* (July 1976), pp. 519–521.

3. Ibid., pp. 520–521.

4. Ibid., pp. 522–523.

5. Ibid.

6. Financial Accounting Standards Board, "Qualitative Characteristics: Criteria for Selecting and Evaluating Financial Accounting and Reporting Policies," Exposure draft (Stamford, Conn.: FASB, 1979).

7. American Accounting Association, *A Statement of Basic Accounting Theory* (Evanston, Ill.: AAA, 1966), p. 9.

8. American Accounting Association, Committee on Concepts and Standards for External Financial Reports, *Statement of Accounting Theory and Theory Acceptance* (Sarasota, Fla.: AAA, 1977), p. 16.

9. American Accounting Association, *A Statement of Basic Accounting Theory*, p. 10.

10. "Conceptual Framework for Financial Accounting and Reporting: Elements of Financial Statements and their Measurements," FASB Discussion Memorandum (Stamford, Conn.: FASB, 1976), p. 1.

11. Robert H. Haveman, "On Estimating Environmental Damage: A Survey of Recent Research in the United States," in Organization for Economic Cooperation and Development, *Environmental Damage Costs* (Paris: OECD, 1976), p. 102.

12. Alien V. Kneese, Robert U. Ayres, and Ralph C. d'Arge, *Economics and the Environment: A Materials Balance Approach* (Baltimore: Johns Hopkins University Press, 1970).

13. Ibid., p. 107.

14. Office of Service and Technology, "Cumulative Regulatory Effects on the Cost of Automotive Transportation (RECAT): Final Report of the *ad hoc* Committee" (Washington, D.C.: Office of Service and Technology, February 28, 1972). Programmers Analysis Unit, *Economic and Technical Appraisal of Air Pollution in the United Kingdom* (Chilton: Berkes, 1971).

15. R. C. Ridker, *Economic Costs of Air Pollution* (New York: Praeger, 1967); P. G. Lave and N. T. Seskin, "Air Pollution and Human Health," *Science* 169 (1968), p. 723.

16. R. T. Stickney, N. P. Mueller, and A. S. Spence, "Pollution vs. Rubber," *Rubber Age* 45 (September 1971); Midwest Research Institute, *Systems Analysis of the Effects of Air Pollution on Materials* (Chicago: Midwest Research Institute, January 1970).

17. Ridker also attempted to estimate soiling and deterioration damages by relying on two other approaches: survey of consumers, and survey of the cleaning industry.

18. P. Benedict, M. Miller, and T. Olson, *Economic Impact of Air Pollution Plants in the United States* (Stanford, Calif.: Stanford Research Institute. November 1971); S. Millecan, *A Survey and Assessment of Air Pollution Damage to California Vegetation in 1970* (Sacramento: California Department of Agriculture, June 1971).

19. T. Landau, "Statistical Aspects of Air Pollution as It Applies to Agriculture." Paper presented at the 1971 meeting of the Statistical Societies. Fort Collins, Colo.

20. R. Diffey, "An Investigation into the Effect of High Traffic Noise on House Prices in a Homogeneous Submarket." Paper presented at a Seminar on House Prices and the Micro-economics of Housing, London School of Economics, December 1971.

21. P. Plowden, *The Cost of Noise* (London: Metra Consulting Group, 1970).

22. R. E. Wyzga, "A Survey of Environmental Damage Functions," in *Environmental Damage Costs* (Paris: Organization for Economic Co-Operation and Development, 1974).

23. M. Clawson and J. L. Knetsch, *Economics of Outdoor Recreation* (Baltimore: Johns Hopkins University Press, 1971).

24. Organization for Economic Co-Operation and Development, *Economic Measurement of Environmental Damage* (Paris: OECD, 1976), p. 6.

25. Ibid., p. 52.

26. A. Myrick Freeman III., *The Benefits of Environmental Improvement: Theory and Practice* (Baltimore: Johns Hopkins University Press, 1979), p. 4.

27. Ibid., p. 82.

28. M. Kurtz, "An Experimental Approach to the Determination of the Demand for Public Goods," *Journal of Public Economics* 3 (1974), pp. 329–348; Peter Bolrun, "An Approach to the Problem of Estimating Demand for Public Goods," *Swedish Journal of Economics* I (March 1971), pp. 94–105.

29. H. R. Bowen, "The Interpretation of Voting in the Allocation of Economic Resources," *Quarterly Journal of Economics* 58 (1963), pp. 27–48.

30. James L. Barr and Otto A. Davis, "An Elementary Political and Economic Theory of the Expenditures of Local Government," *Southern Economic Journal* 33 (October 1996), pp. 149–165; T. E. Borcherding and R. T. Deacon, "The Demand for Services of Nonfederal Governments," *American Economic Review* 67 (December 1972), pp. 891–901; T. C. Bergstrom and R. P. Goodman, "Private Demands for Public Goods," *American Economic Review* 63 (June 1973), pp. 280–296.

31. Ridker, *Economic Costs of Air Pollution*, p. 25.

32. A. R. Prest and R. Turvey, "Cost-Benefit Analysis: A Survey," *Economic Journal* (December 1965), pp. 683–735.

33. PPBS rests essentially on cost-benefit analysis.

34. Another test for potential Pareto improvements is that everyone in society could be made better off by means of a costless redistribution of the net benefits.

35. Otto Eckstein, "A Survey of the Theory of Public Expenditure Criteria," in James M. Buchanan, ed., *Public Finances: Needs, Sources and Utilization* (Princeton: Princeton University Press, 1961).

36. Jesse Burkhead and Jerry Miner, *Public Expenditure* (Chicago: Aldine-Atherton, 1971), p. 225.

37. R. N. McKean, *Efficiency in Government through Systems Analysis* (New York: Wiley, 1958), ch. 8.

38. George A. Steiner. "Problems in Implementing Program Budgeting," in David Novick, ed., *Program Budgeting* (Cambridge: Harvard University Press, 1965), pp. 87–88.

39. William J. Baumol, "On the Discount Rate for Public Projects," in Robert Haveman and Julius Margolis, eds., *Public Expenditures and Policy Analysis* (Chicago: Markham, 1970), p. 274.

40. Burkhead and Miner, *Public Expenditure*, p. 232.

41. U.S. Bureau of the Budget, *Standards and Criteria for Formulating and Evaluating Federal Water Resources Development* (Washington, D.C.: U.S. Government, 1961), p. 67.

42. A. C. Pigou. *The Economics of Welfare*, 4th ed. (London: Macmillan, 1932).

43. R. A. Musgrave, *Fiscal Systems* (New Haven: Yale University Press, 1969), pp. 797–806.

44. Prest and Turvey, "Cost-Benefit Analysis," pp. 729–731.

45. U.S. House of Representatives, Committee on Interstate and Foreign Commerce, Subcommittee on Oversight and Investigations, *Federal Regulation and Regulatory Reform*, 94th Cong., 2d sess., 1976, ch. 15 (subcommittee print).

46. Michael S. Baram, "Cost-Benefit Analysis: An Inadequate Basis for Health, Safety, and Environmental Regulatory Decision Making," *Ecology Law Quarterly* 8 (1980), pp. 473–531.

47. Barry G. King, "Cost-Effectiveness Analysis? Implications for Accountants," *Journal of Accountancy* (May 1970), p. 43.

48. M. C. Houston and G. Ogawa, "Observations on the Theoretical Basis of Cost Effectiveness," *Operations Research* (March-April 1966), pp. 242–266.

49. King, "Cost-Effectiveness Analysis" p. 44.

50. William A. Niskanen, "Measures of Effectiveness," in Thomas A. Goidman, ed., *Cost-Effectiveness Analysis* (New York: Praeger, 1967), p. 20.

51. Neil M. Singer, *Public Microeconomics* (Boston: Little, Brown, 1976), p. 320.

52. King, "Cost-Effectiveness Analysis," pp. 48–49.

SELECTED READINGS

Toward a Theory of Microsocial Accounting

Beams, Floyd A., and Paul E. Fertig. "Pollution Control through Social Cost Conversion." *Journal of Accountancy* (November 1971), pp. 37–42.

Bendock, C. M. "Measuring Social Costs." *Management Accounting* (January 1975), pp. 13–15.

Chastain, Clark E. "Corporate Accounting for Environmental Information." *Financial Executive* (May 1975), pp. 45–50.

Churchill, Neil C. "Toward a Theory for Social Accounting." *Sloan Management Review* (Spring 1974), pp. 1–16.

Churchman, C. W. "On the Facility, Felicity and Morality of Measuring Social Change." *Accounting Review* (January 1971).

Linowes, David F. "The Accountant's Enlarged Professional Responsibilities." *Journal of Accountancy* (February 1973), pp. 47–57.

Mason, Alister K. "Social Costs: A New Challenge for Accountants." *Canadian Chartered Accountant Magazine* (June 1971), pp. 390–395.

Ramanathan, Kavassen V. "Toward a Theory of Corporate Social Accounting." *Accounting Review* (July 1976), pp. 516–528.

Ronen, J. "Accounting for Social Costs and Benefits." In J. J. Cramer, Jr., and G. H. Sorter, eds. *Objectives of Financial Statements* (New York: American Institute of Certified Public Accountants, May 1974), pp. 317–342.

Sawin, Henry S. "The CPA's Role in Restoring the Ecological Balance." *Management Advisor* (March–April 1971), pp. 23–29.

Shulman, James S., and Jeffrey Gale. "Laying the Groundwork for Social Accounting." *Financial Executive* (March 1972), pp. 38–52.

Evaluating Social Programs: Cost-Benefit Analysis

Anderson, Lee G., and Russel F. Settle. *Benefit-Cost Analysis: A Practical Guide* (Lexington, Mass.: Heath, 1977).

Bailey, Duncan, and Charles Schotta. "Private and Social Rates of Return to the Education of Academicians." *American Economic Review* (March 1972).

Baram, Michael S. "Cost-Benefit Analysis: An Inadequate Basis for Health, Safety, and Environmental Regulatory Decision Making." *Ecology Law Quarterly* 8 (1980), pp. 473–531.

Baumol, William J. "On the Discount Rate for Public Projects." In Robert Haveman and Julius Margolis, eds. *Public Expenditures and Policy Analysis* (Chicago: Markham, 1970).

———. "On the Social Rate of Discount." *American Economic Review* (September 1968).

Eckstein, Otto. "A Survey of the Theory of Public Expenditure Criteria." In James M. Buchanan, ed. *Public Finances: Needs, Sources and Utilization* (Princeton: Princeton University Press, 1961).

Gramlich, Edward M. *Benefit-Cost Analysis of Government Programs* (Englewood Cliffs, N.J.: Prentice-Hall, 1981).

Hanke, Steve H. "On the Feasibility of Benefit-Cost Analysis." *Public Policy* 29, no. 2 (Spring 1981), pp. 147–157.

Kendall, M. G., ed. *Cost Benefit Analysis* (New York: American Elsevier, 1971).

McKean, R. N. *Efficiency in Government through Systems Analysis* (New York: Wiley, 1958).

Mishan, E. J. *Cost-Benefit Analysis* (New York: Praeger, 1976).

Novick, David, ed. *Program Budgeting* (Cambridge: Harvard University Press, 1965).

Prest, A. R., and R. Turvey. "Cost-Benefit Analysis: A Survey." *Economic Journal* (December 1965), pp. 683–735.

Sassone, Peter G., and William A. Schaefer. *Cost-Benefit Analysis: A Practical Guide* (Lexington, Mass.: Heath, 1977).

Weisbrod, Burton A. "Costs and Benefits of Medical Research: A Case Study of Poliomyelitis." *Journal of Political Economy* (May–June 1971); pp. 527–544.

Evaluating Social Programs: Cost-Effectiveness Analysis

Committee on Accounting for Not-for-Profit Organizations. "Report of the Committee." *Accounting Review*, supplement, 46 (1971), pp. 81–164.

Committee on Measures of Effectiveness for Social Programs. "Report of the Committee." *Accounting Review*, supplement, 47 (1972), pp. 337–398.

Committee on Nonfinancial Measures of Effectiveness. "Report of the Committee." *Accounting Review*, supplement, 46 (1971), pp. 165–212.

Committee on Not-for-Profit Organizations, 1972–73. "Report of the Committee." *Accounting Review*, supplement, 49 (1974), pp. 225–249.

Goidman, Thomas A. *Cost-Effectiveness Analysis* (New York: Praeger, 1967).

Heuston, M. C., and G. Ogawa. "Observations on the Theoretical Basis of Cost Effectiveness." *Operations Research* (March–April 1966), pp. 242–266.

King, Barry G. "Cost-Effectiveness Analysis: Implications for Accountants." *Journal of Accounting* (May 1970).

Singer, Neil M. *Public Microeconomics* (Boston: Little, Brown, 1976).

Sorenson, James E., and Hugh D. Grove. "Cost-Outcome and Cost-Effectiveness Analysis: Emerging Nonprofit Performance Evaluation Techniques." *Accounting Review* (July 1977), pp. 658–675.

Measurement in Microsocial Accounting

Barr, James L., and Otto A. Davis. "An Elementary Political and Economic Theory of the Expenditures of Local Government." *Southern Economic Journal.* (October 1966), pp. 149–165.

Bergstrom, T. C., and R. P. Goodman. "Private Demands for Public Goods." *American Economic Review* 63 (June 1973), pp. 280–296.

Bohn, Peter. "An Approach to the Problem of Estimating Demand for Public Goods." *Swedish Journal of Economics* I (March 1971), pp. 94–105.

Borcherding, T. E., and R. T. Deacon. "The Demand for Services of Nonfederal Governments." *American Economic Review* 67 (December 1972), pp. 891–901.

Bowen, H. R. "The Interpretation of Voting in the Allocation of Economic Resources." *Quarterly Journal of Economics* 58 (1963), pp. 27–48.

Clawson, M., and J. L. Knetsch. *Economics of Outdoor Recreation* (Baltimore: Johns Hopkins University Press, 1971).

Feenberg, D., and E. S. Mills. *Measuring the Benefits of Water Pollution Abatement* (New York: Academic Press, 1980).

Freeman, A. Myrick III. *The Benefits of Environmental Improvement: Theory and Practice* (Baltimore: Johns Hopkins University Press, 1979).

———. "On Estimating Air Pollution Control Benefits from Land Value Studies. *Journal of Environmental Economics and Management* I (May 1974), pp. 74–83.

Hause, John C. "The Theory of Welfare Cost Measurement." *Journal of Political Economy* 6 (December 1975), pp. 1145–1182.

Kapp, K. William. *Social Costs of Business Enterprise* (New York: Asia Publishing House, 1963).

Kneese, Alien V.; Robert U. Ayres; and Ralph C. d'Arge. *Economics and the Environ-*

ment: A Materials Balance Approach (Baltimore: Johns Hopkins University Press, 1970).

Kurtz, M. "An Experimental Approach to the Determination of the Demand for Public Goods." *Journal of Public Economics* 3 (1974), pp. 329–348.

Organization for Economic Co-Operation and Development. *Economic Implication of Pollution Control* (Paris: OECD, 1974).

———. *Economic Measurement of Environmental Damage* (Paris: OECD 1976).

———. *Environmental Damage Costs* (Paris: OECD, 1974).

Plowden, P. *The Cost of Noise* (London: Metra Consulting Group, 1970).

Ridker, R. G. *Economic Costs of Air Pollution* (New York: Praeger, 1967).

Appendix 7.1: George E. Pinches and Diane M. Lander, "The Use of NPV in Newly Industrialized and Developing Countries: a.k.a. What Have We Ignored?" *Managerial Finance* 23, 9 (1997), pp. 24–45.

Abstract

Interviews in South Korea, Taiwan, Singapore, and India indicate net present value (NPV) is not widely employed in making capital investment decisions in these newly industrialized and developing countries. It is not from lack of knowledge about net present value: rather, it is due to (1) widespread violation of the assumptions underlying NPV, (2) the high risk/high return nature of the capital investments, and (3) the decision-making process employed in making capital investment decisions. These same three conditions exist for many capital investment decisions made by firms in developed countries. Only by abandoning the static NPV approach, building in real options, and understanding and building in the decision-making process will further advances be made in capital budgeting decision-making.

One of the key paradigms in finance is net present value (NPV). In order to maximize value, managers should accept all positive NPV investment projects, and reject all negative NPV projects. The issue becomes more complex when uncertainty is introduced, or, as in recent years, when real options to defer, abandon, expand, etc. are incorporated into the decision-making process [e.g., Dixit and Pindyck (1994) and Trigeorgis (1995 and 1996)]. However, with these exceptions, the state of the art in capital investment decision-making revolves around the simple statement—take all positive NPV projects.[1] In practice, evidence from surveys[2] and discussions with corporate executives indicates the message taught for the last 30 years in business schools has been heard and, to a large extent, acted upon by larger U. S., Canadian, and British-based firms.

While larger firms in North America, and to a lesser extent Western Europe, generally employ the static, or traditional, NPV framework for making, or assisting in making, capital investment decisions, less is known about the decision-making process employed by firms in other parts of the world. The question addressed in this study is: "Do firms in other parts of the world, especially in newly industrialized or developing countries in the Asia Pacific region, employ NPV for making capital investment decisions?"

The purposes of this study are threefold: (1) to report the results of a series of open-ended interviews conducted in South Korea, Taiwan, Singapore, and India about the capital investment decision-making process employed; (2) to understand why NPV is not widely employed in making capital investment decisions in these newly industrialized and developing countries; and, most important, (3) to indicate that NPV and the capital budgeting decision-making process need rethinking and refocusing to make them more effective—in all countries, whether developed, newly industrialized, or developing.

The paper proceeds in the following manner. Section I provides an introduction to the study. In Section II the results of the interviews are presented. In Section III patterns that emerged during the interview process are presented, along with a number of specific examples of the types of capital investment decisions being considered. In Section IV the assumptions underlying NPV are examined, and then risk/return and the decision-making process are considered. Section V contains the discussion and conclusions.

I. Introduction: Capital Budgeting Decision-Making

A fundamental paradigm in financial economics specifies how firms *should* make capital investment decisions. Specifically, the focus of the decision process

■   is on net present value (NPV),

■   is on cash flows, and

■   takes project risk into account.

By accepting positive net present value projects the value of the firm is maximized. This is reasonable, intuitive, and, in theory, workable and is employed by many larger firms in developed countries. The question addressed in this paper is: "Does the same approach to capital investment decision-making—stressing cash flows, risk, and net present value—exist in other countries, especially newly industrialized or developing countries in the Asia Pacific region?"

This question arose when one of the authors spoke with the chief financial officer (CFO) of the chemical division of a major Asia Pacific firm. During the discussion the CFO commented that *he and his firm know all about net present value, but they did not use it when making capital investment decisions.* Subsequent investigation indicated that information on the use of NPV in the Asia Pacific region is available only for Japan. Hodder (1986) examined how Japanese firms made capital investment decisions. He found that while some firms used discounted cash flow and net present value, they were in the minority. Rather "...the vast majority of Japanese firms appear to assess a project's 'profitability' based on cash flow projections that include imputed interest charges on their investment in that project" (p. 18). Likewise, Scarbrough, et. al. (1991) noted that 71 percent of advanced manufacturing companies in Japan justified investments on the basis of difficult-to-quantify benefits, while Hiraki (1995) indicated discounted cash flow techniques are not widely employed in Japan. Beyond these studies, we are unaware of any others indicating how firms in the Asia Pacific region—especially in newly industrialized and developing countries—make capital investment decisions.

II. The Use of Net Present Value in Capital Investment Decision-Making

Population and gross domestic product (GDP)/capita information for South Korea, Taiwan, Singapore and India, along with the United States, is provided in Table 1. Examining the table we see the tremendous size differences in these countries, with India having a huge and expanding population that is approaching one billion. In terms of GDP/capita, Singapore had the highest rate of growth from 1979 to the present, while India had the lowest. In South Korea the growth has been driven by the planned development of export-oriented heavy industry companies, characterized by 30 or so large *chebols* (affiliated groups of firms) that dominate the economy. Taiwan, on the other hand, has achieved its economic progress through a less-planned system that focused primarily on smaller labor-intensive firms. In recent years the traditionally smaller firms are being replaced with larger more capital- and technology-intensive firms. In Singapore, the emphasis has been on policy transparency and economic stability and has focused on service, manufacturing and taking advantage of Singapore's unique location. Finally, historically socialist-oriented India is a mixture of traditional village farming, supplemented by large and often inefficient government companies, and an increasing number of modern for-profit firms. South Korea, Taiwan and Singapore are newly industrialized countries, with the GDP/capita of Singapore projected to surpass that of the United States early in the twenty-first century. India, on the other hand, while making economic progress, is still a developing country that suffers from over population, and many basic services remain underdeveloped.

In order to assess the capital investment decision-making process in newly industrialized and developing countries in the Asia Pacific region, a series of open-ended interviews were conducted in South Korea, Taiwan, Singapore, and India. In total, over 30 formal interviews were undertaken with the interviewees selected on a convenience basis. These interviews were conducted at three or more large firms in each country and a number of smaller firms. In addition, informal interviews were conducted with government officials, development officers, and professors knowledgeable and interested in capital budgeting.[3]

Table 1									
Population and GDP/Capita for South Korea, Taiwan, Singapore, India and the United States									
Population (in millions)					*GDP/Capita ($)*				
Year	South Korea	Taiwan	Singapore	India	United States	South Korea	Taiwan	Singapore	India	United States
1979	40.1	18.0	2.4	686.1	223.2	$ 1,600	$ 1,830	$ 3,810	$170	$10,745
1984	42.0	19.1	2.5	746.4	236.4	2,000	2,980	7,000	240	11,338
1989	43.3	20.2	2.7	833.4	248.2	4,600	6,000	10,300	400	21,082
1994	45.1	21.3	2.9	919.9	260.7	11,270	12,070	19,940	1,360	25,850
Note: Until 1992 the United States reported gross national product, GNP.									
Source: Central Intelligence Agency. *World Fact Book.* Washington, D.C., various years.									

To understand the capital budgeting decision-making process in these four countries, the question asked in the formal open-ended interviews was: "How does your firm make capital investment decisions?" Except for very small firms, the interviewees indicated they knew and understood net present value, and that their firms generally estimated expected cash flows. However, when asked for details, the interviewees were concerned with specific aspects of the NPV process. One issue was how to realistically estimate the incremental cash flows associated with a project. Some firms simply projected accounting numbers and then took net income and added back depreciation to obtain an estimate of cash flow. A second issue was the appropriate discount rate to employ. More often than not the discount rate used was the cost of debt. Sometimes it was the after-tax cost of debt but, generally, the before-tax cost of debt was employed.[4] The explanation given was that since the primary financing employed was debt, the cost of debt was the relevant discount rate. Another issue, this time for multinationals, was the issue of the "appropriate" perspective, i.e., the home country versus the host country. A final issue was how to estimate incremental cash flows for foreign projects. Whatever the issues, the interviewees indicated net present value was not of primary importance in the capital investment decision-making process employed by their firm. Either NPV was not employed at all or, if it was employed, it did not play a major role in the decision-making process.

The next question asked was: "If net present value does not play a significant role, what factor or factors are of primary importance?" All firms interviewed, except for a few small ones, calculated the payback period.[5] About 20 percent of the firms calculated payback simply in accounting terms. Also, all of the large firms worked with balance sheets and income statements, and calculated some variation of an accounting-based return on investment. Finally, most of the large firms knew about and used sensitivity analysis, either on cash flows or on accounting numbers.

III. Why is NPV not Employed in Capital Investment Decision-Making?

How do we explain why net present value is not important in the capital investment decision-making process for firms in four newly industrialized or developing counties in the Asia Pacific region? In order to better understand this lack of focus on net present value, we looked at the following factors:

- Role of Strategic Decisions

- Role of the Home Government

- Role of the Banks

- Role of the Company Founder

Role of Strategic Decisions

Many of the capital investment decisions faced by the firms can loosely be called "strategic decisions." We found that strategic opportunities were generally not subjected to a formal capital investment analysis which employed net present value. The first type of strategic decision is a one-shot, or now-or-never, opportunity. A firm interviewed in South Korea made the decision to bet at least a tenth of the total firm value on a major petrochemical complex. Petrochemical prices were high, there was sufficient demand, and, at that time, an integrated petrochemical complex did not exist in South Korea. The argument was that if the firm was going to get into the business, now was the time. Unfortunately, by the time the complex came on stream: (1) other petrochemical producers around the world had added capacity, and (2) the worldwide economy was weak. When probed about how profitable the petrochemical complex was going to be, the answer was that the firm might not make much the first 10 years, or even the second 10, but they hoped to make a lot of money the last 10 years.

Another example of a strategic decision is where firms were trying to build market share. That is, they wanted a bigger market share. Sometimes they would say it a little differently; they were trying to drive down production costs so they could be a low-cost producer. Or, they were trying to establish market leadership so they would be number one or number two in the country. But, in essence, these capital investment decisions were based on the premise of building market share. In general, the focus was long term in nature.

Another "strategic" capital investment being made involved substituting capital for labor. Three specific examples indicate the motivation for these capital investment decisions. First, the cost of labor in South Korea, Taiwan, and Singapore has increased dramatically as they have industrialized. Many firms are moving labor intensive industries off-shore into countries like China, the Philippines, and Vietnam, while investing in more capital intensive industries at home. Second was the question of how reliable or how militant was the labor force. This was especially true in South Korea. One firm interviewed had concentrated almost all of its production facilities in a small geographic region. Over time the work force for a major division of the firm had become militant, causing higher labor costs and making the firm subject to strike-related work stoppages. In retrospect, the interviewee admitted the centralization of operations had caused the firm to become more vulnerable to work stoppages. One partial solution for this firm was to become more capital intensive.

India provided a third example. Although labor is inexpensive in India, there still is substitution of capital for labor. The problem in India is almost the reverse of that experienced in South Korea, Taiwan, and Singapore—there are too many employees and, due to government policy, it is almost impossible to lay them off. In one instance a firm had twice as many employees as needed. Since the employees could not be laid off, as the firm became more efficient, it established a procedure where when labor was freed up, the employees were designated as "excess." The excess employees still had to report for work to remain on the payroll and maintain their pension benefits, but they were kept physically separate from the operations of the firm. The advantages to the firm were three-fold: (1) the firm could work with employees who were productive and make the operation more efficient, (2) if anyone was absent, the firm had workers readily available who could be brought in to fill the absent employees place, and (3) if unions questioned the firm about their employment level, the firm could say, "Look at all the excess employees we are paying who are sitting over there." Thus, while there is substitution of capital for labor in India, it is for an atypical reason.

A final "strategic" capital investment decision encountered was the same one faced by firms in many parts of the world: "How do you run capital budgeting numbers on a total quality control manufacturing operation, or a high-tech capital investment?" Typically, it is almost impossible to have any reasonable idea of the source, magnitude or timing of the benefits expected from investments such as these. As in the United States, Japan, and other developed countries, these capital budgeting decisions are generally made more on faith, as opposed to formal economic analysis.[6]

Role of the Government

A second major issue is the role played by the government in South Korea, Taiwan, Singapore, and India. In all of these countries governmental policies significantly impacted the capital investment decision-making process. Governments in newly industrialized and developing countries in the Asia Pacific region have had a tendency to be coordinated in terms of industrial policy. So, if the government wanted firms to get into certain kinds of industries, it spurred development by providing tax credits, cheap financing, and sometimes even cheap land. With respect to land, if the government wanted to encourage firms to develop certain areas of expertise, the government might even purchase land and then resell it to the firms at abnormally low prices. While government action can create important advantages leading to highly profitable projects, government action can also lead to additional uncertainty—especially if government policy changes rapidly without warning. Hence, the role of the government can cut both ways.

Role of the Banks

A third major trend evident in the capital investment process was the role of the banks. By banks we mean domestic banks, multinational banks, and others such as the World Bank, International Monetary Fund, and Import Export Banks. In terms of the analysis and documentation prepared for capital budgeting purposes, the initial standards used by firms in all these countries were dictated by the banks. In fact, the bankers often drew up the capital investment evaluation forms employed by the firms, based on what the banks themselves needed.

Two additional points should be noted about banks, and their role relative to the capital investment process. The first is that the banks played a very large role in determining the kinds of capital investments made by firms in these countries. The second, and related, point is that both historically, and even now, banks have been the major provider of capital in these countries. While substantial changes are occurring in the capital markets in many newly industrialized and developing countries [see, for example, Demirguc-Kunt and Maksimovic, (1995)], the public equity and debt markets do not supply nearly the amount of funds provided by the capital markets in North America and Western Europe. In these countries the comment was that, "The capital investment decisions we made in the past were largely a function of what the banks allowed us to make. That is, the banks dictated the capital investments made."

Role of the Company Founder

The fourth, and final, issue we became aware of concerns the role of the founder, or founders, of the firm. The role of founders is important because they were the risk takers and the ones who provided both the direction and the dream of what the firms have now become. In most of the interviews, the aggressive, risk-taking orientation of the firms' founders was mentioned. Also the founders tended to be more intuitive in terms of how they went about making decisions. While the numbers may have been examined in a cursory manner, the business decisions were based on intuition. If there was any formal capital investment analysis, it was undertaken because the firms needed bank financing.

In recent years, changes have occurred once the role of the founders diminished, and the operating reigns of the business were turned over to professional managers. Invariably we were told, "Professional managers are more conservative than the founders were." This conservatism was particularly evident in terms of taking major capital investment risks.[7] One of the firms interviewed had faced what it perceived to be a severe capital rationing environment. As part of a number of responses to this capital rationing problem, a formal capital investment process based on net present value was implemented. The goal of the firm was to develop a more procedural and logical way of *rejecting* projects. Thus, a formal capital investment procedure, employing net present value, provided the firm's managers a formal system to communicate to divisions why their projects were rejected.

IV. The Appropriateness of NPV in Newly Industrialized and Developing Countries

After interviewing decision makers in South Korea, Taiwan, Singapore, and India, our findings with respect to the role of NPV in the capital investment decision-making process can be summarized as follows. Overwhelmingly, the individuals interviewed knew of NPV: however, while cash flows were important, except in rare instances, NPV was not directly employed in the capital investment decision-making process. Why did these firms not employ NPV? In the previous section we saw some of the reasons why NPV was not employed. Another possible reason is that both managers and academicians have been myopic about the capital investment decision-making process [Pinches (1982)]. However, that does not appear to be an issue for decision makers in newly industrialized and developing countries. In order to more fundamentally answer the question of why NPV is not employed, it is necessary to (1) examine the assumptions underlying net present value, (2) consider risk/return issues, and (3) examine the decision-making process employed by decision makers.

The Appropriateness of the Assumptions Underlying NPV

The basic assumptions underlying NPV are embodied in Fisher's theory of consumer's choice. These assumptions are:

■   *Competitive capital markets*: there are no barriers that prevent access to the capital markets and no one participant is sufficiently dominant to have a significant impact on prices.

■   *No transactions costs or frictions*: transactions can be made instantaneously, they are costless, and no frictions preventing the free trading of securities exist.

■   *Certainty*: there is complete certainty regarding present and future consumption possibilities.

■   *No taxes:* there are no taxes.

In effect, a perfectly competitive capital market is assumed. With the Fisher separation theorem, and the development of complete capital markets, an individual's savings and consumption decisions are effectively uncoupled and the optimal investment decision is to accept the highest net present value projects [see, for example, Fisher (reprinted, 1965) or Hirshleifer (1958)]. Once uncertainty is assumed and firms, instead of individuals are the focus, the basic rule remains the same: firms should accept all positive net present value capital investments. By doing so, the firm is making decisions that maximize the market value of the firm and the wealth of its shareholders.

Although not primary assumptions of classical investment theory, three other points (i.e., implied assumptions or other factors impacting the use of NPV) are also important:

■   *Temporary competitive opportunities*: for firms to capitalize on positive net present value projects, i.e., to capture economic rents, they have to exploit temporary competitive advantages [Brealey and Myers (1991) or Pinches (1995)].

■   *Highly structured, low risk and/or low growth*: evidence exists that net present value is less effective in highly unstructured, risky, and/or dynamic growth situations [Myers (1987) and Sundam (1975)].

■   *Neutrality of governments*: the NPV paradigm implicitly assumes governments do not exist, or if they exist, they do not impose in such a way as to impact the capital investment decisions made by firms.

Based on what we learned from the interviews, along with our understanding of the economic and social/political conditions in South Korea, Taiwan, Singapore, and India, we conclude that:

1.   In all cases (1) the capital markets are not competitive, (2) there are transactions costs and frictions, (3) certainty does not exist, and (4) there are taxes. Hence, the primary assumptions of Fisher's theory of consumer's choice are violated. The absence of sufficiently, or effectively,

complete and competitive markets remains one of the major issues faced even today by firms in newly industrialized and developing countries.

2.   The implied assumption of temporary competitive opportunities did not exist in these countries. Going back 10, 20 and even 30 years, when tremendous growth was occurring in all these countries, obtaining the necessary capital and/or permission to produce provided firms with long-term competitive advantages. This point was mentioned a number of times during the interviews. For example, one executive stated that: "Obtaining a license to produce was like being given the opportunity to print money. Demand was so great that goods produced could be sold at a substantial profit." Hence, many of the capital investments made by firms in newly industrialized and developing countries are made in an environment where the competitive opportunity is long-term, instead of temporary.

3.   Given the unsettled and growing nature of the economies in newly industrialized and developing countries, many of the opportunities faced are not highly structured, do involve high levels of risk, and/or are dynamic growth situations. By it's very nature, NPV is less effective in highly unstructured, risky, and/or dynamic growth situations.

4.   Finally, neutrality of governments, even today, does not exist in many newly industrialized and developing countries.

In retrospect, all of the assumptions underlying traditional, or static, NPV are violated—most to a great degree—in the newly industrialized and developing countries of South Korea, Taiwan, Singapore, and India. Accordingly, it is not surprising NPV has been directly employed only infrequently in the capital investment decision-making process by firms in the Asia Pacific region.

Options, Risk, and Capital Budgeting

A second fundamental reason why NPV is not as widely employed in newly industrialized and developing countries may be due to their stage of development and the risks and returns experienced. The real option, or dynamic NPV, approach to capital investment decision-making[8] recognizes in a formal manner that many capital investment decisions are themselves options and also may incorporate a series of options. The initial capital investment is an option: by deciding to exercise the option and make the capital investment, the firm "kills" the option that exists. Likewise, by making an initial capital investment, firms may have options to expand, contract, abandon, etc. at a later point in time. Ignoring any foregone cash flows (i.e., cash dividends, for an option written on common stock), the value of an option on a financial asset is a function of five factors: the exercise price, the current value of the underlying asset, the time to maturity, the risk-free rate of interest, and the risk (standard deviation) of the underlying asset. In a capital budgeting framework, these same values for an initial investment in real assets are as follows:

For a financial option	**For a real option**
exercise price	investment required to undertake the capital investment
current value of the underlying asset	present value today of the expected cash inflows from making the capital investment
time to maturity	time until real asset option can be exercised
risk-free rate	risk-free rate
standard deviation of the underlying stock price	standard deviation of the cash flows from the capital investment

For example, assume all of the necessary items required for the real option approach to capital investment decision-making have been estimated for a proposed capital investment in a newly industrialized or developing country. The fifth variable for determining the value of this real asset option is the amount of risk; the standard deviation of the cash flows from the capital investment. What is the risk of most capital investments in newly industrialized or developing countries? When compared to the risk of capital investment projects in developed countries, the risk of capital investment projects in developing countries often may be higher. While additional risk in a static NPV framework results in a lower value, in an option pricing framework higher risk leads to a higher value of the option. Viewed from this perspective, the static NPV approach is not appropriate in newly industrialized and developing countries because it provides the wrong message; entrepreneurs and executives intuitively know that the high risk of potential capital investments increases the value of the proposed project. Thus, in the presence of high risk, static NPV substantially underestimates the potential value of capital investment projects. The real option, or dynamic NPV, approach must be employed.

Risk and Decision Making

Finally, let's consider another factor that is omitted when the focus is strictly on the use of NPV—the interaction of the risk involved in capital investment decisions and how executives make decisions. To introduce decision making under uncertainty, consider the action-outcome model[9] shown in Figure 1. Along the horizontal axis is the action, or selection, dimension, while along the vertical axis is the outcome. In the selection dimension, at time t_0 a critical value x_i is determined. If the *ex-ante*

Figure 1

An Action-Outcome Decision Model

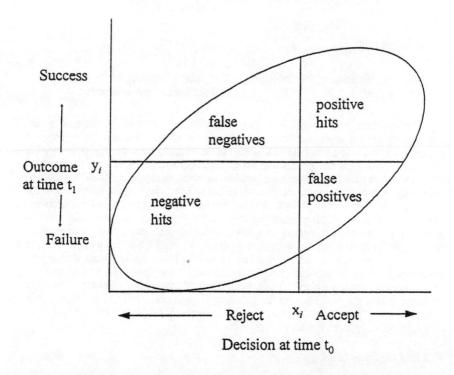

Decision at time t_0

evaluation of the capital investment yields a value x, such that $x \geq x_i$, the project will be accepted. In the case of using NPV, a positive net present value results in the action of accepting a proposed capital investment. After acceptance, the performance of the project is evaluated relative to some critical dimension, y_i, at some future point in time, t_1. If the *ex-post* realized outcome, y, is greater than the critical value, y_i, the capital investment project is considered a success. In any given capital investment decision the degree to which the *ex-post* realization of the project is predicted by the *ex-ante* evaluation is described by the correlation coefficient, xy. The higher the correlation coefficient, the thinner the ellipsoid in Figure 1; the lower the correlation, the thicker the ellipsoid.

There are four possible action-outcome combinations for any capital investment decision in this framework. If a project is accepted ($x \geq x_i$) and it succeeds ($y \geq y_i$) the action-outcome combination is a *positive hit*. If the accepted project fails, it is a *false positive*. On the other hand, if a project is rejected ($x \leq x_i$), there are also two possible action-outcome combinations. If the project eventually becomes a success (that is, if another firm decides to go ahead with a project rejected by the initial firm, and it succeeds), it is a *false negative*. Finally, if the project eventually fails, it is a *negative hit*. It should be clear that firms can make two kinds of errors in making capital investment decisions—they can reject a good project (a *false negative*), or they can accept a bad project (a *false positive*). These two mistakes correspond to Type I and Type II errors in statistical inference.

Using the framework depicted in Figure 1, consider the capital investment decision faced by firms, and especially the founders of firms and subsequent professional management, in developing and newly industrialized countries.[10] First, consider the selection dimension. Entrepreneurs and founders are typically viewed as risk takers, who tend to view risk as manageable, or controllable [Adler (1980) and Keyes (1985)]. This tendency is characterized by the attitude of the president of a highly successful high technology firm, who said: "In starting my company I didn't gamble; I was confident we were going to succeed."[11] The argument he and others make is that by knowing so much about the project and the endeavor, the selection risk is diminished, and therefore the selection point is moved to the left, as depicted in Figure 2a.

Another way the selection point may be impacted is due to the incentives and compensation anticipated. As Shapira notes (1995, p. 111): "It is clear that the tendency of managers to shift the decision criterion is strongly affected by their incentive scheme. The more a manager is worried about the consequences of failure the more he will shift the decision criterion to the right ... and, hence, become more conservative." Entrepreneurs and founders (1) believe they have more information relative to the capital investment decision, and (2) see the potential rewards as large; hence, they move the selection decision criterion to the left as depicted in Figure 2a. A third possible cause of a shift to the left in the decision criterion for entrepreneurs and founders is a function of their total accumulated resources, aspiration goals, and survival focus [Bowman and Kunreuther (1988), MacCrimmon and Wehrung (1986), and March and Shapira (1987 and 1992)]. When professional management takes over, the tendency is for them to become more conservative, and, hence, firms become less

Figure 2

Impact of Changes in Risk Taking and Changes in the Outcome on the Capital Budgeting Process

a. Greater Risk Taking

b. More Successful Projects

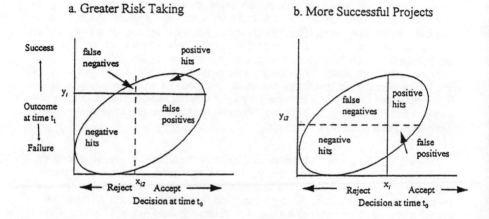

c. Combination of Greater Risk Taking and More Successful Projects

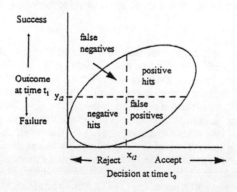

risk-taking. Thus, entrepreneurs and founders tend to increase the potential number of *positive hits*, and *false positives*, relative to professional managers.

Now let us turn to the outcome criterion (as depicted on the vertical axis in Figures 1 and 2) to determine whether the capital investment project is a success or a failure. How can founders and entrepreneurs impact the outcome of capital investment decisions? Two factors exist. First, given the state of economic development over the last 30 years in South Korea, Taiwan, Singapore, and India, exclusive rights to produce, restrictions on competition, and even outright bribes and/or kickbacks (as bribery scandals in South Korea and other countries attest occur), often created a competitive advantage that, in effect, lowers the level needed to declare the capital investment a success, as shown in Figure 2b.

A second factor also exists among successful executives—this is the belief that they can control some of the post-selection outcome. As Shapira notes (1995, p. 80): "Managerial thinking about risk taking is strongly linked to the possibility of postde-cision control. Granted, the belief in control may be fraught with problems ... and ... there is a chance of a bad ending. Nevertheless, more often than not managers believe in their ability to reverse errors after a decision is made." In the terms of prospect theory, Kahneman and Tversky (1979) showed how individuals edit and frame choice problems.[12] In his study of executive decision making, Shapira notes (1995, p. 104): "The picture that emerges from the current study suggests that editing is often done *after* the choice is made. The process appears to be one of editing, choosing, and re-editing, to use prospect theory terms. Thus, managerial risk taking can be described as a prolonged process of editing and restructuring."

In the context of the action-outcome model, the ability to impact the ultimate success of a capital investment results in a lowering of the outcome aspiration level, as indicated in Figure 2b, leading to more *positive hits* and *false negatives*. When accompanied with the previously argued lowering of the acceptance criterion in Figure 2a in newly industrialized and developing countries, the acceptance level is lower (i.e., a propensity to take more risks) and the acceptance criterion is lower (i.e., by impacting or controlling the outcome), leading to a greater percentage of *positive hits* (see Figure 2c). In such an environment, seat of the pants capital investment decision-making by knowledgeable, risk-taking, highly energetic, connected and focused founders may have a far higher probability of *positive hits* than in developed countries. The conclusion is that the decision making environment actually faced in making capital investment decisions in newly industrialized and developing countries is often far removed from that envisioned for net present value.

V. Discussion and Conclusions

The Main Findings

Traditional net present value has been a key paradigm in financial economics since the 1950's. It's message is clear: for firms to maximize value, and the wealth of their shareholders, take all positive NPV capital investment projects and reject all negative NPV projects. However, in newly industrialized and developing countries in the Asia Pacific region we found that, while consideration of possible cash flows was important, net present value was employed only infrequently in making capital investment decisions. Further probing determined it was not a lack of knowledge about net present value that leads to its infrequent use. Instead, more fundamental reasons exist.

First, an analysis of the assumptions underlying NPV indicates all of the assumptions appear to be severely violated in newly industrialized and developing countries. Second, given the high degree of risk, and the very unstructured nature of the capital investment decisions being considered in newly industrialized and developing countries, the option pricing (i.e., dynamic NPV) approach to making capital investments indicates higher risk and higher return go hand-in-hand. This is exactly opposite the relationship between risk and return embodied in the traditional net present value approach. Finally, an analysis of the decision-making process used by founders and entrepreneurs suggests the actual process is far more complicated than envisioned by NPV. All three factors—the failure to meet the assumptions of NPV, the unstructured and highly risky environment, and the actual decision-making process—taken individually or collectively, indicate why traditional NPV is not a widely employed framework for making capital investment decisions in newly industrialized and developing countries.

Applicability of the Findings to Developed Countries

While our analysis focused on capital investment decision-making in newly industrialized and developing countries, reflection suggests many of the same conditions that render traditional NPV inappropriate for making capital investment decisions in these regions also operate—to a greater or lesser extent—in North America, Western Europe, and other developed regions of the world. Specifically, consider the complete markets assumption that underlies net present value. While complete markets generally exist for larger firms, they do not for smaller, more entrepreneurial, firms. Hence, it is not surprising that studies[13] and discussions with executives indicate NPV is used much less in smaller firms in developed countries.

Next, consider the recent developments in the telecommunications industry, the information superhighway, and the internet. How many of the capital investments being made in these highly volatile areas can effectively be modeled using the static NPV approach? Discussion with managers indicates the financial analysis undertaken is often somewhat rudimentary, given the high level of uncertainty that exists with these decisions. While real option approaches to capital investment decision-making are not widely employed in practice, only by modeling the options built into capital investment projects via dynamic NPV can the NPV framework be effectively employed for making wealth maximizing decisions in the face of multiple options and high risk.

Finally, consider the decision-making process employed by managers in making capital investment decisions. Substantial evidence exists that the actual decision-making process is far different from that envisioned in the net present value framework. In the Asia Pacific region their culture and managerial approach emphasizes thinking strategically, and viewing both flexibility and the long-term as important elements in any business decision. Moving to more developed countries, a number of years ago

Pinches (1982) cited a substantial body of literature indicating managerial preferences have a significant impact on capital investment decisions. Statman and Caldwell (1987) examined the tendency for managers to hold on to losers too long. Likewise, Antle and Eppen (1985) and Harris and Raviv (1996) all examine the internal decision-making processes of firms for making capital investment decisions. They address, in part, the decentralization of information and incentive problems which must be taken into consideration when capital investment decision-making is examined.

Therefore, many, if not most, of the same problems that exist with the use of net present value in newly industrialized and developing countries, also exist in developed counties. The changes needed apply to all counties and situations where capital investments are made.

Changes are Needed

Based on the findings of this study, a reexamination of much of the past research on capital investment decision-making, and visiting with numerous executives and professors, we believe it is time to face the music:

- The academic financial economic focus on traditional net present value only captures part of the information needed to understand and implement an effective capital budgeting decision-making process.

- The decision making environment actually faced in firms must be brought into the capital budgeting decision-making environment and process. Consider the following comments recently made to the authors:

- Thomas A. Copeland, formerly of the University of California, Los Angeles, and now partner with McKinsey and Co.: "In order to understand and impact capital budgeting decision-making we must bring the behavioral aspects of how firms actually make capital budgeting decisions into play. The behavior aspects, which we tend to ignore in finance, must be considered."[14]

- Randolph A. Pohlman, formerly vice president at Koch Industries and now Dean at Nova Southeastern University: "... after being around for quite some time, doing some consulting work and spending five years at Koch Industries ... oftentimes decisions were made by individuals or at least were pursued by individuals when, in fact, they were not in the best interest of the company using an NPV type of calculation. In other words, egos and politics intervene."[15]

- Meir Statman, Santa Clara University: "You hit the nail in the last paragraph of your paper; '... capital investment analysis is a process.' ... Formal NPV analysis is a way for finance managers to climb the ladder and compete with the marketing and R & D people. What we need is a positive theory of the capital budgeting process *with an emphasis on the process.*"[16]

Capital investment analysis is a process; it's a process which focuses attention on certain kinds of issues and information that must be considered before projects are accepted or rejected. Only by abandoning the static NPV approach, building in real options, and understanding the actual decision-making process, will financial economists be able to make substantial further contributions to capital budgeting—whether in developing, newly industrialized, or developed countries. Now is the time to cast off the narrow, time-worn, shackles financial economists have worn for so long. Only by significantly shifting and broadening our focus will we add further value for executives faced with making wealth maximizing capital investment decisions.

We thank the following individuals who provided helpful comments on earlier drafts of this paper: Ashish Arora, Larry Gordon, Keith Howe, Larry Hwang, Karyl Leggio, V. K. Narayanan, Randy Pohlman, Margaret Reed, David Shafer, Srinivasan Sundaram, Chin-Chin Soh, Meir Statman, Jim Wood, and Mridu Vashist.

Notes

1. While we discuss net present value, by implication we are also referring to internal rate of return (IRR).

2. See, for example, Cooper, Cornick, and Redmon (1992), Gilbert and Reichert (1995), Gitman and Forrester (1977), Jog and Srivastava (1995), Mukherjee and Henderson (1987), Pike (1989 and 1996), Stanley and Block (1984), and Trahan and Gitman (1995).

3. There are two possible biases in the sample of firms. First, there is a bias toward large firms, since they were the primarily source of the formal interviews. Second, there is a survival bias. While these biases exist, we believe they do not negate the findings or conclusions of this study. A list of firms and organizations is available from the authors.

4. While the specifics of the tax code differ among the countries, interest is a tax deductible expense in all the countries, so differing tax consequences do not explain the tendency to use the cost of debt as the discount rate, or why some firms use the before-tax cost while others use the after-tax cost of debt.

5. This tendency to employ the payback period mirrors its use in more developed countries, as indicated by Cooper, Cornick, and Redmon (1992), Gilbert and Reichert (1995), Gitman and Forrester (1977), Mukherjee and Henderson (1987), Pike (1989 and 1996), and Trahan and Gitman (1995).

6. See, for example, Accola (1994), Grenadier and Weiss (1995), Kaplan (1986), or Wilner, Koch, and Klammer (1992).

7. This change may result in "timid choices," as noted by Kahneman and Lovallo (1993). An alternative explanation may be a tendency by managers to adopt capital investment policies that maximize managerial reputation. See, for example, Cooper and Petry (1994) and Hirshleifer (1993).

8. See, for example, Brealey and Myers (1991), Dixit and Pindyck (1994), Pinches (1995), or Trigeorgis (1995 and 1996). Recently Sercu and Uppal (1994) have applied option pricing theory to making international capital expenditure decisions.

9. This model has been employed by Einhorn and Hogarth (1987) and Shapira (1995), among others.

10. These same arguments can be made for small, start-up, ventures or high tech capital investments made in developed countries.

11. Shapira (1995), p. 73.

12. Prospect theory also forms a foundation for explaining why managers may be reluctant to terminate capital investment projects, even when they have turned bad [Statman and Caldwell (1987)].

13. See, for example, Cooper and Petry (1994), Stanley and Block (1984) and Trahan and Gitman (1995)

14. Thomas A. Copeland, paraphrased from a talk given at the Midwest Finance Association, March 21, 1996, Chicago, Illinois.

15. Randolph A. Pohlman, personal correspondence, January 9, 1996.

16. Meir Statman, personal crrespondence, January 9, 1996. Emphasis added.

References

Accola, W. L., 1994. "Assessing Risk and Uncertainty in New Technology Investments," *Accounting Horizons* (September), 19-35.

Adler, S., 1980. "*Risk Making Management,*" Business Horizons (23), 11-14.

Antle, R., and G. D. Eppen, 1985. "Capital Rationing and Organizational Slack in Capital Budgeting," *Management Science* (February), 163-174.

Bowman, E. H., and H. Kunreuther, 1988. "Post-Bhopal Behavior at a Chemical Company," *Journal of Management Studies* (July), 387-402.

Brealey, R. A., and S. C. Myers, 1991. *Principles of Corporate Finance.* New York: McGraw-Hill, 4th ed.

Cooper, D., and G. Petry, 1994. "Corporate Performance and Adherence to Shareholder Wealth-Maximizing Principles," *Financial Management* (Spring), 71-76.

Cooper, W. D., M. F. Cornick, and A. Redmon, 1992. "Capital Budgeting: A 1990 Study of Fortune 500 Company Practices," *Journal of Applied Business Research* (Summer), 20-23.

Demirguc-Kunt, A., and V. Maksimovic, 1995. "Capital Structures in Developing Countries: Evidence from Ten Country Cases," working paper, World Bank and University of Maryland-College Park.

Dixit, A. K., and R. S. Pindyck, 1994. *Investment Under Uncertainty.* Princeton: Princeton University Press.

Einhorn, H., and R. Hogarth, 1987. "Confidence in Judgement: Persistence of the Illusion of Validity," *Psychological Review* (September), 395-416.

Fisher, I., 1965. *The Theory of Interest.* New York: Augustus M. Kelly, reprint of 1930 edition.

Gilbert, E., and A. Reichert, 1995. "The Practice of Financial Management among Large United States Corporations," *Financial Practice and Education* (Spring/Summer), 16-23.

Gitman, L. J., and J. R. Forrester, Jr., 1977. "A Survey of Capital Budgeting Techniques Used by Major U. S. Firms," *Financial Management* (Fall), 66-71.

Grenadier, S. R., and A. M. Weiss, 1995. "Investment in Technological Innovations: An Option Pricing Approach," working paper, Stanford University.

Harris, M., and A. Raviv, 1996. "The Capital Budgeting Process, Incentives and Information," *Journal of Finance* (September). 1139-1174.

Hiraki, T., 1995. Corporate Governance, Long-term Investment Orientation, and Real Options in Japan," in L. Trigeorgis (editor), *Real Options in Capital Investment: Models, Strategies, and Applications*. Westport, CT: Praeger.

Hirshleifer, D. 1993. "Managerial Reputation and Corporate Investment Decisions," *Financial Management* (Summer), 145-160.

Hirshleifer, J., 1958. "On the Theory of Optimal Investment Decision," *Journal of Political Economy* (August), 329-352.

Hodder, J. E., 1986. "Evaluation of Manufacturing Investments: A Comparison of U.S. and Japanese Practices," *Financial Management* (Spring), 17-24.

Jog, V. M., and A. K. Srivastava, 1995. "Capital Budgeting Practices in Corporate Canada," *Financial Practice and Education* (Fall/Winter), 37-43.

Kahneman, D., and D. Lovallo, 1993. "Timid Choices and Bold Forecasts: A Cognitive Perspective on Risk Taking," *Management Science* (January), 17-31.

Kahneman, D., and A. Tversky, 1979. "Prospect Theory: An Analysis of Decisions Under Risk," *Econometrica* (March), 263-291.

Kaplan, R. S., 1986. "Must CIM be Justified by Faith Alone?" *Harvard Business Review* (March-April), 87-93.

Keyes, R., 1985. *Chancing It*. Boston: Little, Brown.

MacCrimmon, K. R., and D. A. Wehrung, 1986. *Taking Risks: The Management of Uncertainty*. New York: Free Press.

March, J. G., and Z. Shapira, 1987. "Managerial Perspectives on Risk and Risk Taking," *Management Science* (November), 1404-1418.

March, J. G., and Z. Shapira, 1992. "Variable Risk Preferences and the Focus of Attention," *Psychological Review* (January), 172-183.

Mukherjee, T. K., and G. V. Henderson, 1987. "The Capital Budgeting Process: Theory and Practice," *Interfaces* (March/April), 78-90.

Myers, S. C., 1987. "Finance Theory and Financial Strategy," *Midland Corporate Finance Journal* (Spring), 6-13.

Pike, R., 1996. "A Longitudinal Survey on Capital Budgeting Practices," *Journal of Business Finance & Accounting* (January), 79-92.

Pike, R. H., 1989. "Do Sophisticated Capital Budgeting Approaches Improve Investment Decision-Making Effectiveness?" *Engineering Economist* (Winter), 149-161.

Pinches, G. E., 1995. *Financial Management*. New York: Harper Collins.

Pinches, G. E., 1982. "Myopia, Capital Budgeting and Decision Making," *Financial Management* (Autumn), 6-19.

Scarbrough, P., A. J. Nanni, and M. Sakurai, 1991. "Japanese Management Accounting Practices and the Effects of Assembly and Process Automation," *Management Accounting Research* (March), 27-46.

Sercu, P., and R. Uppal, 1994. "International Capital Budgeting Using Option Pricing Theory," *Managerial Finance* (No. 8), 3-21.

Shapira, Z., 1995. *Risk Taking: A Managerial Perspective*. New York: Russell Sage Foundation.

Stanley, M. T., and S. B. Block, 1984. "A Survey of Multinational Capital Budgeting," *Financial Review* (19), 36-54.

Statman, M., and D. Caldwell, 1987. "Applying Behavioral Finance to Capital Budgeting: Project Terminations," *Financial Management* (Winter), 7-15.

Sundam, G. L., 1975. "Evaluating Capital Budgeting Models in Simulated Environments," *Journal of Finance* (September), 977-992.

Trahan, E. A., and L. J. Gitman, 1995. "Bridging the Theory-Practice Gap in Corporate Finance: A Survey of Chief Financial Officers," *Quarterly Review of Economics and Finance* (Spring), 73-87.

Trigeorgis, L. (editor), 1995. *Real Options in Capital Investment: Models, Strategies, and Applications*. Westport, CT: Praeger.

Trigeorgis, L., 1996. *Real Options: Managerial Flexibility and Strategy in Resource Allocation*. Cambridge, MA: MIT Press.

Wilner, N., B. Koch, and T. Klammer, 1992. "Justification of High Technology Capital Investment—An Empirical Study," *Engineering Economist* (Summer), 341-353.

Chapter 8 _____

Wealth Measurement and Distribution: The Behavioral and Cognitive Implications

INTRODUCTION

Because the shareholders are considered the ultimate owners of the firm, wealth measurement has consisted in various ways of income measurement that include schemes of earnings management and/or income smoothing. If the corporation was instead perceived as an alliance of a concerned team that includes the shareholders, the bondholders, the employees, and the government, then the measurement of wealth is reduced to the determination of the value added that is ultimately distributed as dividends to the shareholders, interest to bondholders, wages to employees, taxes to the government, and undistributed value added as retained earnings.

Because accounting focused on shareholders' wealth and changes in wealth with the resulting measurement of profit, empirical research does not report any overwhelming use of value added by decision makers. The belief is that decision makers tend to ignore or underweigh value-added information. The omission of value added in wealth measurement and distribution affects the decision-making process by associating wealth with profit rather than with the total value added resulting from the activities of the firm. The reasons for the omission of the value added in wealth measurement and distribution are either ignored or totally misunderstood. Accordingly, it is the objective of this chapter to develop and test predictions about the tendency of decision makers to omit value-added information out of their wealth measurement and distribution, and, in the end, help decision makers improve the quality of their decision. The chapter uses Holland et al.'s[1] theoretical framework of cognitive processing to examine the effects of accounting knowledge on the omission of value added in wealth measurement and distribution.

The cognitive processing literature suggests that people rely on knowledge structures stored in memory to guide their decision. The higher the knowledge in the given area, the higher the likelihood of the recall of a familiar knowledge structure considered suitable for a given decision context. Because the accounting knowledge structure stored in memory does not emphasize the use, or the relevance, of value-added information, it is possible to hypothesize that decision makers with high accounting knowledge will have a greater tendency to ignore value added in wealth measurement than decision makers with low accounting knowledge because the former group of decision makers will recall accounting knowledge structures that do not incorporate value-added information.

The impact of accounting knowledge on the use of value-added information in wealth measurement and distribution was examined in a between-analysis laboratory experiment. Subjects in the experiment assumed the role of a preparer of accounting reports asked by a superior to determine the wealth of an entity on the basis of a given set of accounting. Accounting knowledge was measured (a) as a discrete variable by classifying the subject into high-and low-accounting-knowledge classes based upon the program of business study in which the subject was enrolled, and (b) as a continuous variable by classifying the subject on the basis of the number of accounting courses he had completed. The effect of analytical ability on income measurement and distribution performance was also controlled.

The result of the experiment showed that contrary to intuitive expectation, high accounting knowledge interferes with a decision maker's ability to rely on value added rather than profit as a measure of wealth. In particular, the subject's ignorance of value added in wealth measurement and distribution increased significantly with increases in the subject's accountancy knowledge. Validity tests rule out differential knowledge about value-added reporting as a potential explanation of their average tendencies not to rely on value added in wealth measurement.

This study presents the first formal attempt to provide an explanation for why decision makers may ignore value-added information in wealth measurement and distribution by focusing on the role of knowledge structures. Where knowledge structures do not include information on the role of value added in wealth measurement and distribution, the result is an ignorance and/or avoidance of the concept and a fixation on income measurement as the only concept of wealth measurement. This result was obtained even after controlling for analytical ability as a potential explanation.

Finally, this study adds to the emerging studies that focus on the dysfunctional effect of knowledge of a subject matter by an examination of specific conditions where high accounting knowledge may hinder performance.[2,3,4]

The findings of this study suggest that the benefits of high knowledge or experience may be hampered by the incongruence between the knowledge structure stored in memory and the decision problem faced by the decision maker.[5,6,7]

THEORETICAL CONSIDERATIONS

Use of Value-Added Information in Wealth Measurement

By definition value added is the economic measure of wealth. While the economist relies on value added for measurement of the wealth of a nation, the accountant relies on income as the measurement of wealth. In effect, generally accepted accounting principles are primarily used in the case of the income statement for measurement of the income of a period as an expression of the wealth generated for that period. Alternative uses of information used for income measurement can be easily used to construct a value-added statement containing the net value added or the gross value added generated by the activities of the firm in a given period. Because value-added reports are not mandated in the United States, the reconstruction of value added from the information used to determine income is not accomplished for either external disclosure or internal uses. While optimal wealth measurement incorporates value added, externally reported financial accounting data do not include value added. Empirical research on why decision makers may tend to ignore value-added information in wealth measurement when it is not explicitly provided is practically nonexistent. The current study starts this research by examining whether differential knowledge of generally accepted accounting principles (GAAP) is the main cause for the ignorance and/or avoidance of value-added information in wealth measurement. As will be discussed later, the knowledge structures created by the mental storage of GAAP-based information may explain the role of accounting knowledge in wealth measurement that includes value-added information.

A Cognitive View of the Judgment/Decision Process in Accounting

In what follows, a model of the judgment/decision process in accounting is proposed as an exercise in social perception and cognition, requiring both formal and implicit judgment.[8] The primary input to this process is an accounting problem or phenomenon that needs to be solved and requires a judgment preceding either a preference or a decision. The model consists of the following steps:

1. Observation of the accounting phenomenon by the decision maker
2. Schema formation or building of the accounting phenomenon
3. Schema organization or storage
4. Attention and recognition process triggered by a stimulus
5. Retrieval of stored information needed for the judgment decision

6. Reconstruction and integration of retrieved information with new information
7. Judgment process
8. Decision/action response

Observation of the Accounting Phenomenon by the Decision Maker

The decision maker is assumed to have the opportunity to observe the accounting phenomenon. To understand the accounting phenomenon, the decision maker may be given some information that is deemed diagnostic. If this information is not provided, the decision maker may seek the information and test available information judged most relevant to the phenomenon. Following H. H. Kelly's approach to casual attribution,[9] the search behavior may concentrate on these types of available information:

1. *Consensus information*: how this accounting phenomenon and other accounting phenomena were rated or performed on given dimensions.
2. *Distinctiveness information*: how this accounting phenomenon was rated or performed on various other dimensions.
3. *Consistency information*: how this accounting phenomenon was rated or performed on important dimensions in the past.

Evidence shows that subjects tend to focus more on distinctiveness or consistency information than on consensus information.[10] Studies examining search behavior in reaction to an accounting phenomenon are very limited.

The search behavior is not misguided. It is fair to assume that the decision maker has some expectations about the accounting phenomenon that may determine the type of information sought. These expectations are termed *preconceived notions* in De Nisi et al.'s model.[11] They result from the decision maker's previous experiences with the accounting phenomenon. These expectations or preconceived notions may bias the decision maker toward choosing some information rather than other information. Providing background information prior to observation contributes to this phenomenon.[12,13] R. S. Wyer and T. K. Srull maintain that prior information predisposes the subject to select one of a number of frames of references.[14] Bias is a result of the tendency to seek evidence confirming preconceived notions rather than neutral or disconfirming evidence.[15,16,17]

Schema Formation or Building

Once the accounting phenomenon has been observed, the relevant information is encoded in the sense that it is categorized on the basis of experience and organized in memory along schemata or knowledge structures. As stated by R. E. Nisbett and L. Ross:

Few, if any, stimuli are approached for the first time by the adult. Instead, they are processed through pre-existing systems of schematized and abstracted knowledge—beliefs, theories, propositions and schemas. These knowledge structures label and categorize objects and events quickly and, for the most part, accurately. They also define a set of expectations about objects and events and suggest appropriate responses to them.[18]

A schema can be simply an update of a template that exists prior to the occurrence of a known accounting phenomenon or a new template generated by the occurrence of a new accounting phenomenon. In the first case, little ambiguity is assumed to exist and therefore the encoding follows an automatic process.[19] In the second case, no immediate available schema exists, and a controlled categorization process is triggered to determine which schema is consistent with the dimensions of the accounting phenomenon. Both processes are suggested in the case of the encoding of information or performance appraisal:

Thus, both the automatic and controlled processes have the same end result: the assignment of a person to a category based on prototype-machine process. The difference is whether the stimulus person's behavior is sufficiently consistent with other cues to allow the categorization to proceed automatically or whether a controlled process must be used to determine which category is consistent with the individual's behavior. The actual category assignment is a function of contextual factors influencing the salience of pare ocular categories and stimulus characteristics, as well as individual differences among perceivers that render some categories and their prototypes more available than others and some stimulus features more salient than others.[20]

Basically, an accounting phenomenon may be categorized in a given schema by virtue of its possession of obvious or salient attributes known to the perceiver. When no salient category prototype or schema provides a natural framework, the automatic process is superseded by a controlled process or a consciously monitored process.[21]

The controlled process can be triggered by either a new accounting phenomenon or new features of a known phenomenon that are inconsistent with a previous categorization. In the latter case a recategorization is invoked until the inconsistency is resolved and a new schema is used to describe the accounting phenomenon, causing a reconstruction of memories about the phenomenon such that memories consistent with the new categorization are more available.

Schema Organization and Storage

After information about a given phenomenon is encoded to form a representation or schema, it is stored and maintained in long-term memory. E. Tulving distinguishes between episodic and semantic memory.[22] Basically, a person's episodic memories are personal while semantic memory is knowledge of words and symbols, their meanings and referent knowledge of the relations among words, and the rules or algorithms for manipulating words, symbols, and the relations among them. R. C. Atkinson and R. M. Shiffrin maintain that the basic structural features of episodic memory are three memory stores: the sensory register, the short-term store, and the long-term store.[23] Information enters the memory system through the various senses and goes first to the sensory register, whose function is to preserve incoming information long enough for it to be selectively transmitted into the memory system. It is kept there less than a second and is lost through either decay or erasure by overwriting.

The information then goes to the short-term store, "working in memory where conscious mental processes are performed." It is where consciousness exercises its function. Information can be kept indefinitely here provided it is given constant attention; if not, it is lost through decay in twenty to thirty seconds.

The information next goes to the long-term store through a conscious or unconscious process where it can be held indefinitely and often permanently (although it can be lost due to decay or interference of various sorts). The long-term store is assumed to have unlimited capacity. In this multistore model, information about the accounting phenomenon moves through different and separate memory systems, ending with a long-term store where semantic information is maintained along meaning-based codes or schemata. It is important to realize at this stage that if the person intends to remember the accounting phenomenon for all time, he/she must perform a different analysis on the input than when his/her intentions are temporary.[24] A person's intention determines whether the storage of the information on the accounting phenomenon is permanent or temporary. A different coding is used: a memory code for permanent storage and a perceptual role for temporary storage.

Different codes have different permanence. Codes of the sensory aspects of an input, such as appearance, are short lived. Hence, a person who looked at a word to decide whether it was printed in red or green would not remember the word's name very long because his coding would have emphasized color, not meaning. In contrast, a person who looked at a word to decide whether it was a synonym for some other word would form a semantic code, and he/she would remember the name of the examined word for quite a while.[25]

Stimulus and Attention and Recognition Process

Upon observation of a triggering event or stimulus, the schema in the accounting phenomenon is activated. The activation, as a process of detection, search, and attention, can be either a controlled or an automatic processing.[26]

Basically, automatic detection, triggered by the recognition of a stimulus, operates independently of the person's control. Automatic processing is the apprehension of stimuli by the use of previously learned routines that are in the long-term storage.

Automatic processing as learned in long-term store, is triggered by appropriate inputs, and then operates independently of the subject's control. An automatic sequence can contain components that control information flow, attract attention, or govern over responses. Automatic sequences do not require attention, though they may attract it if training is appropriate, and they do not use up short-term capacity.[27]

In these automatic processes, no conscious effort is involved in the search as well as in demanding attention due to the learned sequence of the elements composing the schemata. On the other hand, controlled processes involve a temporary activation of novel sequences of processing steps that require attention, use short-term memory, and involve a conscious effort.

It is important to realize that in both processes, the use of a schema for encoding or retrieving information depends on accessibility in memory, where the accessibility of a schema is the probability that it can be activated, either for use in storage of incoming information or for retrieval of previously stored information.[28,29]

Accessibility of a schema depends upon such factors as the strength of the stored information, the extent of the overlap or match between input and schema, and the recency and frequency of previous activations. The instrumental effect of an activation on the accessibility of a schema is presumably a decreasing function of its prior strength. That is, a weak schema benefits more from an activation than a strong one.[30]

Empirical evidence on the increased accessibility of information with the frequency of activation is available.[31,32]

Retrieval of Stored Information Needed for Judgement/Decision

Either the automatic or controlled search process activates the appropriate schema for the accounting phenomenon and allows the retrieval of information on the phenomenon. It is, however, the schema, a representation of the phenomenon, that is recalled rather than the actual phenomenon.[33,34,35] The effect becomes stronger as the time between observation and recall increases.[36]

The potential for different types of biases exists at this stage. For example, people may be more likely to recall information consistent with a schema confirming an expectation[37] or may recall schema-consistent information that they never saw.[38] A good deal of evidence also suggest that schema-inconsistent information is more likely to be recalled[39] because of its novelty, saliency, and difficulty of incorporation into a schema.[40]

What is more likely to be recalled when faced with an accounting phenomenon, what types of biases affect the recall of schemata of accounting phenomenon, and what can be done to reduce or eliminate the distortions in recall are some of the important questions in need of investigation. This model will assume that familiarity with the accounting phenomenon through constant record keeping and other forms of monitoring may result in less biased recall. The solution, in fact, is more complex and depends on the type of relationship between memory and judgment. Reid Hastie and Bernadette Park investigated these relationships and distinguished between two types of judgment tasks, memory-biased and online. They also identified five information-processing models that relate memory for evidence to judgment based on the evidence: (1) independent processing, (2) availability, (3) biased retrieval, (4) biased encoding, and (5) incongruity-biased encoding.[41]

With regard to the five information-processing models, the distinction is three-fold: (1) cases where there is no relation between judgment and memory processes, which include the independent processing models; (2) cases where memory availability causes judgment, which include the availability-based information-processing model and the automatic search process described earlier; and (3) cases where judgment causes memory, which include the biased retrieval, the biased encoding, and incongruity-biased encoding models. The biased retrieval model is selective in the sense that traces that "fit" the judgment are more likely to be found at the memory decision stage. Such biases have been termed *selective recall, confirmatory memory*, and *access-biased memory*.[42,43,44,45]

The biased encoding model assumes that biasing takes place at the time of the encoding of evidence information and memory search will locate a biased sample of information reflecting the initial encoding bias. The incongruity-biased encoding model assumes that after the initial encoding, incoming information that is incongruent or contradictory is given special processing to enhance its memorability by being placed in "special tags" that strongly attach to memory. In memory search, the subject is more likely to find the incongruent information.[46,47]

This model assumes that where the accounting phenomenon calls for an online task, the availability or automatic search model will characterize the retrieval of stored information needed for judgment decision. Selection of a processing model will depend on the individual objectives of the subject and the perceived consequences of his/her judgments on his/her economic and psychological welfare.

Reconstruction and Integration of Retrieved Information with Other Available Information

At this stage the process involves the integration of the information retrieved from memory and other available information into a single evaluation of the accounting phenomenon.

Where familiarity with the phenomenon is present and previously learned routines are retrieved, active integration will not take place. An earlier integration is recalled from past stored output on the phenomenon. "What was once accomplished by slow, conscious, deductive reasoning is now arrived at by fast, unconscious perceptual processing."[48]

Where the phenomenon presents challenging and novel dimensions and where controlled processes were involved in attention and recognition, a cognitive integration of all the information is required to reach a single evaluation of the accounting phenomenon. G. Mandler describes the process of "response learn-ing" as follows:

First, the organism makes a series of discrete responses, often interrupted by incorrect ones. However, once errors are dropped out and the sequence of behavior becomes rel-atively stable—as in running a maze, speaking a word, reproducing a visual pattern—the various components of the total behavior required in the situation are "integrated." Integration refers to the fact that previously discrete parts of a sequence come to behave functionally as a unit; the whole sequence is elicited as a unit and behaves as a single component response as in the past; any part of it elicits the whole sequence.[49]

Brunswick's lens model and Anderson's weighted average model provide sup-port to the types of integration of information that take place.[50] The integration process is, however, also subject to various biases:

1. People may attach and give great weight to some type of information. For example, evidence in the employee appraisal literature shows that negative information has greater weight than positive information.[51,52]
2. There is evidence in both psychology and accounting of an underutilization or un-derweighting of base rate or consensus information.[53]
3. There is ample evidence in psychology and accounting of the effect of various heu-ristics involved in decisions on and about accounting phenomena. They include: (1) representativeness, (2) availability, (3) confirmation bias, (4) anchoring and adjust-ment, (5) conjunction fallacy, (6) hindsight bias, (7) illusory correlation and contin-gency judgment, (8) selective perception, (9) frequency, (10) concrete information, (11) data presentation, (12) inconsistency, (13) conservation, (14) nonlinear extrapo-lation, (15) law of small numbers, (16) habit/"rule of thumb," (17) "best-guess" strat-egy, (18) complexity in the decision environment, (19) social pressure in the decision environment, (20) consistency of information sources, (21) question format, (22) scale effects, (23) wishful thinking, (24) outcome-irrelevant learning structures, (25) mis-perceptions of chance fluctuations (gambler's fallacy), (26) success/failure attributions, and (27) logical fallacies in recall.[54]

The Judgment Process

The judgment process is the result of the integration process of information and the forming of a single evaluation of the accounting phenomenon if the attention, recognition, and integration processes are the result of controlled proc-ess. The judgment made in this case requires a conscious access to all the mental processes implied in the model. If, however, the attention, retrieval recognition, and integration process were the result of automatic processes, the judgment is not the mental process implied in this model.[55,56] It is a routine judgment. Rou-tine judgment involves the rapid matching of immediate perceptions to a tem-plate that provides, and executes, a specific response: "if total debts do not equal total credits, re-add the total balance."

In the above example, there is no awareness of how the brain actually decides that the debits do not equal the credits. Even if awareness were possible, it is not normally necessary—a great many of our routine activities, such as keeping our eyes open or holding our pencils, are done without any particular conscious awareness, at least until something causes us to become aware.[57]

Decision/Action (Response)

The final step of the model is the decision or selection of a response to the accounting phenomenon. It is a conscious response preference resulting from the judgment process. It is an output of the judgment process and is clearly influenced by all the mental processes and biases described earlier. As a result, a new schema on the phenomenon will develop that will be part of the knowledge structure or the phenomenon stored in long-term memory.

The move from judgment to decision is a bridging process. It assumes that no obstacles stand in the way. The decision/action has been investigated in various accounting environments and using various accounting phenomena. It has been found to differ from various normative decision models, including Bayesian-decision theory and expected value model.[58,59]

The bridging process, however, will be influenced by the cognitive steps described in this model as well as by other factors, including the possible consequences of the decision on the accounting phenomenon. Gibbins, for instance, cites the following factors:

Personal attitudes may play a direct role, such as determining priorities within the search process. For example, some public accountants may use financial return as their first selection criterion; others may use moral propriety as their first. Personal attitudes can also play an indirect role, limiting past actions and thus limiting the experiences on which judgment guides are built. The applications of such attitudes to the judgment process need not be conscious—particularly for deeply ingrained beliefs.[60]

The Role of Accounting Knowledge Structure in the Use of Value Added

The essence of cognitive relativism in accounting is the presence of a cognitive process that is assumed to guide the judgment/decision process. The model, outlined earlier, shows that judgments and decisions made about accounting phenomena are the products of a set of social cognitive operations that include the observation of information on accounting phenomena and the formulation of schemata or knowledge structures that are stored in memory and later retrieved to allow the formulation of judgments and/or decisions when needed.[61] It is the steps of (a) retrieval of stored information needed for judgment/decision, and (b) the reconsideration and integration of retrieval information with other available information that are important to this study. Basically, it is the steps where information from external sources is combined with knowledge structures recalled from long-term memory. Because cognition is highly knowledge- and context-dependent, a specific context will induce the recall of knowledge structures that are expected to be relevant to the context. Because the formal accounting training focuses on GAAP, the end result is that the knowledge structures stored and recalled will not include value- added-based knowledge for wealth measurement and distribution.

The same phenomenon of a lack of fit between the knowledge structures recalled from memory and the given problem-solving structure has been observed in a chess context,[62] a tax context,[63] and an opportunity cost context.[64] In all these contexts the studies show evidence of the dysfunctional effects resulting from the lack of fit between the knowledge structures recalled from memory and the decision situation examined.

What may be concluded from the above studies is a similar situation for value-added information in wealth measurement and accounting knowledge. Basically decision makers with high accounting knowledge who are faced with a wealth measurement task may be more inclined to recall GAAP-based knowledge structures that fail to incorporate value-added information. Accordingly, the following hypothesis is proposed:

H1: The amount of value-added information ignored in a wealth measurement task will be greater for decision makers with high accounting knowledge than for decision makers with low and no accounting knowledge.

RESEARCH DESIGN

Subjects

Three groups of subjects were asked to participate in a wealth measurement task. The three groups differed in the level of accounting knowledge possessed. The level of accounting knowledge was measured both as a discrete variable of classifying subjects into high- and low- and no-accounting-knowledge classes based on the program of business study in which the participants were enrolled and the number of accounting courses taken.

A total of 180 students from the graduate and undergraduate accounting program of a large university participated in the experiment. The subject received a flat compensation payment of $5.00 plus a performance-contingent bonus, paid after the experiment was conducted. The bonus was based on a composite score that includes the number of value-added information used by the subjects in their wealth measurement tasks, plus their scores on an analytical ability test. Participants whose scores were in the top quartile received a bonus of $3.00, the second quartile received $2.00, and the third quartile received $1.00. The bottom quartile did not receive a bonus.

Case Materials and Procedures

An experiment phase and a postexperiment phase characterized the study. In the experiment phase, the subjects were provided with the instruments, the as-

Exhibit 8.1
Experimental Procedures

A: Experiment Phase

Procedure	Description
1. Read general instruction	Information about the study, tasks, and compensation
2. Read assignment and memorandum	Description of the wealth measurement task and detailed financial information
3. Complete response memorandum	Compute the wealth, with supporting calculation and a brief explanation of the rationale used

B: Post-Experiment Phase

Procedure	Description
1. Complete reaction questionnaire	Debriefing question
2. Complete reasoning exercise	Analytical ability and value added knowledge tests
3. Complete background questionnaire	Academic background and work experience questions
4. Receive monetary compensation	Flat compensation upon completion of both parts of the experiment

signment, and data memorandum and a response memorandum. In the postexperiment phase, the subjects were provided with a reaction questionnaire, a combined test of analytical ability and value-added knowledge, and a background questionnaire. Both phases are summarized in Exhibit 8.1. For part one, in the response memorandum the subjects were provided with revenues and expenses data for a fictional company for a given year and were instructed to (a) compute the wealth generated by the firm for the given year based on the data provided, and (b) indicate how that wealth was distributed. Appendix 3.1 shows the materials used for both part one and part two of the experiment. The case materials were calibrated in a two-stage pilot test. In the first stage three accounting professors evaluated the materials and suggested changes that were later incorporated. In the second stage three graduate students completed the tasks required and provided the comments that were also included in the materials presented to the subjects.

Independent and Dependent Variables

The three knowledge groups formed included a high-accounting-knowledge group, a low-accounting-knowledge group, and a no-accounting-knowledge group. The subjects in the high-accounting-knowledge group (1) were enrolled in the Master of Science in Accounting program and (2) had completed more than the minimum six accounting background courses required before being admitted to the program. The subjects in the low-accounting-knowledge group (1) were enrolled in the undergraduate accounting group and (2) were in the first week of taking the second required accounting course, giving them a maximum of one accounting course taken. The no-accounting-knowledge group (1) were enrolled in the undergraduate business program and (2) were in the first week of taking the first required financial accounting course, giving them a maximum of zero accounting courses taken.[65]

Value added can be defined by either the subtractive method as sales minus bought-in materials and services, or the additive method as wages + interest + depreciation + dividends + taxes + retained earnings. Therefore, there are two value-added information options that can be provided by the subjects: (1) when the subjects used the subtractive method for wealth measurement and (2) when they used the additive method for wealth distribution.

The information provided to the subjects included revenues and expenses that can be used in either the subtractive or the additive methods. The subjects were instructed to compute wealth and indicate how it was distributed. The expectation is that subjects in the no- and low-accounting-knowledge groups will intuitively think of the situation in terms of value-added measurement and distribution. Subjects in the high-accounting-knowledge group are expected to think of the situation in terms of profit measurement and dividend distribution.

The key feature of the design is the presentation of sufficient information on both revenues and expenses for a given year to permit either a profit-based or a value-added-based wealth measurement and distribution. The memorandum is silent on both profit and value added as accounting concepts of wealth. This omission makes it possible to test whether the subjects in the zero- and low-accounting-knowledge groups intuitively rely on value added as a measurement of wealth before being socialized differently by a heavier exposure to GAAP. The two different variables of wealth measurement and distribution were coded by two trained graduate research assistants, completing their last semester in the Masters program. They were adequately compensated and trained with facsimile wealth measurement and distribution cases. There were no differences in the results provided by the two coders.

RESULTS

Validity Test

Validity tests focused on task difficulty and familiarity, value-added reporting knowledge, and analytical ability.

To test the assumption of similar perceptions of task difficulty, subjects were asked to evaluate the task on a ten-point scale ranging from "not difficult" (1) to "very difficult" (10). The mean scale for high- (5.22), low- (5.85), and no (5.81) accounting-knowledge subjects did not differ significantly ($F = 0.062$; $p = 0730$).

To test the assumption of similar familiarity with the tasks, subjects were asked if they had encountered analogous wealth measurement and distribution situations within the last two years that helped them perform the tasks on a ten-point scale ranging from "Nothing analogous" (1) to "Completely analogous" (10). The mean score for high- (4.38), low- (4.21), and no- (3.44) accounting-knowledge-subjects did not differ significantly ($F = 1.275$; $p = 0.346$).

To test the assumption of constant knowledge of value-added reporting, all the students in the three groups provided answers indicative of complete ignorance of value-added reporting. The result is not surprising as value-added reporting is neither taught nor used in practice in the United States.

To test the assumption of similar analytical ability, the subjects were given the same eight questions indicative of analytical ability selected from a prior Graduate Record Examination[66] and used by Vera-Munoz.[67] Analytical ability is composed of analytical reasoning and logical reasoning. Analytical ability is the ability to analyze a given structure of arbitrary relationships and to deduce new information from that structure. Logical reasoning is the ability to analyze and critique argumentation by understanding and assessing relationships among arguments or parts of an argument.[68] The mean scores for high- (7.89), low- (7.32), and no- (7.23) accounting-knowledge subjects did not differ significantly.

Tests of Accounting Knowledge

Descriptive statistics and planned, comparison tests for the average number of value-added information omitted by accounting knowledge groups are presented in Exhibit 8.2. The descriptive statistics for the average number of value-added information omitted by the subjects are shown in Panel A, which shows that the overall mean number of value-added information omitted by the subjects was 0.785. The mean number of omissions was higher for subjects with high accounting knowledge than for subjects with low accounting knowledge (0.937 vs. 0.858, respectively) and no accounting knowledge (0.937 vs. 0.560, respectively).

The total number and percentage of subjects who omitted value-added information in both wealth measurement and wealth distribution is presented in Panel B of Exhibit 8.2, which shows two important results. First, the percentage of subjects who omitted value-added information is higher for high-knowledge and low-knowledge groups than for the no-accounting-knowledge group. It also shows that the number of omissions for the three groups is smaller for wealth distribution than for wealth measurement.

The result of the planned comparison for the purpose of testing H1 after controlling for analytical ability are shown in Panel C of Exhibit 8.2. H1 predicts that high-accounting-knowledge decision makers are more likely to ignore value

Exhibit 8.2

Descriptive Statistics and Planned-Comparisons Tests for the Number of Value-Added Information Omitted, by Accounting Knowledge

Panel A: Descriptive Statistics (Standard Deviation in parenthesis: the maximum possible number of value added information omission was two, and the minimum was zero.)[a]

Accounting Knowledge	Average Value Added Omissions
High	0.937 n=64[b]
Low	0.858 n=148
No	0.560 n=148
Overall	0.785 n=360

Notes: a: Results of the statistical analysis that control the analytical ability are qualitatively similar to those that do not control the analytical ability. Thus, for presentation purposes, the means reported here are the raw (observed) means (i.e., not adjusted for analytical ability).

b: n = number of subjects in a group x two decisions (one on wealth measurement and one on wealth distribution).

Panel B: Total Number (Percentage) of Value Added Information Omitted, by accounting knowledge[c]

Value Added Information	Accounting Knowledge	Data
1. Value Added Measurement	High	30 (93.7)
	Low	63 (85.1)
	No	43 (58.1)
2. Value Added Distribution	High	28 (87.5)
	Low	63 (85.1)
	No	23 (31.08)

Note: c: Entities are number (and percentage) of subjects omitting the value added information. The percentages are the ratio of the number of subjects omitting the value added information in the total number of subjects in each category.

Panel C: Planned Comparison (dependent variables is the number of value added information omitted)

Groups	Mean	Standard Deviation
High Accounting Knowledge	1.812	0.4709
Low Accounting Knowledge	1.698	0.5447
No Accounting Knowledge	0.888	0.3582

Notes: F-statistics $= 71.61$, $p = 0.0001$.

240   Evaluating Capital Projects

Exhibit 8.3
Regression Results for the Effects of Accounting Knowledge
$$Y_i = \beta_1 AK_i + \beta_2 AA_i + \beta_3 PE_i + E_i$$

Variable	Expedition	Coefficient	t-statistic	Probability (one-tailed)
Intercept		3.486	8.557	0.0001
AK	(0)	0.035	1.994	0.0401
AA	(-)	-0.990	-5.741	0.0001
PE	(0)	0.004	2.429	0.0172

Notes: F-statistic 96.355 ($p = 0.01$).
   R: 0.3452 (adjusted = 0.3321).
   Variable definitions:
   Y_i = the number of value-added information omitted by subject
   AK_i = accounting knowledge, measured by the number of accounting courses completed
      by subjects
   AA_i = analytical ability, measured by subject i's score on analytical ability test
   PE_i = number of months of practical experience in accounting for subject i
   E_i = error term for subject i

added-information in wealth measurement and distribution than low-accounting-knowledge decision makers. The planned comparison for testing H1 shows that, as predicted, the effect of accounting knowledge after controlling for analytical ability is positive and significant ($F = 71.61; p = 0.00001$). This result indicates that, on average, the number of value-added information omitted is higher for subjects with high and/or low accounting knowledge than for subjects with no accounting knowledge.

To test the effects of accounting knowledge on the tendencies to ignore value-added information, the following regression analysis was conducted:

$$Y_i = \beta_1 AK_i + \beta_2 AA_i + \beta_3 PE_i + E_i$$

where Y_i is the number of value-added information omitted by subject i; AK_i is accounting knowledge measured by the number of accounting courses reported by subject i; AA_i is the analytical ability; and PE_i is the number of months of practical experience of accounting of subject i. Exhibit 8.3 shows that the regression equation is significant ($F = 26.355; p = 0.0001$) and explains 37.21 percent of the variation in the number of value-added information omitted. The significant and positive coefficient for β's indicates that the effects of accounting knowledge were, as predicted, significant ($t = 1.994; p = 0.040$). It shows that more value-added information is omitted by those subjects with greater accounting knowledge (as measured by the number of accounting courses completed). Also as expected, the negative and significant coefficient for β_3 indicates that the value-added information omissions increase with analytical ability increase

$(t = -5.741; p = 0.2201)$. Finally, the practical experience in accounting, as another surrogate of accounting knowledge, indicates a positive and significant coefficient (33). It shows that more value-added information is omitted by those subjects with greater practical experience in accounting $(t = 6.409; p = 0.017)$.

DISCUSSION AND IMPLICATIONS

This study provides empirical evidence that both high and low accounting knowledge interferes with a decision maker's ability to incorporate value-added information in wealth measurement and distribution decisions. The evidence supports the cognitive-processing-literature suggestion that people rely on knowledge structures stored in memory to guide their decision. Basically students with high and low accounting knowledge make their wealth measurement and distribution decisions as if they access from memory GAAP-based rules, which do not include value-added information. The subjects with no accounting knowledge at all seem to have intuitively thought of using value-added information in their wealth measurement and distribution decisions. The results imply that while the use of value-added information may be the most intuitive way of measuring and distributing wealth, the accounting knowledge as based on GAAP rules led the subjects to rely on profit measurement and dividend distribution. This is another case showing the dysfunctional effect of accounting knowledge where accounting knowledge seems to hinder performance in wealth measurement and distribution. The lack of fit between the accounting knowledge structures based on GAAP recalled from memory and the wealth measurement and distribution decisions that require consideration of value-added information contributes to the erosion of decision quality.

NOTES

1. J. Holland; K. Holy; R. Nisbett; and P. Thagard, *Induction: Process of Inference, Learning, and Discovery* (Cambridge, MA: MIT Press, 1986).

2. W. Chase and H. Simon, "The Mind's Eye in Chess," in *Visual Information Processing*, W. G. Chase, Ed. (New York: Academic Press, 1973).

3. G. Marchant; J. Robinson; W. Anderson; and M. Schadewald, "Analogical Transfer and Expertise in Legal Reasoning," *Organizational Behavior and Human Decision Process* 48 (1991), pp. 277–290.

4. C. Vera-Munoz, "The Effects of Accounting Knowledge and Context on the Omission of Opportunity Costs in Resource Allocation Decisions," *Accounting Review* (January 1998), pp. 47–72.

5. P. Frensch and R. Sternberg, "Expertise and Intelligent Thinking: When Is It to Know Better?" in *Advances in the Psychology of Human Intelligence*, R. Sternberg, Ed. (Hillsdale, N.J.: Erlbaum, 1989), p. 5.

6. M. Nelson; R. Libby; and S. Bonner, "Knowledge Structures and the Estimation of Conditional Probabilities in Audit Planning," *Accounting Review* (January 1995), pp. 804–824.

7. R. Libby and J. Luft, "Determinants of Judgement Performance in Accounting Settings: Ability, Knowledge, Motivation and Environment," *Accounting, Organizations and Society* (July 1993), pp. 425–450.

8. Similar models have been proposed for the performance appraisal process. See, e.g., A. S. De Nisi; T. P. Cafferty; and B. M. Meglino, "A Cognitive View of the Performance Appraisal Process: A Model and Research Proposition," *Organizational Behavior and Human Performance* 33 (1984), pp. 360–396; J. M. Feldman, "Beyond Attribution Theory: Cognitive Processes in Performance Appraisal," *Journal of Applied Psychology* 66, no. 2 (1981), pp. 127–48.

9. H. H. Kelly, "Attribution in Social Interactions," in *Attribution: Perceiving the Causes of Behavior*, E. E. Jones et al., Eds. (Morristown, N.J.: General Learning Process, 1972).

10. B. Major, "Information Acquisition and Attribution Processes," *Journal of Personality and Social Psychology* 39 (1980), pp. 1010–1023.

11. De Nisi, Cafferty, and Meglino, "Performance Appraisal Process," pp. 367–368.

12. H. I. Tajfel, "Social Perception," in *Handbook of Social Psychology*, G. Lidzkey and E. Aronson, Eds., vol. 1 (Reading, Mass.: Addison-Wesley, 1969).

13. P. Slovic; B. Fischoff; and S. Lichtenstein, "Behavioral Decision Theory," *Annual Review of Psychology* 28 (1977), pp. 119–139.

14. R. S. Wyer and T. K. Srull, "Category Accessibility: Some Theoretical and Empirical Issues Concerning the Processing Social Stimulus Information," in *Social Cognition: The Ontario Symposium*, E. Higgins; C. Herman; and M. Zarma, Eds., vol. 1 (Hillsdale, N.J.: Erlbaum, 1981).

15. M. Snyder and N. Cantor, "Treating Hypotheses about Other People: The Use of Historical Knowledge," *Journal of Experimental Social Psychology* 15 (1979), pp. 330–342.

16. M. Snyder, "Seek and Ye Shall Find: Testing Hypotheses about Other People," in *Social Cognition: The Ontario Symposium*, M. Higgins; E. C. Herman; and M. Zarma, Eds., vol. 1 (Hillsdale, N.J.: Erlbaum, 1981), p. 33.

17. E. B. Ebbensen, "Cognitive Processes in Inferences about a Person's Personality," in *Social Cognition: The Ontario Symposium*, M. Higgins; E. C. Herman; and M. Zarma, Eds., vol. 1 (Hillsdale, N.J.: Erlbaum, 1981), p. 55.

18. R. E. Nisbett and L. Ross, *Human Inference: Strategies and Shortcomings of Social Judgement* (Englewood Cliffs, N.J.: Trent and Hall, 1980), p. 7.

19. Wyer and Srull, "Category Accessibility."

20. Feldman, "Beyond Attribution Theory," p. 129.

21. M. Snyder and W. Uranowity, "Recontracting the Past: Some Cognitive Consequences of Person Perception," *Journal of Personality and Social Psychology* 37 (1979), pp. 1660–1672.

22. E. Tulving, "Episodic and Semantic Memory," in *Organization of Memory*, E. Tulving and W. Donaldson, Eds. (New York: Academic Press, 1972).

23. R. C. Atkinson and R. M. Shiffrin, "Human Memory: A Proposed System and Its Control Process," in *Advances in the Psychology of Learning and Motivation Research and Theory*, K. W. Spence and J. T. Spence, Eds., vol. 2 (New York: Academic Press, 1968).

24. R. I. Craig, and R. S. Lockart, "Levels of Processing: A Framework for Memory Research," *Journal of Verbal Learning and Verbal Behavior* 11 (1972), pp. 671–684.

25. R. Lachman; J. L. Lachman; and Earl C. Butterfield, *Cognitive Psychology and Information Processing: An Introduction* (Hillsdale, N.J.: Erlbaum, 1979), p. 274.

26. Walter Schneider and Richard M. Shiffrin, "Controlled and Automatic Human Information Processing: I. Detection, Search, and Attention," *Psychology Review* (January 1977), pp. 1–53.

27. Ibid., p. 51.

28. E. Tulving and Z. Parlstone, "Availability versus Accessibility of Information in Memory for Words," *Journal of Verbal Learning and Verbal Behavior* 5 (1966), pp. 381–391.

29. B. Hayes-Roth, "Evolution of Cognitive Structures and Processes," *Psychological Review* 84 (1977), pp. 260–278.

30. P. W. Thorndyke and B. Hayes-Roth, "The Use of Schema in the Acquisition and Transfer of Knowledge," *Cognitive Psychology* 11 (1979), pp. 86–87.

31. J. Pealmutter; P. Source; and J. L. Myers, "Retrieval Process in Recall," *Cognitive Psychology* 8 (1976), pp. 32–63.

32. B. Hayes-Roth and F. Hayes-Roth, "Plasticity in Memorial Networks," *Journal of Verbal Learning and Verbal Behavior* (1979), pp. 253–262.

33. Ibid.

34. A. G. Greenwald, "Cognitive Learning, Cognitive Response to Persuasion, and Attitude Change," in *Psychological Foundations of Attitudes*, A. Greenwald; T. Brock; and T. Ostron, Eds. (New York, Academic Press, 1960).

35. R. Shanke and R. Abelson, *Scripts, Plans, Goals, and Understanding* (Hillsdale, N.J.: Erlbaum, 1977).

36. T. K. Srull and R. S. Wyer, "Category Accessibility and Social Perception: Some Implications for the Study of Person, Memory and Interpersonal Judgements," *Journal of Personality and Social Psychology* 38 (1980), pp. 841–856.

37. K. P. Sentis and E. Burnstein, "Remembering Schema Consistent Information; Effects of Balance Schema on Recognition Memory," *Journal of Personality and Social Psychology* 37 (1979), pp. 2200–2211.

38. C. E. Cohen, "Person Categories and Social Perception: Testing Some Boundaries of the Processing Effects of Prior Knowledge," *Journal of Personality and Social Psychology* 40 (1981), pp. 441–452.

39. S. E. Taylor et al., "The Generalizability of Salience Effects," *Journal of Personality and Social Psychology* 37 (1979), pp. 357–368.

40. R. I. Craig and E. Tulving, "Depth of Processing and the Retention of Words in Episodic Memory," *Journal of Verbal Learning and Verbal Behavior* 11 (1972), pp. 671–684.

41. R. Hastie and Bernadette Park, "The Relationship between Memory and Judgement Depends on Whether the Judgement Task Is Memory-Biased or On-Line," *Psychological Review* 93, no. 3 (1986), pp. 258–268.

42. E. J. Learner; A. Blank; and B. Chanowitz, "The Mindlessness of Ostensibly Thoughtful Action; The Role of Placebo Information in Interpersonal Interaction," *Journal of Personality and Social Psychology* 36 (1978), pp. 635–642.

43. E. E. Learner, "False Models and Post-Data Model Construction," *Journal of the American Statistical Association* 69 (1974, pp. 122–131.

44. E. E. Learner, "Explaining Your Results as Accent-Biased Memory," *Journal of the American Statistical Association* 70 (1975), pp. 88–93.

45. M. Synder and W. Uranowitz, "Reconstructing the Past: Some Cognitive Conse-

quences of Person Perception," *Journal of Personality and Social Psychology* 36 (1978), pp. 941–945.

46. A. C. Graesser and G. V. Nalsamura, "The Impact of Schema on Comprehension and Memory," *Psychology of Learning and Memory* 16 (1982), pp. 60–102.

47. P. Graesser; T. Gordon; and S. Sawyer, "Memory for Typical and Atypical Actions in Scripted Activities," *Journal of Verbal Learning and Behavior* 18 (1979), pp. 319–332.

48. W. Chase and H. Simon, "Perception in Chess," *Cognitive Psychology* 4 (1973), pp. 55–87.

49. G. Mandler, "From Association to Structure," *Psychological Review* 69 (1962), pp. 415–427.

50. Ahmed Belkaoui, *Human Information Processing in Accounting* (Westport, Conn.: Quorum Books, 1989).

51. D. L. Hamilton and L. J. Huffman, "Generality of Impression Formation for Evaluative and Non-evaluative Judgements," *Journal of Personality and Social Psychology* 20 (1971), pp. 200–207.

52. R. S. Wyer and H. L. Hinlele, "Information Factor Underlying Inferences about Hypothetical People," *Journal of Personality and Social Psychology* 34 (1976), pp. 481–495.

53. Belkaoui, *Human Information Processing in Accounting.*

54. Ibid.

55. J. Jaynes, *The Origin of Consciousness in the Breakdown of the Bicameral Mind* (Toronto: University of Toronto Press, 1978).

56. R. E. Nisbett and T. D. Wilson, "Telling More than We Can Know: Verbal Reports on Mental Processes," *Psychological Review* (May 1977), pp. 231–259.

57. M. Gibbins, "Propositions about the Psychology of Professional Judgement in Public Accounting," *Journal of Accounting Research* (Spring 1989), p. 103.

58. Belkaoui, *Human Information Processing in Accounting.*

59. R. M. Hogarth, *Judgement and Choice: The Psychology of Decision* (Chichester: Wiley, 1980).

60. Gibbins, "Propositions about the Psychology of Professional Judgement in Public Accounting," p. 114.

61. Ahmed Belkaoui, *Judgement in International Accounting: A Theory of Cognition, Cultures, Language, and Contracts* (Westport, Conn.: Greenwood Publishing, 1990), p. 15.

62. Chase and Simon, "Perception in Chess."

63. Marchant, Robinson, Anderson, and Schadewald, "Analogical Transfer and Expertise in Legal Reasoning."

64. Vera-Munoz, "The Effects of Accounting Knowledge and Context on the Omission of Opportunity Costs in Resource Allocation Decision."

65. Ibid.

66. Ibid., pp. 47–72.

67. Ibid.

68. Ibid.

SELECTED READINGS

Bartlett, F. C. *Remembering* (London: Cambridge University Press, 1932).

Belkaoui, Ahmed. *Human Information Processing in Accounting* (Westport, Conn.: Quorum Books, 1989).

Bobrow, D. G., and D. A. Norman. "Some Principles of Memory Schemata." In *Representations and Understanding: Studies in Cognitive Science*. D. G. Bobrow and A. M. Collins, Eds. (New York: Academic Press, 1975).

Brewer, W. F., and G. V. Nalsamura. "The Nature and Functions of Schemas." In R. S. Wyer, Jr., and T. K. Srull, Eds. *Handbook of Social Cognition* (Hillsdale, N.J.: Erlbaum, 1984), pp. 139–150.

Canton, N., and W. Mischel. "Prototypes in Person Perception." In *Advances in Experimental Psychology*. L. Berkowitz, Ed. Vol. 12 (New York: Academic Press, 1979).

Chase, W. G., and H. A. Simon. "The Mind's Eye in Chess." In *Visual Information Processing*. W. G. Chase, Ed. (New York: Academic Press, 1982).

———. "Perception in Chess." *Cognitive Psychology* 4 (1973), pp. 55–87.

Chi, M. T. H., and R. Koeske. "Network Representations of Child's Dinosaur Knowledge." *Developmental Psychology* 19 (1983), pp. 29–35.

Chiesi, H. L.; G. J. Spilich; and J. F. Voss. "Acquisition of Domain-Related Information in Relation to High and Low Domain Knowledge." *Journal of Verbal Learning and Verbal Behavior* 18 (1979), pp. 257–273.

Cohen, C. E. "Pearson Categories and Social Perception: Testing Some Boundaries of the Processing Effects of Prior Knowledge." *Journal of Personality and Social Psychology* 40 (1981), pp. 441–452.

Craig, R. I., and R. S. Lockart. "Level of Processing: A Framework for Memory Research." *Journal of Verbal Learning and Verbal Behavior* 11 (1972), pp. 671–684.

Craig, R. I., and E. Tuvling. "Depth of Processing and the Retention of Words in Episodic Memory." *Journal of Verbal Learning and Verbal Behavior* 11 (1972), pp. 671–684.

De Nisi, A. S.; T. P. Cafferty; and B. M. Meglino. "A Cognitive View of the Performance Appraisal Process: A Model and Research Proposition." *Organizational Behavior and Human Performance* 33 (1984), pp. 360–396.

Ebbesen, E. B. "Cognitive Processes in Inferences about a Person's Personality." In *Social Cognition: The Ontario Stmposium*. M. Higgins; E. C. Herman; and M. Zarma, Eds. (Hillsdale, N.J.: Erlbaum, 1984), pp. 52–59.

Emby, C., and M. Gibbins. "Good Judgment in Public Accounting: Quality and Justification." *Contemporary Accounting Research* (Spring 1988), pp. 287–313.

Feldman, Jack M. "Beyond Attribution Theory: Cognitive Processes in Performance Appraisal." *Journal of Applied Psychology* 66, no. 2 (1981), pp. 127–148.

Ferguson, T. J.; B. G. Rule; and D. Carlson. "Memory for Personally Relevant Information." *Journal of Personality and Social Psychology* 44 (1983), pp. 251–261.

Vera-Munoz, Sandra C. "The Effects of Accounting Knowledge and Context on the Omission of Opportunity Costs in Resource Allocation Decisions." *Accounting Review* (January 1998), pp. 47–72.

Selected Bibliography

Agmon, Tamir. "Capital Budgeting and Unanticipated Changes in the Exchange Rate." *Advances in Financial Planning and Forecasting*, vol. 4, part B (1990), pp. 295–314.

Ang, James S., and Tsong-Yue Lai. "A Simple Rule for Multinational Capital Budgeting." *Global Finance Journal* (Fall 1989), pp. 71–75.

Baker, James C., and Laurence J. Beardsley. "Multinational Companies' Use of Risk Evaluation and Profit Measurement for Capital Budgeting Decisions." *Journal of Business Finance* (Spring 1973), pp. 38–43.

Bavishi, Vinod B. "Capital Budgeting Practices at Multinationals." *Management Accounting* (August 1981), pp. 32–35.

Booth, L. D. "Capital Budgeting Frameworks for the Multinational Corporation." *Journal of International Business Studies* (Fall 1982), pp. 113–123.

Hendricks, James. "Capital Budgeting Decisions: NPV or IRR?" *Cost and Management* (March-April 1980), pp. 16–20.

McIntyre, A. D., and N. J. Coulthurst. "Theory and Practice in Capital Budgeting." *British Accounting Review* (Autumn 1985), pp. 24–70.

Mills, R. W. "Capital Budgeting—The State of the Art." *Long Range Planning* (August 1998), pp. 76–81.

————. "Capital Budgeting Techniques Used in the UK and the USA." *Management Accounting* 61, no. 1 (1998), pp. 22–28.

Riahi-Belkaoui, Ahmed. *Accounting in the Developing Countries* (Westport, Conn.: Quorum, 1994).

Riahi-Belkaoui, Ahmed. *Handbook of Cost Accounting: Theory and Techniques* (Westport, Conn.: Quorum, 1991).

Riahi-Belkaoui, Ahmed. *The New Foundations of Management Accounting* (Westport, Conn.: Quorum, 1991).

Index

About the Author

AHMED RIAHI-BELKAOUI is CBA Distinguished Professor of Accounting in the College of Business Administration, University of Illinois at Chicago. Author of more than 45 Quorum books, published or forthcoming, and coauthor of several more, he is also a prolific contributor to the scholarly and professional journals of his field, and has served on numerous editorial boards that oversee them.